Making the News,
Taking the News

Making the News,
Taking the News

From NBC to the
Ford White House

RON NESSEN

Wesleyan University Press

Middletown, Connecticut

Wesleyan University Press

Middletown CT 06459

www.wesleyan.edu/wespress

© 2011 Ron Nessen

All rights reserved

Manufactured in the United States of America

Wesleyan University Press is a member of the Green Press Initiative.
The paper used in this book meets their minimum
requirement for recycled paper.

Library of Congress Cataloging-in-Publication Data

Nessen, Ron, 1934–

Making the news, taking the news : from NBC to the Ford White House / Ron Nessen.

p. cm.

ISBN 978-0-8195-7156-4 (cloth : alk. paper) — ISBN 978-0-8195-7157-1 (e-book)

1. Nessen, Ron, 1934- 2. Television journalists—United States—Biography.

3. Presidential press secretaries—United States—Biography. 4. United States—

Politics and government—1945–1989. I. Title.

PN4874.N2957A3 2011

070.92—DC23

[B]   2011017892

5 4 3 2 1

Contents

CONTENTS

Introduction

The fifteen years from 1962 to 1977 were a historic and tumultuous time: the civil rights revolution in the American South; the assassinations of John F. Kennedy and Robert Kennedy, of Martin Luther King Jr. and Malcolm X; President Lyndon B. Johnson's progressive Great Society social program; Che Guevara stirring revolution in Latin America; the indictment and resignation of a corrupt vice president, Spiro T. Agnew; the Watergate break-in scandal, which forced President Richard Nixon to resign; the ascendancy of an appointed vice president, Gerald R. Ford, to the White House; the Yom Kippur War in the Middle East, followed by an embargo on oil shipments and a resulting deep economic recession; a cultural and social revolution that brought rock-and-roll music, women's rights, widespread drug use, and more-relaxed standards of sexual conduct; the Vietnam War and the widespread public demonstrations against that war; and the end of that war, with the dramatic helicopter evacuation of the remaining Americans and the desperate efforts of thousands of Vietnamese to escape Communist conquest.

I had a front-row seat at most of the events of those tumultuous years, first as a globe-trotting NBC News correspondent from 1962 to 1974 and then as President Gerald R. Ford's White House press secretary from 1974 to 1977.

During those fifteen years, I grew and matured as a journalist. I also grew and matured as a man.

And I recognized some unpleasant truths about myself.

Winston Churchill, also a journalist before he entered politics, once proclaimed, "It's better to be making the news than taking the news, to be an actor rather than a critic." Churchill is a hero of mine. A framed copy of that quote hangs in my office. But I disagree with him on that point.

Having worked at both taking the news and making the news, I prefer the journalist's role. I'm more comfortable as an observer than as a participant.

I was born during the Great Depression, a member of the small In-Between Generation—too young to be in the Greatest Generation that fought World War II, too old to be a baby boomer. I've never quite fit into either cohort. That's one reason why I've always felt like an outsider, which is the role of a professional journalist.

The years 1962 to 1977 also were tumultuous and tragic times in my personal life. I stood at a hospital bedside and watched my six-year-old son die of brain cancer. My wife divorced me because I was too immature to know how to be a caring husband to a grieving mother. I entered into an ill-considered second marriage with a Korean woman I met in Saigon. I later left her and our child. I didn't understand the need for faithfulness in marriage. I repeatedly cheated on my wives, perhaps to prove to myself that I was manly, to overcome a coddled upbringing by my mother.

Is it possible for a person to be ashamed of some of the things he has done in his life—the people he has hurt, the mistakes he has made—and at the same time to be proud of his accomplishments? That's the way I feel about my life.

Not that I haven't written about such a man before. I wrote a quickie book about my time in the Ford White House, but it was mostly a chronology and self-justification without much introspection or analysis. And I had written or cowritten five novels. All of them featured a main character whose life and attitudes were tidied-up versions of my own life and attitudes. I started yet another novel featuring the professional and romantic adventures of yet another nicer me. I got eighty-five pages into the book and stalled.

That's when my psychiatrist—who had helped me through some hard times, some dark times, some confused times, who had helped me to grow up, to mature, to become a man—finally enabled me to see that I had been writing sanitized, novelistic accounts of my own life, accounts that excised events and behavior and character flaws I wanted to hide from the world, and from myself. It was time, the psychiatrist persuaded me, to stop writing fictionalized versions of my life and to start writing the factual version of my life, flaws and all—a memoir. And so, after decades of being a professional observer of other people's lives, and then a creator of fictionalized versions of my own life, it's time to tell, examine, and make sense of my real life story.

And it's time to put aside the journalist's principle of reporting just the facts and to offer some opinions, of myself and of others.

My recollections in this book are not based just on memory, but primarily on contemporaneous notes, press releases, newspaper clippings, copies of letters I wrote to friends, family, and my psychiatrist, and especially on almost fifty hours of oral diary entries I tape recorded almost every night when I got home from the White House. Reading through and listening to all that material for this memoir, I felt regret for many things I did in my personal life and in my professional life. I was chastened. I think I'm a better person now.

This book recounts what I saw, what I learned, what I did, and what I'm sorry I did during fifteen years of taking the news and making the news.

Making the News,
Taking the News

The *Mal Jaune*

On April 29, 1975, as the victorious North Vietnamese army swept toward final victory in Saigon and as the last Americans were evacuated by helicopter from the U.S. embassy compound, I stood on the stage in an auditorium in the Old Executive Office Building and read to the White House press corps this statement from President Ford:

> During the past week, I had ordered the reduction of American personnel in the United States mission in Saigon to levels that could be quickly evacuated during an emergency, while enabling that mission to continue to fulfill its duties. During the day on Monday, Washington time, the airport at Saigon came under persistent rocket as well as artillery fire and was effectively closed. The military situation in the area deteriorated rapidly. I therefore ordered the evacuation of all American personnel remaining in South Vietnam. The evacuation has now been completed. I commend the personnel of the Armed Forces who accomplished it, as well as Ambassador Graham Martin and the staff of his mission, who served so well under difficult conditions. This action closes a chapter in the American experience. I ask all Americans to close ranks, to avoid recrimination about the past, to look ahead to the many goals we share, and to work together on the great tasks that remain to be accomplished.

The war was over.

My voice was unnaturally high and quivering. I fought to control my emotions. Ten years earlier, in the summer of 1965, as a young White House correspondent for NBC News, I covered President Lyndon B. Johnson's announcement that he was ordering the first large contingent of American combat soldiers to South Vietnam, to try to prevent the North Vietnamese and the Vietcong from conquering that country.

Then NBC News dispatched me to Vietnam to cover the ever-increasing American role in the war. Over the next eight years I served five reportorial tours in Vietnam, covering the deployment of more and more American troops, the Tet offensive in 1968, the siege of Khe Sanh, many bloody battles, including Pleiku and An Khe, Da Nang and the Mekong Delta, and, finally, the cease-fire that ended America's military involvement.

Vietnam dominated my life for nearly a decade. I came of age as a journalist there. I gained confidence in myself, as a reporter and as a man. I witnessed horrifying things there. I saw friends and colleagues—and innocent children and adults—killed there. I met a woman there whom I later married. I won praise and journalistic awards for my coverage. I almost bled to death while reporting on the war in Vietnam when a fragment from an exploding hand grenade pierced my lung.

Until I went to Vietnam, I doubted my physical abilities, my capacity to cope in a harsh world. I doubted my manliness. My mother, Ida Nessen—a typical Jewish mother—had raised me to believe that I was too frail for sports or playground games. She was a plain woman with dark hair and dark eyes who sewed and knitted many of her own clothes. She had worked in the credit office of a department store before her marriage, and worked as a bookkeeper for my father's five-and-ten-cent store after their wedding.

Growing up, I frequently heard my father, Fred Nessen—a handsome, athletic, dapper man with slicked-back hair and a neatly trimmed mustache—arguing with my mother about her overprotectiveness. He regularly accused her of turning me into a "mama's boy." When they fought over my upbringing, he often shouted that she was making me a "sissy."

My father's family immigrated to America from Brest-Litovsk, on the Russian-Polish border, when he was five years old. His father opened a junkyard in Somerville, Massachusetts. I sometimes excuse my bad behavior with the explanation, "What do you expect from the grandson of a Russian peasant?" (My mother's father, David Kaufman, also was an immigrant "Russian peasant," born in Kiev.) Like many immigrants, my father changed his name, from Nissenbaum to something less ethnic, more American—Nessen.

The great lessons I learned from my father were determination, perseverance, and resolution in the face of adversity. During World War II, he prospered from a rented variety store he operated in Washington, D.C., near the bustling navy yard and marine barracks, a neighborhood jammed in those years with sailors and marines with money to spend. But after the war, the owner of the store declined to renew my father's lease. My mother urged my father to take a salaried job as a salesman. He had too much pride, too much determination, for that.

He refused to give up. Instead, he bought a vacant lot in the same block as his leased store, built his own store, and worked hard for more than twenty years to get back to where he had been in 1945.

In 1968, parts of Washington were swept by riots set off by the assassination of Martin Luther King Jr. Many white-owned businesses were set afire. My father's store was not burned, but it was looted. My mother persuaded him to rent the store to another merchant and to retire.

By then, I was an award-winning network TV correspondent. I considered myself a successful achiever in the wider sophisticated world. I looked down on my parents, embarrassed by their middle-class Jewish lifestyle— my mother played mahjong, my father was a Shriner, they belonged to the Book of the Month Club, they vacationed in Miami Beach. And then, when I went through my father's papers after his death, I discovered that he had expressed his feelings by secretly writing poetry.

> My awakening these mornings is only a make believe of exuberance.
> Oh, for those days of not so long ago when happiness was not false pretense.
> In the mirror of my bathroom, I see a face that truly shows its age.
> I realize that what I see is the payment of a life I have lived.
> For different from vintage wine, I do not improve—I just grow old.

Not Longfellow. But not what I expected from the man I had considered a stereotypical uncultured immigrant merchant.

One morning before dawn, in the winter of 1971, I was awakened by a phone call. It was my mother, calling from Florida, where my parents lived in retirement. She was crying hysterically. My father had died, of cancer and a heart attack. He was sixty-eight years old. At the time, absorbed in events of my own life, I experienced no grief. I felt no emotional loss. I do now. I wish I had known my father better. I wish he had spent more time with me. Before he died, I did not yet appreciate what my father had made of his life. I did not yet comprehend the traits I had inherited from him and from his father, the junkman. I was not yet able to understand or to tell my father about my feelings for him. And I have regretted it ever since.

In the summer of 1965, facing my first day in combat in Vietnam as a TV correspondent, I recalled that during my childhood my mother had told me repeatedly that I was too weak, that I was too prone to illness, to join the Boy Scouts or to go on camping trips. She instructed my summer camp counselor not to let me participate in strenuous activities because I had a heart problem. (I didn't.) And here I am bedding down with troops of the 101st Airborne Division, some of the toughest soldiers in the world, hours away from battle. My last thought before falling into an anxious sleep the night before my baptism by fire was: "If my mother could only see me now!"

Some of my thoughts about my mother during those first days in Vietnam were definitely uncharitable. I wrote to a friend: "I keep looking in my mailbox every day, waiting impatiently for a letter from my mother which I know will say how worried she is about me. . . . I have had a little fantasy that she collapsed or had some kind of seizure when she read and heard about my close calls." It would be my revenge for her raising me to believe I was too frail to face physical challenges. Some of my journalistic colleagues and competitors in Vietnam thought I deliberately placed myself in risky situations, to the point of being foolhardy, in order to advance my career. No doubt that was part of the reason I courted danger again and again. But I also was trying to prove to my mother, and to prove to myself, that I was a man.

Covering the war, I also developed a deep attachment to Vietnam and the Vietnamese people, who had suffered so much, in the French Indochina war, and then in the American war against the Vietcong and North Vietnamese. The French writer Bernard Fall—whose Vietnam coverage went back to the 1950s—accused me one night over dinner at a Saigon café of coming down with the *mal jaune*—the "yellow sickness," an incurable affection for Vietnam and its people. I pleaded guilty.

So it was no wonder that my voice quivered, no wonder I was so overcome with emotion when it fell to me, as Ford's White House press secretary, to announce the end of the Vietnam War. That war had shaped who I was—personally and professionally—what I thought of myself, what others thought of me.

2

Golf in Palm Springs, Death in Saigon

Incongruously, the beginning of the end of the war occurred as President Ford was flying to an Easter golfing vacation in lush and wealthy Palm Springs, California, in April 1975. Aboard Air Force One, the radio operator handed me a brown envelope. Inside was a message: Da Nang, a major South Vietnamese city and former U.S. Marine base, had fallen to the North Vietnamese. I passed the note to the president. He read it, shook his head, and said nothing.

Ford's vacation was a horror. Every night the TV newscasts featured film of South Vietnamese soldiers throwing away their weapons and uniforms, fleeing from the invading North Vietnamese. The Saigon troops, trying to get away from the approaching Communist forces, were shown clubbing women and children with rifle butts in their desperation to get aboard evacuation helicopters.

These scenes were followed by pictures of Ford playing golf while reporters shouted questions at him. The worst moment came when Ford interrupted his vacation to make a public appearance in Bakersfield, California. When reporters approached the president as he disembarked from Air Force One to ask him about the chaos in Vietnam, he literally ran away from them. Virtually every nightly newscast and newspaper front page displayed pictures of him sprinting across the airfield, fleeing the pursuing pack of journalists.

At my next press briefing, one reporter sneered: "He ran almost as fast as the South Vietnamese Army." At that point, there was almost nothing the United States could do to stave off a Communist victory. The last American combat troops had been withdrawn by President Nixon more than two years earlier. Congress had forbidden any more American aid to Vietnam.

As a symbolic gesture of his continuing support and sympathy, Ford flew from Palm Springs to the San Francisco airport one night in a rainstorm to welcome a planeload of South Vietnamese infants who had been evacuated from Saigon. The babies were supposed to be orphans, but we learned later that some were actually the children of South Vietnamese military and government officials who had paid bribes to get their offspring on the plane. Ford joined volunteers carrying the babies to ambulances and buses.

One day, Tom DeFrank, then the *Newsweek* magazine White House correspondent—a longtime friend of mine who had covered Ford when he was vice president—came to visit me in my temporary press office in a Palm Springs motel. He was gathering material for an article on the impending end of the Vietnam War. He asked me to recall my years in Saigon. I told him about my near-death experience there. I told him about friends and colleagues who had been killed there. I told him about the Vietnamese cameramen and sound technicians with whom I had shared danger. Now they were caught in the chaos of the collapsing South Vietnamese government. I was worried about what would happen to them.

I told DeFrank about witnessing indescribable horrors that I could never get out of my mind. And now South Vietnam was about to be taken over by harsh conquerors. I knew more horrors awaited that beautiful country and its beautiful people. America would not, could not save them from that fate.

The greatest influence on who I was as a person, aside from my mother, was what I had seen and lived through in Vietnam.

DeFrank could see I was in turmoil. "There is nothing you can do, is there?" he asked sympathetically.

"No," I replied. Then I was overwhelmed by emotion. I put my head down on my desk and cried.

I was anguished. My wife, Cindy—a Korean woman I first met in Vietnam—had just left me. She left because I was rarely home, and when I was home, I was too irritable from the long hours and pressures of my job to be a loving husband. I was too harried to seek solace from her. And I was too preoccupied with my problems to listen to her problems. I believed we would never understand each other because we came from two such different cultures and backgrounds. Finally, one night, I was overwhelmed by all these pent-up pressures and conflicts. I had exploded at Cindy in anger and helplessness. She moved out. It was too much for me to bear. That's why I cried during my conversation with DeFrank. (Cindy and I later reconciled for a time, but later divorced.)

President Ford dispatched the army chief of staff, General Frederick Weyand, to Saigon to assess the deteriorating situation and to recommend what, if anything, the United States could do to save South Vietnam.

The irrepressible young official photographer to the president, David Hume Kennerly, who had spent two and a half years as a photographer in Vietnam for *Time* magazine, asked for and received Ford's permission to accompany the general.

Weyand returned with a pessimistic report on South Vietnam's ability to survive. He recommended that Ford request from Congress an additional $722 million in aid to the South Vietnamese Army, primarily for ammunition. He also suggested that Ford use American air power to prevent North Vietnamese troops from overrunning Saigon. Kennerly's much more terse summation of the situation: "I don't care what the generals are telling you. They're bullshitting you if they say that Vietnam has got more than three or four weeks left."

Back from his Palm Springs vacation, Ford focused on what to do about Vietnam. He sought recommendations from senior staff people on what to say in a speech to the nation and in proposals to Congress.

By then I had become a dove on the war. I suggested Ford begin his speech this way: "I have decided it is time to put the divisions and the horrors of this war behind us and to lead this nation and the world in a new direction. . . . None of my advisers was able to assure me that . . . additional money would enable South Vietnam to stabilize the military situation and continue the fight. When the outcome is so doubtful, I cannot in good conscience ask the American people to bear a further burden after they have given so much."

White House Chief of Staff Donald Rumsfeld commented that my speech draft sounded like I had "vomited out" all my feelings about Vietnam and its people.

The president, of course, rejected my approach. Instead, he made a speech to Congress asking the members to provide another $722 million in military aid to South Vietnam, to allow U.S. military forces to evacuate

Americans and Vietnamese from the country, and to launch a humanitarian effort to help the refugees.

One member of Congress booed Ford loudly. Another hissed. Half the members stayed away from the speech entirely to demonstrate their opposition.

The Senate Foreign Relations Committee asked for a meeting with Ford, which was granted. One senator after another urged the president to immediately end all U.S. involvement in Vietnam, to get all Americans out of the country right away, except perhaps for a small rear guard that could be evacuated with one helicopter lift, and to deny all help to the refugees. Ford rejected these proposals. After the meeting, Secretary of State Henry Kissinger came to my office and commented, "Have you ever heard such bullshit in your life?"

As the situation in Vietnam continued to deteriorate, Ford flew to New Orleans to deliver two long-scheduled speeches. In the afternoon, he would speak to the Navy League, an organization of family members and other supporters of the U.S. Navy. In that speech, largely composed by the hawkish Kissinger, Ford would call for a strong national defense and reiterate continued American support for the South Vietnamese.

On the flight to New Orleans, I read the text of Ford's evening speech to be delivered to thousands of students at Tulane University. It was very different from the Navy League address. At Tulane, Ford would acknowledge for the first time that for America, the Vietnam War was over. I learned that the Tulane speech had been drafted by Ford's chief speechwriter, Robert Hartmann, and a colleague, Milton Friedman. They had deliberately not informed Kissinger of its contents.

On the elevator carrying Ford and his party to the Tulane auditorium, I was worried that the president might stumble through this important speech after a long and tiring day—and after sipping a cocktail at a reception. I tried to express my concerns to him in a diplomatic way, suggesting that he read the speech slowly, that he follow the text carefully.

Ford's outspoken young photographer, David Kennerly, translated my carefully crafted words: "Mr. President, what he's trying to tell you is 'Don't screw it up.'"

And he didn't screw it up.

"America can regain the sense of pride that existed before Vietnam,"

Ford told the students and the TV audience. "But it cannot be achieved by refighting a war that is finished as far as America in concerned."

The student audience roared its approval.

Aboard Air Force One, on the flight back to Washington from New Orleans, the staff was in a celebratory mood after Ford's declaration. Rumsfeld's young assistant Dick Cheney raised his glass and offered a toast, "Fuck the war!"

In telling the Tulane audience that the Vietnam War was over for America, Ford was accepting reality. Within days, the Communist forces were swarming southward in their final conquest of Vietnam. As the end drew near, Kissinger commented to me, "Why don't these people die fast? The worst thing that could happen would be for them to linger on."

But linger on they did, for another month. During that month, the United States evacuated thousands of South Vietnamese refugees, including many who had worked for or cooperated with the U.S. government.

If the United States had not evacuated them, they would have been killed or imprisoned by the North Vietnamese victors. Nevertheless, I was barraged daily at my White House briefing by reporters demanding to know by what authority President Ford had ordered the evacuation of Vietnamese citizens, since Congress had cut off all funding for any further American involvement in Indochina.

"Does he feel he broke the law?" one reporter demanded. At the same time that I was being barraged by such hostile questions from reporters for networks, wire services, newspapers, and magazines, demanding to know what authority President Ford had to evacuate Vietnamese civilians, I was being barraged by phone calls from executives of those same networks, wire services, newspapers, and magazines begging me to help evacuate their Vietnamese employees.

One lesson I've learned from my years in Washington is that hypocrisy is the leading product of the place.

During this difficult period when I was being pounded by the press, some friends at the Justice Department sent me a blue brocade bullet-proof vest to symbolically repel the barrage of media criticism. I wore it to my next briefing as a joke.

My spirits were raised during those difficult days when Ford unexpectedly said to me during an Oval Office meeting, "You know, you're doing a hell of a job." I demurred. But the president continued that he knew what a hard week it been in the Press Room. He said he was grateful to me for taking the heat.

I replied, "Well, that's what you pay me for."

And Ford said, "Yeah, I know, but you're doing a damned good job, and I really appreciate it."

I don't know what motivated him to say those things that day. But I was grateful. His words bolstered my spirits.

A television news clip from those emotional last days of the Vietnam War still haunts me. It showed a weeping Vietnamese woman holding up her naked, paralyzed baby to the camera, the child's arms and legs flopping uncontrollably. The baby had apparently been wounded by a bomb or grenade blast. The mother begged the cameraman to help the infant. But the cameraman could do nothing for that helpless baby, any more than America could save South Vietnam. I almost cried watching that scene.

Finally, on April 28, 1975, during a meeting in the Cabinet Room on energy and economic issues, Deputy National Security Adviser Brent Scowcroft slipped in and handed Ford a folded sheet of white paper. The president opened and read the note. It said, "Airport in Saigon being rocketed. Two U.S. Marines killed."

The president and his national security advisers assembled at 7:30 p.m. It was dawn in Saigon. Ford ordered C-130 military transport planes to land at Saigon's Tan Son Nhut Airport to evacuate the remaining Americans. Later that night, Scowcroft, looking frail and exhausted, took the elevator to the president's living quarters on the second floor of the White House to report that the planes were unable to land because the runways were blocked by abandoned Vietnamese warplanes and by thousands of panicked South Vietnamese trying to escape.

Graham Martin, the U.S. ambassador in Saigon, requested that "Operation Frequent Wind," the evacuation by helicopter of himself, his staff, and the other Americans remaining in the doomed city, be commenced. Ford agreed. It was 11 p.m. A short time later, the president came to the Situation Room for a briefing. On the way back to his residence, he stopped at the office of his chief of staff Don Rumsfeld, where Rumsfeld, his deputy Dick Cheney, and I were waiting for the next developments.

The four of us stood in silence for a few minutes. No one could think of anything appropriate to say. Everyone was lost in his own thoughts. Finally, the president turned and walked away.

"Sleep well," I called after him. ". . . if you can," I added softly.

And then the long wait began.

The evacuation was expected to last two hours. It actually went on for more than sixteen hours. Ambassador Martin was given authority to determine who should be evacuated. More than 5,500 panicky Vietnamese, half of them children—who were in danger from the Communists if they remained in Saigon—were allowed to clamber aboard the choppers, along with the remaining 1,300 Americans. Thirty-four helicopters ferried the evacuees to U.S. aircraft carriers stationed off the coast in the South China Sea.

While we waited in the White House, a good deal of black humor was exchanged to try to ease the stress and raise our spirits. Kennerly, the irreverent photographer, cracked, "There's good news and bad news. The good news is—the war is over. The bad news is—we lost." Even Kissinger, not known for his sense of humor, joked that he had lost two countries in two weeks—first Cambodia and now Vietnam—one for each of his titles, secretary of state and national security adviser.

"Give me another title and I will lose another country," Kissinger growled in his heavily accented English. Later, in a more reflective mood, Kissinger said, "Vietnam would find more ways of breaking one's heart than anyone could ever have conceived."

I didn't always agree with Kissinger. But I did on that.

At 3 a.m., while the evacuation dragged on, I lay down on the sofa in my West Wing office and slept fitfully.

At 7:30 a.m., Ford returned to the Oval Office. He looked very tired.

Finally, the choppers extracting Americans and endangered South Vietnamese from Saigon began developing mechanical problems from hour after hour of nonstop flights. It was time to end the evacuation. Ford instructed Kissinger to direct Ambassador Martin to make sure all the Americans were out, then terminate the flights and leave on the last helicopter. Word came back from the embassy: Martin, who must have been under enormous emotional stress, would not leave on Kissinger's instructions. He insisted on receiving the evacuation order directly from the president himself. Ford sent the order.

Martin replied by teletype: "I will go out on the last chopper. This is our last communication. I'm destroying the communications equipment."

It was 4:45 p.m. in Washington, dawn in Saigon. The war was over.

From the moment I became White House press secretary, I felt a persistent anxiety that someday I would be the one who would have to stand up in public and announce that the war was over, that the Communists had won. And now that nightmare was coming true.

Kissinger and I went to the auditorium in the old Executive Office Building next door to the White House for a press briefing on the final pullout. It was sparsely attended. Most newspaper and television reporters were back in their offices, writing their stories for the morning newspapers and the evening newscasts, watching the briefing on TV.

I began by announcing, "The evacuation has now been completed."

But it had not been completed.

As Kissinger and I walked out after the briefing, a worried-looking Scowcroft was waiting just offstage to tell us that a contingent of 129 marines was still in the U.S. embassy compound in Saigon. They were a rear guard to protect the helicopter landing zone. Three large choppers were on their way back to extract the marines. So my declaration that the evacuation was "completed" was not true. Kissinger exploded in anger.

"How could this happen!" he shouted. "It's unbelievable! This is the most botched, incompetent operation I've ever seen!"

There ensued a debate among senior presidential aides about whether to publicly correct our misstatement or not. I argued for doing nothing. In a few hours, the marines would be gone and our declaration that the evacuation had been completed would be true. But Rumsfeld countered, "This war has been marked by so many lies and evasions, it's not right to have it end on one last lie. We ought to be perfectly honest and say that at the time we said the evacuation was over, it really wasn't over."

And so that's what we did.

A few days later, Congress wrote one last, sad chapter in the history of America's involvement in Vietnam. The House of Representatives defeated a bill to provide $327 million in humanitarian aid to the Vietnamese refugees. When I showed Ford the Associated Press bulletin reporting the House rejection, he exploded, "God damn it! Those sons of bitches!" I had never heard him curse before.

Ford wanted to issue a strongly worded statement condemning the House rejection of humanitarian aid to the Vietnamese refugees. But it took hours of wrangling among a dozen White House staffers—Rumsfeld, Cheney, me, the speech-writing staff, the NSC staff, and others—before we could agree on the language of the statement. I showed the final draft to Ford for his approval. He was in the White House barbershop getting a haircut. Kennerly, the photographer, was in the barbershop at the time. He commented that we ought to refer to the House members who had voted against refugee aid as "those pricks." I had never heard anyone use that word in the president's presence. Ford laughed. We didn't include that word in the statement.

Ford launched a vigorous lobbying campaign to overcome congressional opposition to providing aid to the Vietnamese refugees. "It was a matter of principle," he told members of Congress. "To ignore the refugees in their hour of need would be to repudiate the values we cherish as a nation of immigrants." As part of his lobbying campaign, Ford made a personal visit to a refugee camp at Fort Chafee, Arkansas.

At one White House meeting during which Ford implored members of Congress to approve funding for the Vietnamese refugees, then-Senator, now-Vice President, Joseph Biden informed the president that he would not vote "to pay any money to get Vietnamese out unless we can't get any Americans out without buying 174,000 Vietnamese [refugees]. In that case, I'm willing to buy the 174,000 Vietnamese."

Congress eventually relented and provided funding to establish refugee camps in the United States for the Vietnamese, despite objections from Biden and others.

Given what I had witnessed and lived through in Vietnam, my deep affection and sympathy for the people of that county, my dread at what surely awaited the South Vietnamese at the hands of their conquerors, I was glad that Ford had overcome opposition like Biden's and had persuaded Congress to appropriate money to help the refugees who had reached America. I was happy to be working for a leader with character who fought to accomplish what he believed in. I thought then, and I still think, that taking in the Vietnamese refugees and providing funds for them to start new lives in America was one of the great examples of Ford's moral leadership.

3

"You Lied to Me!"

Journalism was not my first career choice. Around the end of World War II, when I was about to enter my teens, my mother asked me one day what I wanted to be when I grew up. "A writer," I replied, meaning the kind of writer whose novels I devoured: Ernest Hemingway, Graham Greene, Somerset Maugham, James T. Farrell.

"But what are you going to do to make a living?" my mother countered. And thus she steered me toward becoming the kind of writer who could make a living: a journalist.

Another reason for choosing journalism as a career was that it would take me to interesting and important events in far-off places. Each night back then, just before going to sleep, I tuned into the fifteen-minute radio newscast of Lowell Thomas, who traveled to the most remote corners of the world reporting from the scene of important events.

Listening on my little white Bakelite art deco bedside radio to the sing-songy voice of Lowell Thomas reporting from exotic places, I decided *that* was the kind of journalist I wanted to be when I grew up. What I couldn't know as a child was that traveling to the most remote corners of the earth to cover exciting and memorable stories imposed a price, required a sacrifice—I would be away from home for long periods, and those absences would strain and break relationships with family and friends.

Broadcast journalism suited two contradictory aspects of my personality— my desire for public recognition and my desire for privacy. The audience could see and hear me on television, but I couldn't see or hear them.

After my freshman year at American University, a school with an excellent campus radio station and journalism program—Willard Scott and Eddie Walker were classmates—I became impatient with *studying* how to be a broadcast journalist. I wanted to actually *be* a broadcast journalist. I was hired by a little 250-watt radio station in the small town of Martinsburg, West Virginia. After a year and a half, I moved to a larger station in the Washington suburbs. Then I decided I wanted to write lengthier stories, so I took a job at a weekly newspaper in another Washington suburb.

An editor at United Press International liked an investigative story I wrote for the weekly paper and hired me for the wire service. I learned a valuable journalistic lesson on my very first assignment at the UPI.

I was sent to the Washington Zoo to cover a horrific story—a lion had reached out of his cage, grabbed a little girl who had wandered too close, and killed her. I rushed to the zoo in a cab. But by the time I got there, the victim and most of the eyewitnesses were gone. I interviewed second-hand, third-hand, and fourth-hand sources. I found a pay phone, called the UPI, and began dictating my story.

A gruff-voiced editor named Milt Magruder cut in on the line and growled repeatedly, "How do you know?" He insisted I convince him that every quote and assertion in my story was accurate. It was a journalism lesson I never forgot. Another thing I learned at the UPI was how to curse. Growing up, I never heard my parents utter a swear word. As a result, I never said "shit" or "fuck" or even "damn" until I joined the wire service, where those words seemed to make up half the vocabulary of some of the editors!

I discovered in my years at the UPI that a journalist sometimes has to choose between being a good reporter and being a decent human being. I first confronted that dilemma at about three o'clock one morning when I was working the overnight shift, writing stories for the next day's early afternoon newspapers. The chief news editor in New York sent me a telex message saying that the son of a well-known U.S. senator, Bourke Hickenlooper, had been killed in a plane crash. The editor instructed me to phone the senator's home and get his reaction to his son's death.

I knew that I probably would be the one who first gave the senator the news that his son was dead. I decided that in this instance I would rather be a decent human than a good reporter. I waited fifteen minutes, then informed the news editor in New York that there was no answer when I called Hickenlooper's home.

At the UPI, I got my first taste of White House coverage. I sometimes was dispatched to assist the wire service's legendary but frequently inebriated presidential correspondent Merriman Smith. And on Sunday mornings, to earn overtime pay—my salary was just ninety dollars a week—I covered President Dwight Eisenhower's attendance at church services.

Finally, Russ Tornabene, the NBC News bureau chief in Washington, hired me for the network after I took a class in radio-TV news writing that he was teaching in the evenings at American University. My twelve years at NBC News were the best of times in my professional life. If there was a big news story anywhere in the world, NBC often sent me to cover it.

In October 1962 the United States and the Soviet Union were in a confrontation—the Cuban Missile Crisis—that threatened to escalate into nuclear war. The confrontation began when American spy planes discovered that Russia had installed nuclear missiles in Fidel Castro's Cuba, aimed at the United States, less than one hundred miles away. President Kennedy mobilized U.S. military forces and established a naval blockade to stop and inspect all ships on their way to Cuba.

Moscow backed down and agreed to remove the missiles. To ensure that the Soviet Union kept its promise, Kennedy demanded that it openly display the missiles on the decks of the Russian ships removing them from Cuba. He ordered America Air Force planes to fly low over the ships to confirm the presence of the missiles. NBC assigned me and a camera crew to go along on one of the Air Force inspection flights. We took off early one morning from Andrews Air Force Base outside Washington, flew south to the waters off Cuba, and soon spotted one of the freighters.

The pilot steered the plane downward until we were only a few hundred feet above the water so that intelligence officers aboard could confirm the presence of the missiles. The pilot invited me and my camera crew to come forward so we could film the Russian ships through the broad windows in the cockpit. The cockpit was suffocatingly hot from the bright sun above and all the people packed into the small space. The plane was going round and round in tight circles above the Russian ship, one wing high, one wing low. I was feeling more and more dizzy, more and more nauseated. And, to my extreme embarrassment, I threw up.

If my years at NBC News were the best times in my professional life, they were some of the worst times in my personal life. I was married in those days to a second cousin, Sandra Frey. Sandy and I had met and fallen in love as teenagers, when her family came from their home in Chicago to visit my parents and sightsee in Washington. I was an immature twenty-year-old when we married. We had a daughter, Caren, and, several years later, a son, Stephen. I was not a faithful husband. I cheated on my wife at every opportunity. I seemed driven to get every woman I met into bed. Perhaps I pursued other women because neither by instruction nor example did my parents teach me the joys of a close and loving relationship or the need for faithfulness in marriage. Or perhaps my infidelity was part of my never-ending effort to prove to myself that I was man, not a "sissy," not a mama's boy.

In 1963, when my son Stephen was five years old, my wife and I noticed he was having trouble walking. Doctors discovered he had a tumor at the top of his spinal cord, perhaps caused by his head snapping back when my car was rear-ended by another vehicle some months earlier. My son was operated on, and the doctors told us that they had successfully removed the entire tumor. I assured Steve that he had been cured, that he would be fine now. But, as we learned later, the doctors had not been able to successfully remove the entire tumor. They told us they had in order to give us hope, because they didn't think a very young couple could handle the terrible truth.

In a few months, our son's tumor recurred. A second operation was not possible. He began to drift in and out of consciousness. One night, as I stood helplessly beside his bed at Children's Hospital in Washington, Steve mumbled, "You lied to me!" Shortly afterward, he stopped breathing. A nurse began to press on his chest, trying to revive him. I waved her away. I knew it was no use. I went to the window in the hospital room, put my head down, and cried. My wife came to me and said, "You can't do that now. You have to be strong."

And I stopped crying. But I believe that episode was one reason why, for so many years afterward, I had trouble showing or feeling emotion.

The tragedy of my son's death did not stop my philandering. I was too young, too immature, and too devastated by my son's death to be able to console my wife. Night after night, as she wept beside me in bed, I pretended to be asleep. Not long after my son died, my wife became fed up with my infidelities. She hired a detective, who secretly took pictures of me slipping into the home of a woman I was having an affair with, a colleague at NBC News. With that evidence, my wife obtained a quick divorce on grounds of adultery and moved back to her family home in Illinois with our daughter Caren.

My wife had our son Steve's coffin dug up and reburied in Chicago. I've only visited his grave once. I could not handle the reminder of what an awful person I had been during that period. All these years later, I still feel the pain of those losses and the shame of my conduct. For decades after my son's death and my wife's departure, I had periodic dreams in which he was still alive and I was begging her to come back. I still weep when I think of Steve.

My son died on October 21, 1963. Thirty-three days later, President John F. Kennedy was assassinated.

The next few days were a blur of nonstop news coverage: the return of Kennedy's body from Dallas to Andrews Air Force base; Vice President Lyndon Johnson's ascension to the presidency; Kennedy's funeral with the heart-rending scenes of the widow, Jacqueline, and their two children; the killing of Kennedy's assassin Lee Harvey Oswald by Jack Ruby; and finally, after the funeral, the retreat of the Kennedy family to its compound in Hyannis Port, Massachusetts, to mourn.

I was sent by NBC News to Hyannis Port to cover the Kennedy family in its grief. The only one who emerged from the compound was the slain president's mother, Rose. I and a handful of other reporters followed her to Catholic Mass every morning. She never spoke to us, and we were too respectful to shout questions at her. Today's journalists, I think, would have shouted questions at her.

Vice President Lyndon Johnson ascended to the presidency. Sander Vanocur, the NBC News White House correspondent, was a personal friend of the Kennedy family. After JFK was assassinated, Vanocur had no stomach to cover a Johnson White House. I had filled in for Vanocur on weekends and assisted him at other times, and now I was promoted to replace him as NBC News White House correspondent.

4

Weekends in Austin

Lyndon Johnson had many admirable traits, and some not so admirable. One of his traits that affected me and other reporters covering the White House was his desire to keep his travel plans a secret until the last minute.

Johnson generally would fly to his ranch in Johnson City, Texas, for a long weekend about once a month. But he would never reveal in advance which weekend he was going to the ranch. So, every Friday morning, I and the other correspondents covering LBJ had to come to the White House with our suitcases packed for the weekend.

At about 4 p.m., somebody on press secretary George Reedy's staff would announce over the loudspeaker in the Press Room either that the press bus was leaving the White House in fifteen minutes for Andrews Air Force Base, where Air Force One and a chartered plane for reporters would take off for Texas, or that the president was staying in Washington for the weekend and no more news was expected until Monday morning.

On Texas weekends, the press contingent usually only saw Johnson on Sunday mornings, when we would drive to Johnson City to attend church services with the president in case he was in a talkative mood or his pastor said something newsworthy in the sermon. Because of his compulsion to keep his plans secret, LBJ would not even let reporters know in advance which church he was attending. We had to park outside the ranch and follow his motorcade.

Johnson's weekends in Texas were generally news-free. So I and the other reporters spent our time enjoying the pleasures of the Texas state capital, a wonderful city that blended four different cultures—the political, literary, musical, and culinary. I especially enjoyed the culinary. My journalistic colleagues introduced me to Tex-Mex food at El Rancho #1 and Mi Casa Es Su Casa. I was also introduced to Coors beer, a Denver brew not sold on the East Coast in those days. White House reporters—and White House staff members—hauled cases of Coors back to Washington in the cargo hold of Air Force One.

The trips to Texas sometimes brought out Johnson's poor-southern-boy streak of liking to humiliate people. In a celebration at the ranch the day after his landslide victory in the 1964 presidential election, LBJ tied a red cowboy bandanna around the neck of his vice-presidential running mate, Senator Hubert Humphrey of Minnesota, and boosted Humphrey onto the back of a horse. Humphrey—a sophisticated former college professor and doctoral candidate—looked very uncomfortable.

LBJ also had an eye for the ladies. Once, on a weekend trip to the ranch, he invited four women reporters to join him in his Lincoln convertible for a tour of the surrounding Texas Hill Country. With Johnson at the wheel, a paper cup of Pearl Beer in his hand, the Lincoln was clocked at ninety miles per hour.

Yet, for all his roughneck traits—and his dominating, larger-than-life public persona—LBJ privately was haunted by personal insecurities and by doubts about the ability of American troops to prevent the Communists from taking over South Vietnam. In audiotapes of LBJ's phone conversations, secretly recorded by the president and made public long after his death, the macho Johnson can be heard confiding to Senator Richard B. Russell, chairman of the Senate Armed Services Committee, his deep doubts about becoming involved militarily in Vietnam. Johnson told Russell he didn't see how the United States could win in Vietnam. But, he concluded reluctantly, he needed to act tough.

On another tape, Johnson implores his wife, Lady Bird, to come down from the White House residence to stand beside him at a ceremony in the Rose Garden. She begs off because she has a dentist appointment. He pleads with her, even if she can stay only a few minutes, because he needs her reassuring presence.

Normally Johnson liked to keep his thoughts and actions secret from the press and public. But on a few occasions he was shockingly open about normally private matters. The prime example of that was the famous photo of Johnson lifting up his shirt and jacket to show the press the large and ugly scar from his 1965 gallbladder operation.

On the weekends that Johnson did not go to his Texas ranch, he fre-

quently invited reporters and news photographers to join him for peram-
bulating news conferences around and around the circular driveway on
the South Lawn of the White House, sometimes covering four miles.
From firsthand experience, I can say it was not easy trotting to keep up
with the long-legged Texan while straining to hear him, scribbling notes,
and shouting questions.

Johnson bristled at what he considered unfairly critical press coverage—
including mine. In a farewell speech at the National Press Club three days
before the end of his presidency in 1969, LBJ acknowledged that he had
uttered "a few oaths" directed at reporters during his time in the White
House. And he declared, "I would be less than candid if I failed to say that
I am troubled by the difficulties of communicating with and through the
press." Once, just after I had reported some development in the escalating
American intervention in Vietnam, I encountered the president at a White
House event. "Well, look here, it's Ron Nessen," he drawled sarcastically.
"While I was taking a nap, he done gone and started a *war*."

And just as suddenly, the thoughtful, sympathetic Johnson could
emerge. Shortly after I was wounded while covering the war in Vietnam,
I received a letter from the president. "I was very sorry to learn today that
you had been wounded but I was pleased that you are recovering," LBJ
wrote. "I wanted you to know that you have my every good wish for a
speedy recovery. I am sure that you will soon be back doing your usual
good job for NBC News."

Johnson was nominated for a full term as president at the 1964 Democratic convention, held in Atlantic City, but as usual he kept his political
plans secret as long as possible. In fact, for a time, his insecurities and
self-doubts made him uncertain about whether he should run for president. He went so far as to draft a statement declaring, "The times require
leadership . . . and a voice that men of all parties, sections, and color will
follow. I have learned after trying very hard that I am not that voice or that
leader." Lady Bird, LBJ's friends, and White House aides like Bill Moyers
eventually talked Johnson into running in 1964.

In the period leading up to that year's Democratic convention, one of
the topics I and other reporters asked Johnson about on those perambulat-
ing Saturday South Lawn news conferences was his choice for a vice-
presidential running mate. Attorney General Robert Kennedy and his sup-

porters put pressure on Johnson to name Kennedy as his VP candidate. But there was bad blood between the two men, dating back to 1960 when Robert Kennedy had tried to talk his brother John out of choosing LBJ for his running mate. Johnson, the master politician, deftly quashed the Kennedy-for-VP movement by announcing that no member of his Cabinet would be considered for the VP nomination.

LBJ kept his selection of Senator Hubert Humphrey as his running mate a secret until the last minute, not just from the press and the public, but from his own staff. Johnson encouraged speculation that he was also considering Senators Eugene McCarthy of Minnesota and Thomas Dodd of Connecticut, as well as Humphrey. The president went so far as to arrange for Dodd and Humphrey to fly together to Atlantic City to prolong the uncertainty about his choice.

Conservative senator Barry Goldwater of Arizona soundly defeated his moderate GOP opponent, New York governor Nelson Rockefeller, to win the 1964 Republican nomination at that party's convention at the Cow Palace arena in San Francisco, with William E. Miller, a conservative congressman from upstate New York, as his running mate. Goldwater electrified the convention delegates when he proclaimed in his acceptance speech, "Extremism in the defense of liberty is no vice. And . . . moderation in the pursuit of justice is no virtue."

I was designated a "floor reporter" at the 1964 presidential nominating conventions, my first experience covering these quadrennial political events. I was thirty years old. As a floor reporter, I carried a portable transmitter strapped to my back, headphones on my ears, and a microphone in my hand. I roamed the convention floor, looking for news, interviewing delegates, chasing rumors, and trying to persuade the anchormen—David Brinkley, Chet Huntley, and John Chancellor—to put me on the air.

My fellow young and ambitious floor reporters—Dick Valeriani, Chuck Quinn, Peter Hackes, Bob Goralski, Herb Kaplow, and others—were fighting equally hard for airtime. Even in those early years at NBC, I had the reputation for aggressive—or overly aggressive—reporting. At one point during the Democratic convention, when I saw a CBS reporter rushing a delegate into that network's convention studios, presumably to make some newsworthy announcement, I followed them with *my* NBC microphone. A couple of CBS security guards picked me up and threw me out.

After the conventions, NBC News assigned me to cover LBJ's presidential campaign, while another young correspondent, Robert (or "Robin," as he was called then) MacNeil, covered the Goldwater campaign. It was an ironic pairing, since MacNeil and I were both dating the same woman! He later married her.

Those were the days before communications satellites, cellular phones, digital cameras, or the Internet. I filed my radio stories over a pay phone, if I could find one. (And I always had to carry a pocketful of dimes and quarters to feed the coin slots in the phone!) TV stories were shot on sixteen-millimeter film. About three o'clock each afternoon, my cameraman would bundle up the film we had shot so far that day, and I would carry it to a chartered plane, which would fly me to the nearest big city with an NBC-affiliated station.

The film would be processed—or "run through the soup," as we called it—and edited. I would write my script, and if everything worked well, we would transmit the story via leased transmission lines to NBC News in New York, hopefully in time for the Huntley-Brinkley newscast at 6:30 p.m. Then I would write and record a second version of the story for the next morning's *Today* show, get back on the chartered plane, and catch up with the presidential campaign in whatever city it was spending the night.

In the middle of the campaign, NBC News switched assignments for three weeks—sending me to report on Goldwater, and MacNeil to cover LBJ. The idea was to improve our coverage by giving us each an insight into the other campaign, and to prevent us from becoming unwittingly enamored of our assigned candidate and his staff.

Surprisingly, I found I liked covering the Goldwater campaign better than I liked covering the Johnson campaign. Goldwater and his staff knew that the ultraconservative candidate had almost no chance of winning against a sitting president, so they were relaxed and much more fun to be around. One weekend during my stint covering Goldwater, the Republican candidate took a break from campaigning to return to his hometown of Phoenix, Arizona, where he presented his collection of hundreds of Hopi Indian kachina dolls to the Museum of Western Art. I told Goldwater that the speech he gave at the presentation ceremony was the best speech I had ever heard him deliver. "I wish that's all I had to talk about," the candidate replied. I believed him.

[23]

While LBJ traveled the country aboard Air Force One, where meals were served and other services were provided by navy stewards, Goldwater, his staff, and his press contingent traveled aboard a chartered airliner, served by attractive stewardesses. Given my proclivities, I flirted with and even dated one of the stewardesses during my three weeks covering the GOP candidate.

Goldwater often used colorful—and politically harmful—language in his speeches and his interviews. He once said the United States would be better off if the eastern seaboard was sawed off and allowed to float out to sea. He suggested making Social Security voluntary and proposed selling the Tennessee Valley Authority. And he once joked that the United States should "lob" a nuclear bomb "into the men's room of the Kremlin." Yes, covering Goldwater could be a treasure trove for a reporter.

One of Goldwater's campaign slogans was, "In your heart you know he's right." Johnson's supporters parodied this with campaign buttons reading, "In your guts you know he's nuts." Later I covered the Richard Nixon and George Wallace presidential campaigns in 1968, and the Democratic vice-presidential campaign of Sargent Shriver in 1972. But none was as much fun as the Goldwater run or as exhausting as the LBJ campaign.

Lyndon Johnson won that 1964 election in a landslide. And I was given an interesting and unorthodox assignment for his inauguration on January 20, 1965. NBC News had an automobile modified with a platform welded to the roof to hold a TV camera, cameraman, microwave dish, and technician for transmitting pictures while driving alongside LBJ's inaugural parade. And a seat and TV monitor were welded to the front fender, where I sat and delivered a running commentary. My most lasting memory of that assignment? It was cold!

In 1967 I was part of the press corps that accompanied Johnson when he flew to Australia to attend the funeral of that country's prime minister, Harold Holt, who had drowned while swimming in the ocean. On the way home LBJ made an unannounced stop at the American military base at Cam Ranh Bay in Vietnam. The visit came at a time when Johnson was sending more and more American forces to Vietnam, little progress was being made on the battlefield, and opposition to the war was growing in the United States. "This Christmas—like many Christmases—comes at a time of great testing for our nation," LBJ told the troops. "This time it is a test of will, whether we have the vision and the steady hand to see us through a grave challenge to our freedom and our liberty. You have met the test. There is no doubt about it."

From Vietnam the president flew to Rome, where he met with Pope Paul VI for more than an hour. The pontiff expressed hope that negotiations would bring peace to Vietnam. Johnson asked the pope for his help in ending the war.

Lyndon Johnson's reputation in history has been shaped primarily by his role in leading the nation deeper into the unpopular and ultimately unsuccessful Vietnam War. He no doubt would have preferred to be judged by his domestic policy milestones, such as the War on Poverty; Head Start; the Elementary and Secondary Education Act; Medicare; space exploration; and civil rights legislation that prohibited discrimination against African Americans in employment, the use of public facilities, voting, and housing.

5

"We Shall Overcome"

I had been at NBC News only a few months when I was sent to Birmingham, Alabama, to cover my first civil rights story. Four African American girls, attending Sunday school, had been killed when someone set off nineteen sticks of dynamite at the Sixteenth Street Baptist Church. I and my camera crew arrived in Birmingham in time to cover the funeral, addressed by Martin Luther King Jr. and other civil rights leaders.

The northern newspaper and broadcast correspondents who rushed to Birmingham to cover the bombing and its aftermath huddled together self-protectively—mostly staying at the same motels, eating together in the same restaurants—because we were despised by many local residents almost as much as African Americans were. One night I and a few other reporters covering the Birmingham story went out to dinner at a well-known local restaurant—a racially segregated restaurant, of course. Our group included Wallace Terry, an African American reporter for *Time* magazine. We didn't know what reaction our group would get at the restaurant. In fact, we were treated with excessive politeness and attentive service. Sometimes southern hospitality trumped southern racism.

On June 21, 1964—during what was called "Freedom Summer"—three young men disappeared while working to promote voting rights for African Americans in Mississippi. The men were James Cheney, a twenty-one-year-old black civil rights advocate from Meridian, Mississippi; Andrew Goodman, a twenty-year-old white student from New York; and Michael Schwerner, a twenty-four-year old white organizer for the Congress of Racial Equality (CORE).

Outrage over their disappearance persuaded Congress to give final approval to President Johnson's civil rights legislation. The president signed the bill into law on July 2, 1964.

Thirty-two days later, the bodies of the three civil rights workers were found buried under fifteen feet of dirt in an earthen dam near Philadelphia, Mississippi. NBC News dispatched me to cover the story. The discovery of the bodies of Cheney, Goodman, and Schwerner coincided with the annual Neshoba County Fair in Philadelphia, that town's big communal event of the year. Many of Philadelphia's residents spend the week of the fair living in cottages they had built on the fairgrounds.

On my first afternoon in Philadelphia, I was standing outside the fairgrounds filming a story for the next morning's *Today* show when a burly man came up to me and clamped a heavy hand on my shoulder. *Uh-oh*, I thought. *We're about to be run out of town. Or worse.* After all, I was a moderately liberal white Jewish guy wearing a necktie and jacket, holding a microphone and talking into a TV camera. I stood out from the blue-jeaned, plaid-shirted, work-booted, southern-accented crowd attending the Neshoba County Fair, to say the least. But the burly man politely suggested that we should feel free to film inside the fairgrounds. He invited me and my crew to have lunch at his cottage. He said we could use his telephone if we needed to call our office. And that was the reception I and my crew received from many Philadelphia residents.

As I reported later on Frank Blair's Sunday *Today* show: "Philadelphia, Mississippi, has an inferiority complex. The townspeople feel that, thanks to biased reporting, the world looks on them as a whole community of bigoted killers. . . . So, this past week, Philadelphia conducted a kind of informal public relations campaign to change its image . . . the strategy was nothing more than good old southern hospitality. . . . The people of Philadelphia seemed to be saying, 'See how nice we are. We're not killers. Any town that can give a fair as open-hearted as this can't be so bad.'"

Maybe so. But my camera crew was afraid to stay overnight in Philadelphia. And, indeed, there were plenty of Mississippians and other southerners who hated northern journalists for coming to their region and telling the nation and the world about the racial prejudice and discrimination in the region. After each day's coverage, my camera crew insisted on driving forty miles along a dark country road to a motel in Meridian. I thought we were in greater danger from anti-media Mississippians on that dark road than we would have been at the Holiday Inn in Philadelphia, where a contingent of FBI agents was ensconced.

The civil rights revolution in the South in the 1960s was one of the great social, cultural, and political milestones of my generation, or, indeed, of American history. That was one reason why I was so eager to cover the story. The other reason was more personal. I was essentially raised by a woman who was referred to in those days as "a live-in colored girl"—my family's maid, Victoria, half black, half Cherokee Indian, from North Carolina.

When I was a child, my mother was often ill or recovering from one of her frequent operations. And when she was well, she spent much of her time helping in my father's store. Victoria was in reality my surrogate mother. I grew up in Washington, D.C., when the city and suburbs were still divided into all-white neighborhoods and all-black neighborhoods. I went to segregated schools through high school, before the Supreme Court declared them unconstitutional. My parents had no black friends, and I had no black playmates.

Although my parents had often encountered discrimination and anti-Semitism, they had their own prejudices against African Americans. They routinely referred to Victoria and other blacks as *schvartzas*—roughly the Yiddish equivalent of the "N" word. Even though I grew up in that atmosphere, I have never said *"schvartza,"* I have never used the "N" word. Perhaps, having been cursed as a "kike" on the school playground, I was sensitive to the pain that can be caused by racial and ethnic slurs. Or maybe it was because I was raised by Victoria.

As a sheltered little Jewish boy, I found Victoria exotic, mysterious. Her high cheekbones. Her tan skin. Her husky, softly accented voice. The smells of her Pond's cold cream, of her cheap pomade, of her thick black hair as she singed it around a hot curling iron. One day my parents discovered that Victoria had let a man spend the night in her basement room. They fired her.

Twenty years later, when I covered the efforts by African Americans in the South to attend all-white schools, to eat at all-white lunch counters, to vote, to march for their rights, I often thought about "our live-in colored girl." I hoped I might see her again. But I never did. And after all this time, I still think about Victoria.

The last civil rights story I covered before being sent to Vietnam was the Selma-to-Montgomery march in Alabama in March of 1965.

Early in 1965, more than five hundred civil rights advocates set out from

Selma to walk along U.S. Highway 80 to the state capital fifty-four miles away. The march was to protest the denial of voting rights to most black residents in the area, and the beating and shooting of a civil rights worker and his family by state troopers the month before.

The area was home to many fiercely antiblack members of the Ku Klux Klan and the White Citizens Council. Alabama's segregationist governor, George Wallace, said the march was a threat to public safety and declared that he would do whatever was needed to stop it.

The marchers had only gone six blocks when they encountered a contingent of state troopers and Dallas County police, some on horseback, at the Edmund Pettus Bridge spanning the Alabama River. The troopers and police attacked and dispersed the marchers with clubs and bullwhips and sprayed them with tear gas. The day of the failed march became known as "Bloody Sunday."

Two weeks later, Martin Luther King Jr. and other civil rights leaders, armed with a court order from a federal district court judge authorizing the march, set out from Selma at the head of a much larger group of protesters—3,200 when they began, 25,000 by the time they reached Montgomery five days later. The march attracted a glittering array of show business names, who entertained the marchers at a rally the night they reached Montgomery. The stars included Harry Belafonte; Joan Baez; Tony Bennett; Frankie Laine; Peter, Paul, and Mary; Sammy Davis Jr.; and Nina Simone. Simone angrily snarled her famous civil rights protest song, "Mississippi God Damn."

The climax of the march was a speech by King on the steps of the State House in Montgomery. It became known as King's "How Long?" speech. "How long will justice be crucified and truth bear it?" King asked in his soaring voice. "I come to say to you this afternoon, however difficult the moment, however frustrating the hour, it will not be long because 'truth crushed to earth will rise again.'" The crowd cheered. NBC canceled its regular programming for more than one hour to carry King's oration live. I and two network colleagues, Richard Valeriani and Chuck Quinn, reported from the scene.

Early in the morning after King's historic speech, I awoke at my motel in Montgomery and headed for the airport in a cab. The march was over. I was on my way to catch a flight back to my home base in Washington.

The cabdriver asked me if I had heard about the woman who had been killed early that morning. I hadn't. She was Viola Liuzzo, a white Detroit housewife and medical lab technician, mother of five, who had come to Alabama to support the civil rights marchers. In the predawn darkness the morning after King's speech, Liuzzo was driving along a deserted road toward Selma. A car pulled alongside. Two white men in the car—Ku Klux Klan members—shot her to death.

Covering these stories, I had empathy for the plight of African Americans fighting racial discrimination in the South because I had personally encountered anti-Semitic discrimination. Until I was about ten years old, my family were the only Jews living in a working-class Irish and Italian neighborhood along the Anacostia River in Washington. I attended Kingman Elementary School, a square redbrick building about a half mile from my house. My schoolmates derided me as a "kike." I was regularly beaten up on the playground at recess and after school by gentile students, and my mother frequently had to drive me home after class to save me from a gauntlet of jeering boys. She arranged for me to eat lunch each day with a Jewish couple who ran a tiny delicatessen near my school so I wouldn't have to confront physical and psychological hazing in the school cafeteria.

Later, my family moved to a nicer house in a more upscale neighborhood of Washington called Shepherd Park. The couple they bought the house from were moving away because they thought too many Jews were moving into the neighborhood.

So I brought to my coverage of the racial integration stories in the early 1960s a personal knowledge of what it felt like to be the target of irrational prejudice.

Still, I tried to keep my personal feelings out of my coverage and to limit my scripts to the who, what, when, where, and how of each story.

Perhaps my just-the-facts approach was what an editorial writer for the Jackson, Mississippi, *Daily News* had in mind when he published this appraisal of an interview I did on the *Today* show with the attorney general of Mississippi about the state's civil rights clashes: "It is the first time I have ever witnessed a national network 'newsman' interviewing a southern conservative on the race issue without nasty digs, snide remarks, caustic and belligerent questions, and editorial contributions of his own philosophy. Mr. Nessen conducted the interview with intelligence . . . [and] fairness."

6

A Change of Plans

I wasn't supposed to be reporting for NBC News from Vietnam in 1965. After three years in the network's Washington bureau, I was reassigned to the London office. London in the '60s! The Beatles! Carnaby Street! Miniskirts! Having been divorced by my first wife, Sandy, I was a bachelor again. I looked forward to living, working—and playing—in my new swinging home base. In preparation for the assignment, I traveled to NBC headquarters at Rockefeller Center in New York City for a final round of meetings with the network's news executives.

"How would you like to go to London the long way?" Julian Goodman, vice president of NBC News, asked me when I stopped at his office. "What do you mean 'the long way'?" I asked. Goodman explained that two NBC News correspondents assigned to the Saigon bureau were overdue for vacations, and another correspondent's wife was about to give birth in Hong Kong, leaving the bureau seriously short-staffed just as the big American troop buildup was beginning. Goodman asked me to fill in at the Saigon bureau for two months, and then I could move on to my assignment in London.

America was becoming more and more deeply involved in the Vietnam War. It was growing into the biggest news story in the world. TV reports from the war dominated the *Huntley-Brinkley Report*, the network's premier evening news program. If I accepted the assignment to Saigon for two months, I would get a lot of airtime. *Of course* I wanted to make a detour to Vietnam on my way to London! Without hesitation, I told Goodman I would accept the temporary assignment.

Before departing for the war, I wanted to spend some time with my daughter Caren, who was now ten. I had hardly seen her in the years since my divorce from her mother, and I didn't know when I would have an opportunity to see her again. My ex-wife had made it difficult for me to spend time with Caren since our divorce. I had to go to court to obtain a judge's order requiring her to allow visits. But surprisingly Sandy agreed to let me to take Caren on a vacation in Hawaii before I flew to Vietnam. I picked up Caren at the Chicago airport, flew first to Los Angeles, where I took her to Disneyland, and then on to Hawaii for a week. Our relationship seemed distant and strained. During the first few days we were both slightly ill, probably from the stress of the situation. Not used to being with my daughter on a daily basis, I alternated between harshness— spanking her when she misbehaved—and indulgence—inundating her with gifts and attention to assuage my guilt.

At the end of the vacation, I returned Caren to Chicago. Sandy was at the airport to pick her up. The scene was uncomfortable. It made me feel adrift, unattached. My mind churned with mixed feelings, with unspoken emotions, for which there was no resolution. I knew I would not see my daughter again for a long time. I was going to a dangerous place where I had no friends. I literally had no home. Later, in a letter to my psychiatrist, I recalled my feelings that last night: "I was leaving the little worrisome, confusing problems behind and starting with a fresh slate. I was completely free, had confidence in myself." I was closing one chapter in my life and beginning another. I did so with regret and apprehension, but also with excitement and anticipation.

The next morning I took off for Vietnam.

A few days after I arrived in Saigon, I was awakened in my room at the Caravelle Hotel at dawn by a call from one of the NBC cameramen. He told me to get dressed quickly and meet him in the lobby. Three blocks away, in a public park, the South Vietnamese government was about to execute a group of prisoners for buying and selling on the black market. We needed to cover the execution, the cameraman advised.

When we reached the park, we found five Vietnamese black marketers blindfolded and bound to posts, facing a firing squad of soldiers. An officer yelled the Vietnamese equivalent of "Ready. Aim . . ."

I unconsciously raised my right hand and covered my eyes. Again, as with my decision at the UPI not to phone Senator Hickenlooper and inform him of his son's death, I was letting my instincts as a human being overcome my instincts as a journalist. I almost immediately realized that I had to witness the execution in the park if I was going to report on it. I dropped my hand from my eyes just as the officer yelled "Fire!" The South Vietnamese soldiers pulled the triggers on their rifles, unleashing a fusillade of bullets at the prisoners.

The black marketers slumped against their bonds, dead. I scribbled notes in my reporter's pad.

It was my introduction to the horrors of war. I would witness many, greater horrors over the next eight years.

During my first few days in Vietnam, I learned that almost *everything* was available at the many black market outlets openly set up by Vietnamese entrepreneurs on sidewalks all over the city: food, cigarettes, various items pilfered or resold from the U.S. military's PX stores, whiskey, clothes, women. Newly arrived, I was taken by a Vietnamese employee of the NBC News bureau to a black market dealer to buy my combat fatigues—khaki shirts, pants, jackets, and caps, plus belts and boots—to wear while covering the war. Initially, the black market dealer didn't have any pants in my size. He told me to come back the next day. I did, and he had pants in my size, apparently stolen from the PX specifically for me.

Even money was for sale on the black market. Using the official exchange rate in those days, you could buy 73 Vietnamese piastres for one U.S. dollar. But on the black market, you could buy 148 piastres, or more, for a dollar. The Vietnamese had more faith in the value of the American greenback than they did in the value of their own country's currency. Of course, NBC News reimbursed us for our expenses at the *official* exchange rate, meaning we were repaid twice as much as we actually spent!

During those first days in Saigon, I was deluged with a torrent of new experiences, sights, sounds, and smells. Especially smells—garbage, human excrement, sweat, dead bodies, and the omnipresent pungent aroma of *nuoc mam*, fermented fish sauce, from street vendors. When I first arrived in Vietnam, it had been only eleven years since French colonial rule in Indochina ended with the successful siege of the French military base at Dien Bien Phu by Ho Chi Minh's Communist Vietminh guerrillas. The French influence was still strong. Many educated Vietnamese spoke French and sent their children to Paris to be schooled.

There were many good French restaurants in Saigon in 1965, such as La Cigale, which advertised its "Parisian atmosphere." I had breakfast most mornings at a French café, Givral, which would not have seemed out of place in Marseille. The French tradition of *sieste*—an afternoon nap after lunch—was still observed when I first arrived. Many stores and offices were closed from noon to three because of *sieste*. On my first New Year's Eve in Vietnam, I attended a black-tie dinner party at the Saigon apartment of a French correspondent.

I also dined with friends in the Chinese section of Saigon, called Cholon. We often ate at an upscale restaurant and nightclub called the Arc-en-Ciel— the Rainbow—dining on huge platters of cracked crabs cooked in a delicate batter, washed down with fine wine. While enjoying a delicious meal in an upscale restaurant, it was sometimes difficult to remember there was a war on.

But other times, it was all too easy. Once, while I was dining in Cholon with a group of NBC colleagues, the Vietcong set off an explosion in the street close to the restaurant. I rushed to the scene. Ten Vietnamese were killed, forty were wounded. Many of the dead and wounded were children. Bikes and schoolbooks were strewn about. There were pools of blood and chunks of human brains in the street. Another day I was awakened by a Communist bomb going off around the corner from the Caravelle Hotel at dawn.

In those days, the streets were filled with ancient French automobiles; pint-size taxis; military jeeps; motor scooters carrying entire families of mother, father, and several children; and beautiful young Vietnamese woman pedaling their bicycles, wearing white or black gloves, dressed in silky *ao dais*—the ankle-length, high-collared, slit-sided Vietnamese national dress—their long, shiny, straight black hair reaching to their waist.

Across Saigon's main square from the Caravelle was the colonial-era Continental Hotel, where British writer Graham Greene had composed his great novel *The Quiet American*, which foretold the impact of America's involvement on Vietnam. An outdoor terrace encircled the Continental, a favorite place for French colonials, and later American correspondents and soldiers, to gather for drinks at the cocktail hour, and for prostitutes to troll for customers.

In Saigon in those days, a profusion of prostitutes advertised their wares not just on the Continental Palace terrace but in nightclubs, in bars, in hotels, and on the streets. Pedicab drivers pulled alongside American men on the street and hissed, "You want girl? Number one!" Shortly after I arrived in Vietnam, the NBC News bureau chief, Jack Fern, described Saigon to me as "a supermarket of whores."

Perhaps because of my hypochondriac's fear of disease, I did not patronize Vietnam's whores. And, eventually, I met a decent woman in Saigon whom I dated, fell in love with, and married.

7

The Five O'Clock Follies

Across Tu Do Street from the Continental Hotel was the massive Eden Arcade, a multistory, block-square building housing shops, cafés, and restaurants on the ground floor, and the apartments of many American and French correspondents on the upper floors. The offices where the NBC News correspondents, cameras crews, producers, and Vietnamese support staff worked were on the second floor.

Most of the reporters who arrived in Saigon in the early and mid-1960s to cover the growing U.S. involvement—David Halberstam, Neil Sheehan, Malcolm Browne, Peter Arnett, Michael Herr, Gloria Emerson, George Esper, Joe Galloway, and others—were young, in their twenties to thirties. Many shared the sentiments of the young antiwar protesters back home in the United States. The stories written by these correspondents were often critical of the American effort and of the official U.S. account of how the war was going. Their hostile stories, in turn, fed the antiwar sentiment growing in the United States.

I was one of the few reporters who supported the war and believed the United States could win in Vietnam. At least I did at first. In a 1967 speech, between tours in Vietnam, I declared, "The American buildup has turned the tide. South Vietnam is no longer in danger of being conquered militarily." In another talk, I said, "I am upbeat that South Vietnam will win and be a democratic government."

Why did I hold this contrarian view when most reporters opposed the war and thought America would lose? Maybe it was my tendency—carried from childhood—to look at things differently than my contemporaries, to take a contrary course. Maybe, having come down with the *mal jaune*, I didn't want to contemplate a beautiful people and their beautiful country being conquered. Maybe the South Vietnamese, facing conquest by the totalitarian North Vietnamese, reminded me of my Russian immigrant ancestors who fled Russia and came to America to escape the tsar's oppressive regime.

In one speech after returning from a tour in Vietnam, I told the audience, "I am a 'hawk,' but a reluctant and discouraged 'hawk.'" Still, I said, "If we abandon South Vietnam to the Communists, they will surely massacre thousands or tens of thousands of South Vietnamese: government officials, military men, and others sympathetic to America."

But the more time I spent in Vietnam, the more I was exposed to combat, to death, to the horrors of war, the less certain I was in my hawkish stance. Eventually, I began to question whether LBJ was doing the right thing in pursuing the war. I began to doubt we could win the war. Increasingly, I included scenes of dead U.S. troops in my stories. I did this so American viewers could see the real cost of the war and decide whether they wanted to pay that price to save South Vietnam from Communist conquest.

One reason why I and other reporters turned negative on the war—or at least turned skeptical that the United States could win the war—was that major battles often were fought so close to Saigon that correspondents could witness the combat firsthand, then get back to the city in time to attend the official daily American military briefing, where we usually heard a much more upbeat assessment of the fighting than what we had just witnessed with our own eyes. The daily press briefing was held at 5 p.m. at the MAC-V (Military Assistance Command–Vietnam) headquarters in Saigon. This led the press corps to label the sessions "the Five O'Clock Follies." The military tried—unsuccessfully—to shed that derisive tag by moving the briefing to 4:45 p.m.!

I and other correspondents covering the war believed the authorities greatly exaggerated Communist casualties—what was called the "body count"—in order to convince us and the world that the war was going better than it really was. I once filmed the aftermath of a Communist ambush of a U.S. First Infantry Division unit near Saigon. I watched as the bodies of sixteen enemy soldiers were dumped in a hole and covered up. I saw eight more bodies hauled away in a truck. That night at the Five O'Clock Follies, the official spokesmen claimed U.S. troops had killed six hundred Vietcong in that battle. Another time, the marines claimed to have killed six hundred Vietcong in a battle. An intelligence officer told me privately that the total number of Communist troops in the battle was only two hundred.

Most of the large news bureaus maintained a fleet of cars and drivers to take reporters and cameramen to and from the scenes of nearby battles. Some reporters got around on motor scooters. I once hailed a taxi to take me back to Saigon after covering a battle west of the city. To cover the war elsewhere in the country, I and my camera crew would hitch a ride on a military plane or helicopter or would buy a ticket on an Air Vietnam commercial flight, which continued throughout the war. A trip on an Air Vietnam 727 jetliner wasn't exactly first class or even business class. It was more like peasant class. Some of the rural Vietnamese passengers carried live chickens aboard!

Vietnam was the last war in which the Pentagon let correspondents roam freely on the battlefields. The critical press coverage of the Vietnam War and the ability of correspondents to travel on their own to the scene of American defeats or screw-ups taught the Pentagon a lesson. In every conflict since then, the U.S. military has tightly restricted the access of journalists.

Looking back on my days as a correspondent in Vietnam, I am jealous of one aspect of today's war coverage: reporters can file live reports from the most remote battlefields of Iraq and Afghanistan and Africa using tiny digital cameras, satellite phones, and other modern electronic marvels. In Vietnam, sometimes it was easier to get the story than it was to get the film and radio reports of the story back to the United States. For radio, I trekked to a nondescript apartment building in Saigon after the daily Five O'Clock Follies. On those rare occasions when the elevator was working, we rode up to the unimposing old French PTT studios. When the electricity was out, which was often, we walked up. An elderly, plump Vietnamese woman shouted in French through the old-fashioned microphone, trying to establish a shortwave connection to Paris. On those days when we actually got through, our radio reports were then forwarded from Paris to NBC News in New York via the Atlantic underwater cable.

Getting TV stories on the air was much more complicated. When I first started covering the war, most of the network cameramen used heavy, bulky, old-fashioned Auricon cameras, which were adaptations of the cameras used for decades to shoot the "newsreel" film that was shown in movie theaters. Auricons were perfectly fine for setting up on a tripod to shoot a speech or a news conference. They were definitely not fine for keeping a low profile under fire. Lugging a twenty-five-pound Auricon camera, a seventeen-pound battery, and a twenty-pound backpack was barely manageable for hefty American or European cameramen. It was a burden for diminutive Asian cameramen, especially when slogging through rice paddies, leach-filled swamps, and impenetrable jungle, or crouching in a ditch under fire.

Once we had captured a battle on film, we had to ship the film to the United States for airing. First we had to get the film from the battlefield to Saigon's Tan Son Nhut Airport, usually by hitching a ride aboard a military plane or helicopter. Then we had to persuade an Air Vietnam or Air France or Pan Am flight attendant, or a passenger, to carry the film to Hong Kong, Bangkok, or Tokyo, where an NBC News employee would meet the plane, retrieve the film, and transship it on the next commercial flight to the United States. It normally took at least twenty-four hours between the time the film was shot in Vietnam and the time American audiences could watch it on TV.

But that delay in getting our film on the air was not entirely a bad thing. It gave me time to dig for more information about the battle we had captured on film, to do research, to put new developments in context, to make sure I had all the facts. Then I would write my script, record my narration, and forward that via shortwave or the underwater cable to NBC News in New York to be matched up with the film. Today's correspondents, especially those reporting for all-news twenty-four-hour-a-day cable channels or the Internet, are under pressure to file live reports instantaneously from the most remote places on earth via satellite. They don't have the time to do additional research, put developments in context, or make sure they have all the facts. There's a deadline every minute.

8

Baptism by Fire

After I had been in Vietnam for a couple of weeks, I had my baptism by fire. I flew from Saigon to Da Nang, where the marines operated a press compound in a former motel called the Riverside on the banks of Da Nang Bay off the South China Sea. The major news organizations had their own air-conditioned cabins at the compound. The marines who ran the motel provided a dining hall for dinner and beer, and arranged for a Vietnamese "mama-san" to clean the cabins and do our laundry.

I and my camera crew joined the Eleventh Vietnamese Ranger Battalion as it searched along Route 14 and through villages for guerrillas. The five American advisers attached to the battalion kept urging the Vietnamese commander to get off the road and into the rice paddies and sugarcane fields where the Vietcong were hiding. For about an hour we tramped through farms and towns of straw houses without finding any vc.

Just as it seemed as if we were not going to get any useful action film, the Vietcong suddenly started firing at the South Vietnamese troops—and at me and my camera crew—from three sides: snipers from a dry creek bed on the left, carbine and automatic weapons fire from the front, and mortar shells from the right. It was the first time in my life I had been shot at. Like an idiot, I stood up right in the middle of the attack, holding out my microphone to record the sounds of battle on my portable tape machine. The recorder caught this bit of dialogue between me and an American sergeant advising the South Vietnamese:

Me: What have we got?
Sergeant: About a squad of vc out in front of us.
Me: Are they shooting at us?

Sergeant: Yes, sir, they sure are. Didn't you hear the bullets whizzing over
your head?
Me: No, I didn't.

I quickly jumped into a hole to get out of the line of fire. I wasn't
scared, because I was too inexperienced—or too stupid—to realize what
danger I was in. Eventually the firing subsided. An American radio operator, who had asked me shortly before the vc attack how the Milwaukee
Braves baseball team was doing, had a badly mangled arm, a hole in his
chest, and shrapnel in both legs. A Vietnamese major also was wounded
in both legs. And a Vietnamese soldier had part of his face blown away.

For my second venture into combat, I and my camera crew hooked up
with a unit of the 101st Airborne Division in the Central Highlands of
Vietnam near a town called An Khe. The men of the 101st were among the
toughest, most experienced, most resourceful American troops in Vietnam. I thought to myself: "I'm a fat, out-of-shape, thirty-ish little Jewish
man, and I'm keeping up with the best, toughest soldiers in the world!"
Reaching the 101st bivouac after dark one night, I camped out with them
in an abandoned village. We awoke at 3 a.m., climbed a mountain without
the benefit of a trail, pulling ourselves up from one tree trunk to the next,
pushing through heavy tangles of vines spiked with thorns. The troops
engaged in several firefights with Vietcong guerrillas, killing two, before
ending the sweep at 2 p.m.

Covering the 101st Airborne, I did not have the comforts of an air-
conditioned marine press camp. I didn't take a shower for five days. I didn't
take off my boots for two days. I shared a makeshift latrine with the soldiers, or relieved myself behind a tree. I slept in a tent with a dozen other
men, or on a poncho in a field. I ate C rations. One day the temperature
reached 126 degrees. I thought again of my mother telling my camp counselor not to let me engage in strenuous activities because I was too fragile.

The great Associated Press war photographer Horst Faas taught me
early in my Saigon assignment: "If you're lucky, you'll get ambushed."
Meaning, if you're lucky, you'll be with the unit that sees heavy combat,
because that's what produces the most newsworthy stories and pictures.
By that measurement, I was "lucky" when I hooked up with the First Air
Cavalry Division.

If the 101st Airborne was fighting the Communist guerrillas by adopting guerrilla tactics, the First Air Cavalry was fighting the Communist guerrillas an entirely new way. While the original cavalry had ridden into battle on dozens of horses, the new cavalry rode into battle on dozens of helicopters. I and my camera crew went along on the division's first major battle in Vietnam, "Operation Shiny Bayonet," an attack on North Vietnamese and Vietcong troops in the Ia Drang Valley in the Central Highlands region. Specifically, we went along with the First Battalion of the Seventh Regiment—General Custer's old unit.

Riding in fifty-four helicopters, flying just fifteen or twenty feet off the ground, the troops of the First Air Cav swooped over a mountain range and down into the beautiful, fertile valley. The choppers landed in a field; the troops jumped out and began firing into the surrounding trees. I felt like I was on a landing craft coming ashore at Normandy on D-Day. My camera crew was among the first off the choppers so they could film the action. But I didn't immediately jump off, from fear. The helicopter began to lift. If I didn't jump off immediately, I would be flown back to the base, to safety. When the chopper was about a foot off the ground, I jumped off and ran for cover.

I spent my first Christmas in Vietnam with the First Air Cav, camped out near An Khe. Christmas dinner was C rations—crackers, cheese spread, cold meatballs and baked beans out of a can, and tasteless pound cake, washed down with cans of Coke. Then someone came up with a bottle of booze. I, a few other reporters, my camera crew, and some soldiers sat up half the night getting drunk and musing about the war.

One of the cameramen I frequently worked with was a Vietnamese named Vo Huynh, a muscular, mustachioed man of indeterminate age who looked like one of Genghis Khan's Mongol warriors. Vo Huynh was fearless and had a sixth sense about where to place ourselves to film the best action scenes . . . and when to get out of a place because it was too dangerous. Once, while we were filming in the town square of a village near Da Nang, Vo Huynh said, "Let's go." I wanted to capture a few more scenes on film, so I replied "We'll go in a few minutes." He insisted, "Let's go *now*." Reluctantly, I complied. Minutes later, the square where we had been filming came under Communist attack.

How did Vo Huynh know the attack was imminent? I don't know. But after that, I listened to him whenever he said "Let's go."

In my first ventures into combat, I had survived gunfire from Communist troops on several occasions. But on two occasions, I almost didn't survive gunfire from friendly troops. Once, while returning from a patrol in the Ia Drang Valley, the soldiers I was with accidentally wandered somewhat north of where they were supposed to be. American helicopters flying overhead mistook us for Communist guerrillas and began firing down at us. We tried to hide in the brush while the officers frantically radioed the helicopters that we were *not* enemy soldiers. The choppers swung around and headed back for a second strafing run. Just in time, the radio message got through and the pilots turned away.

Another time, I somehow got ahead of the South Vietnamese soldiers trying to drive Communist forces out of a town. I found myself in a no-man's-land between the two sides. I sought safety in a doorway. The photographer Sean Flynn (actor Errol Flynn's son) was cowering in the same doorway. We peeked out. Someone in the South Vietnamese lead tank spotted us and assumed we were enemy soldiers. The turret of the tank swung around until the barrel of its cannon was pointed directly at our doorway. The tank gunner was about to fire at us. To show we were not enemy soldiers, Flynn frantically waved his camera at the tank crew and shouted *"bao chi, bao chi"*—Vietnamese for "press." I waved my white T-shirt. The tank sat there, its gun pointed at us for what seemed an eternity. Then, convinced we were not Vietcong, the crew rolled past. We were safe behind friendly lines!

Flynn was later captured and killed by Communist insurgents while covering the related war in Cambodia.

The French writer Bernard Fall, who wrote the famous book *Street without Joy*, about the fighting along Highway One, and had befriended me when I first arrived in Vietnam, ironically was killed later on Highway One when he stepped on a Communist land mine. Three of my NBC News colleagues—correspondent Welles Hangen, cameraman Roger Coline, and soundman Yoshihiko Waku—were among the many journalists killed while covering the war. Waku—whom I had worked with often and liked very much—had been scheduled to fly home the next day to Tokyo, where his wife was about to give birth to their child.

Facing and surviving danger on an almost daily basis in Vietnam, both correspondents and troops developed a very dark sense of humor to suppress their fears and preserve their sanity. For instance, a favorite souvenir of American GIs and civilians in Vietnam was a jacket embroidered with the legend "When I die I'm going to Heaven because I've already been in Hell." Another joke described Saigon as a place "where they burn the people and throw the garbage in the streets." Someone posted a sign at Tan Son Nhut Airport reading, "Last one out please turn off the lights."

On rare occasions, even real-life episodes in the war made me laugh. For instance, a Special Forces trooper once told me he had given some K-9 watchdogs to a Vietnamese officer to detect guerrillas trying to sneak up on a guard post. A few weeks later, this trooper ran into the Vietnamese officer and asked him how the dogs were. "Delicious!" was the reply.

In the first days of January 1966, I set out with my camera crew to cover the fighting in a part of Vietnam I had never visited before—the Plain of Reeds, an area of marshes, rice paddies, dikes, and canals south and west of Saigon along the Mekong River near the Cambodian border. The effort to break the hold of Communist forces on the Plain of Reeds, code-named Operation Marauder, was conducted by troops of the 173rd Airborne Brigade, accompanied by South Vietnamese soldiers and troops from Australia and New Zealand. The muddy ground and intersecting waterways hampered the allied offensive. Casualties among American troops and their allies were high. My camera crew and I covered these actions, sharing with the troops the difficulties of operating in the water-soaked topography. I still have, hanging on my office wall, a photograph of me delivering my on-camera wrap-up on an Operation Marauder story while hunkered down behind a dike in several inches of water in a rice paddy.

Throughout my coverage of the Vietnam War, whenever I was about to go into battle, I almost always had fantasies of being hit by a bullet. I wondered what the last instant of my life would be like. I usually was able to suppress these apprehensions. Except once. On that occasion, I declined to join a convoy of marines and reporters heading out of Da Nang on a search for Communist troops. For some reason, I was seized by the conviction that the convoy was going to be ambushed and that I would be killed. I stood on the roadside and watched the convoy drive away. My film crew was sympathetic, and I never let my fears interfere with my coverage again.

When I returned to Saigon from covering my first battles, an NBC News producer who was about to return to the network's New York headquarters after directing war coverage told me he would like to recommend that I remain in the Vietnam bureau for a year instead of going on to my London assignment. Was I willing? I knew instantly that my answer was yes. Part of my motivation was selfish. My stories from Vietnam were frequently featured on the Huntley-Brinkley evening news program and on the *Today* show. One night, I had three separate stories on Huntley-Brinkley.

This high visibility was going to my head. After just a few months, I was changing from a young correspondent with self-doubts about my manliness and ability to function in the conditions of war to an insufferably self-absorbed, egotistical, and opinionated jerk. At one point, Reuven Frank, the legendary NBC News executive, who was a mentor to me and many other young correspondents, sent me a note chastising me for injecting so much personal opinion into a story that it amounted to an editorial. "Self-importance is the deepest and most treacherous of all the traps" for TV correspondents, Reuven wrote.

My newfound self-confidence and addiction to TV exposure also made me more competitive. I jockeyed with other NBC News correspondents to cover the most newsworthy war stories. I was even more competitive and unlikable when trying to outdo rival CBS reporters. Once, after covering a battle, I and my camera crew jumped into a departing helicopter with our film. The pilot asked if any other correspondents needed a ride out. I assured him that none did, even though I knew that Dan Rather and his CBS crew were close by, hoping to hitch a ride out on the chopper. Based on my false assurance, the pilot took off without Rather. CBS filed a formal complaint with MAC-V, and I was reprimanded by the NBC Saigon bureau chief.

Rather and I were part a new generation of youngish reporters who established their reputations covering the war in Vietnam: Morley Safer of CBS (my biggest rival!), Bill Cook of *Newsweek*, Charlie Mohr and Johnny Apple of the *New York Times*, Pat Ferguson of the *Baltimore Sun*, as well as my NBC colleagues Garrick Utley and Dean Brelis.

Explaining my motivation for staying on in Vietnam, I wrote to a friend, "I'm really caught up in the war now. I'm beginning to understand it. I want to tell Americans about it. I'm right in the middle of *the* important chapter of the history of this time."

The other part of my motivation for staying was that covering the Vietnam War provided a justifiable escape from the pain of my shattered marriage, rejection by an estranged daughter, grief over a lost son, and the overprotectiveness of a dominating mother.

But my assignment to Saigon also meant that I had to leave behind a lover in Washington. At the time I departed for Vietnam, I was romantically involved with a colleague at NBC News. She was the woman I had been caught visiting by my then-wife's private detective. And she had wept inconsolably when I left for Saigon. After a couple of weeks, I sent her a long letter, trying to ease her pain. "Absence does make the heart grow fonder," I wrote. "All the other little flirtations have faded away."

Well, not quite.

9

Cindy and the Two Apple Troupe

One night, after I had been in Saigon for about a month, I went up to the ninth-floor bar atop the Caravelle Hotel for a drink. At the bar, it was possible to sip a beer or a martini, munch on good Vietnamese and French snacks, and watch the flashes of artillery fire and the blast of bombs on the horizon.

A Korean cameraman for NBC News was there with an attractive young Korean woman, Song Young Hi, who went by the Western name Cindy. She was the lead singer with a group called Cindy and the Two Apple Troupe. They were appearing at a Saigon nightclub and were scheduled to leave in a few days for their next engagement, in Malaysia. Cindy was wearing a traditional Chinese high-collared, tight-fitting dress called a *cheongsam*. She kept staring at me and I kept staring at her. I wouldn't say it was love at first sight. But it was something at first sight.

That first night, Cindy went off with her date, the Korean cameraman. I had another drink, looked out at the flashes on the horizon for a while, and then went down to my two-room suite a floor below the bar and went to sleep. The next morning, when I checked my mailbox in the hotel lobby, I found a message saying Cindy had phoned and wanted me to call her back. I did. She said she would like to see me again. I said I would like to see her again, but we would have to wait until I returned from a reporting trip I was about to undertake to cover a story in another part of Vietnam. She indicated she would postpone her group's next engagement in Malaysia and remain in Saigon until I returned.

Our first date was a double date for dinner and dancing at a French restaurant with one of the "Two Apples" from her singing troupe and a reporter friend of mine. After dinner, we went to my friend's apartment, where Cindy and I did some heavy petting in the bedroom while my

[47]

friend and the other singer did some heavy petting in the living room. There was a midnight curfew in Saigon, and the two women used that as an excuse to leave and go back to their own hotel before things got too far along.

The next day, someone knocked on the door of my suite at the Caravelle. It was Cindy. I was surprised. The Caravelle normally banned Vietnamese women who were not guests from visiting the rooms, to keep the place from being overrun by prostitutes. But because Cindy was Korean, she was allowed above the lobby. I invited her to come in. We did some more heavy petting, but did not have sex. The visits went on for several days and nights. Eventually, we had sex.

Cindy was not just another in my long list of conquests. I was beginning to feel serious affection for her. The real turning point came when I told her I was going to make a trip to Hong Kong for a short vacation from war coverage. When she told me she wanted to go with me, I replied that I preferred to go alone. She began to cry. I was surprised. Until then, I believed Asians did not show their emotions so openly. In that moment, I realized how much I liked her. However, my reluctance to make a commitment persisted. I didn't formally ask Cindy to move into my rooms at the Caravelle, but I didn't object when she gradually did. Over a period of months, she left a few dresses at a time in my closet, a few pairs of shoes, some cosmetics. Eventually, all her stuff was in my suite, and she gave up her own hotel room.

The longer we lived together, the more frequently Cindy asked me when we were going to get married.

She nagged me to buy her an engagement ring. Sometimes I believed we would eventually wed because she was so devoted to me, and because I was so happy with her, and because the sex was so good. Other times I thought that while it was the right relationship for wartime Saigon, I might not feel the same in ten years, when I was a big-time NBC correspondent or anchorman based in New York, hanging out with the elite, and my wife was a poorly educated Korean whose English was not very good, who had never read Hemingway or Salinger, and couldn't keep up her end of a conversation at a Manhattan cocktail party.

When I imagined that scenario, I asked myself why I gave a damn what the New York cocktail circuit thought about my wife. I was happy with her, and that was all that counted. Other times I worried that I didn't have the self-confidence to pull it off. I also wondered what effect marriage to Cindy would have on my career. I had already received a letter from a friend in New York who said the executives at NBC News believed I was acting like an expatriate in a Graham Greene or Somerset Maugham novel, living with a native girl and never intending to leave Vietnam.

Then there was my mother. After I had sent her photographs of Cindy, my mother wrote hysterical letters, saying she hoped I would stop seeing Cindy, that it would ruin my future, that she couldn't stand the thought of my marrying an Asian woman. I told myself I didn't care what my mother thought. But I wondered whether my relationship with Cindy was an ultimate form of rebellion against a domineering Jewish mother, or even a form of punishment for my mother, for raising me to doubt my manhood.

While I was happy—and faithful—living with Cindy, from time to time I still fantasized about sleeping with other women before I settled down. For instance, when executives at NBC News talked to me about my next assignment—perhaps in Paris, perhaps in Rio—one of my first thoughts was: "Oh boy, I can hardly wait to start sleeping with French girls or Brazilian girls." Someone told me there was an expression to describe people like me: I was guided by my penis rather than my brain. I was candid with Cindy about this continuing desire to sleep with other women. And she was amazingly accommodating in her reply: she didn't care if I slept with other women after we married, as long as I didn't take away my love from her.

Cindy and I had a delicately balanced relationship. My fear of getting too deeply involved was compatible with her Asian reserve and shyness. My clinging to her because the relationship was good in a wartime city with few decent choices matched her clinging to me out of love and out of fear that I was her last chance at marriage and at escaping from poverty. We were both thirty-one years old.

I wanted to make Cindy happy, at least partly because of the hard life she had lived. During World War II, her father had been killed by the Japanese. During the Korean War, as sole support for herself, her mother, and her brothers, she had scratched out an existence as a typist during the day and as a singer at night in a USO Club for American GIs. And now she traveled endlessly through Asia singing in second-rate and third-rate nightclubs.

I was happy living with Cindy, I did not want to hurt her, and so I did not pursue other women in Saigon once we became involved. I always made a point of complimenting her on her appearance and her singing. If I promised to phone her at a certain time, I kept my promise, even if it was inconvenient or difficult on Vietnam's unreliable wartime phone system. Still, I did continue to correspond secretly with some of the women I had dated before leaving Washington. One day Cindy found a letter I had received from a former girlfriend. Without my knowing it, Cindy wrote to her, telling her to stop corresponding with me since she planned to marry me. That was the last I heard from that former girlfriend.

Then one day, my relationship with Cindy hit a more serious bump.

I returned to my suite at the Caravelle from the battlefront to find her sitting on the bed reading a letter I was writing to my former psychiatrist. In the letter, I related in considerable detail my mixed feelings about my relationship with Cindy, and I expressed my doubts about marrying a Korean woman who spoke poor English. I commented in the letter that a primary reason I had let her move in with me was that she was the only clean woman in Saigon, that I felt safe having sex with her. Naturally, she was upset by what I had written. But I had to rush to the NBC offices, and I didn't have time to explain the letter to her.

When I got back to the Caravelle later, she was gone. I took a taxi to a hotel in the Cholon section of Saigon, where one of the Two Apples in her troupe was staying. I found Cindy there. I talked and talked, trying to persuade her to come back. I explained to her that it was important for me to be completely candid in the letter to my psychiatrist. I professed my affection for her. I invited her to accompany me on a forthcoming vacation in Hong Kong.

Finally, grudgingly, she agreed to move back to the Caravelle. I was happy—though I still suffered periodic doubts about whether this was a lifetime romance or just a wartime romance. And I still occasionally had fantasies about sleeping with other women.

As Christmas 1965 approached, Cindy let me know that she wanted a puppy for her present. I had one of the NBC drivers take me to the animal market in Saigon, where people shopped for chickens, ducks, geese, cats, and dogs. For the Vietnamese, it was a *food* market. I believe I was the only one at the animal market shopping for a *pet*! I bought Cindy a cute long-haired puppy. Definitely a "mixed" breed.

I needed to persuade the Caravelle Hotel to waive its rule against keeping pets in the rooms. Like most problems in Vietnam, it was solved by paying bribes, in this case to the front desk clerks—the same clerks we had already bribed with money, radios, tape recorders, and liquor to find rooms for NBC staff members.

Cindy and I settled into a pleasant relationship—Chinese dinners in Cholon, French dinners in Saigon, parties at the apartments of friends, vacation trips to Hong Kong, Bangkok, Penang.

And, for once in my life, I was faithful.

10

Tet and Other Horrors

In Vietnam, Tet is the holiday that celebrates the beginning of a new year, based on the lunar calendar—normally late January or early February on the Western calendar. It is the most important holiday of the year, celebrated with the exchange of gifts, lavish meals, special decorations, and visits to relatives. It is roughly equivalent to the Western Christmas and New Year holidays combined. In 1968, Tet fell on January 30. The United States, South Vietnam, the Vietcong, and North Vietnam all announced they would observe a two-day cease-fire to commemorate the holiday.

I and my camera crew were dispatched to Da Nang to report on how the Tet cease-fire was being observed in that seacoast city, home base for the U.S. Marine contingent in Vietnam. Shortly after midnight on the day the cease-fire was supposed to begin, heavy gunfire erupted and continued for a long time. Da Nang was under attack by the North Vietnamese and Vietcong. And, as we soon learned, similar attacks were taking place all over South Vietnam.

I and most of the other reporters and camera crews in Da Nang were spending the night at the marine press compound, where we were relatively safe. It would have been suicidal to leave the compound in the dark, not knowing for sure where the Vietcong and North Vietnamese attackers were or where their mortar shells might land. And to turn on the camera lights amid the chaos would have made us clear targets.

At dawn—the attack having subsided—I and the other reporters and camera crews ventured outside the marine compound. We found a scene of death and devastation—bodies strewn in the streets, houses and shops riddled with bullets, burned down, or blown up, hysterical Vietnamese civilians wailing over the bodies of loved ones. Walking down a road, I passed a large pile of what appeared to be charcoal. "What's that charcoal?" I asked a marine officer walking beside me. "It's what's left of two little Vietnamese girls who burned to death in that house," he replied.

I still see that horrific image in my mind, and I will for the rest of my life.

We soon learned that the Vietcong and North Vietnamese had occupied the city of Hue (pronounced *Way*), the imperial capital of Vietnam before the French colonial occupation. The marines in Da Nang—determined to recapture the city—loaded up their helicopters and headed for Hue, fifty miles to the northwest. I and my camera crew joined them.

The choppers landed on the south bank of the Perfume River, under fire. The troops and my crew leaped out and ran for cover behind a group of marine tanks lined up on a road next to the river. When all the marines were in place, the tanks moved slowly ahead, firing back at the Communist troops shooting at us.

The marine force was fighting literally door to door. It was more like World War II than a guerrilla war. At last, the marines reached their goal, a building housing the MAC-V regional offices, and liberated the Americans inside.

The battle to recapture Hue from the Communists—a battle with great symbolic significance as well as strategic importance—went on for a month. For me, the most memorable moment—almost a fatal moment—occurred when the marines and the South Vietnamese moved into position to expel the Vietcong and North Vietnamese from the Citadel, the former home of Vietnam's emperors, built in the early nineteenth century. This imperial palace was surrounded by a thirty-foot-high wall and a moat.

As far as I knew, no American correspondent had ever interviewed a Communist soldier on the battlefield. I decided I would try. I took off my white undershirt, waved it in the air as a sign of peaceful intentions, walked across a drawbridge over the moat surrounding the Citadel, and presented myself at the gate. It was probably the most foolhardy thing I have ever done. A Communist soldier atop the wall began firing down at me with his automatic weapon. I turned, raced back across the drawbridge, and dove for cover. By some miracle, I wasn't hit.

Having survived that close call, I almost immediately put myself and my camera crew in even greater peril.

We learned shortly after the Tet offensive began that Communist troops had laid siege to the American Special Forces camp at Khe Sanh on the border with Laos, close to the Demilitarized Zone between South and North Vietnam. So I decided that my camera crew and I had to get to Khe Sanh. The camp was surrounded on all sides by Communist troops, who kept it under artillery, mortar, and rifle fire night and day. The only way to deliver supplies and reinforcements to the Special Forces troops in the camp, and to evacuate the dead and wounded, was by helicopter. My camera crew and I rode in on one of the supply choppers.

It was too dangerous for the helicopters to actually land at Khe Sanh—it would give the Communist gunners time to zero in on them. As the chopper carrying me and my crew circled high above the camp, I looked down and saw the wreckage of several choppers that had been hit and destroyed while trying to land at Khe Sanh. Not reassuring. Suddenly, our helicopter dove steeply and hovered briefly a few feet off the ground. The supplies were shoved out. My camera crew and I jumped out. The chopper rose sharply. My crew and I raced for one of the trenches dug around the landing strip. Several Communist mortar rounds exploded on the strip. Too late! We were safely in a hole, and the helicopter was safely aloft.

Yet again, I had let my quest for a good TV story and my brash assumption of immunity from harm overcome commonsense avoidance of such high risk.

After a few days of filming and interviewing troops inside the besieged Special Forces base, I and my camera crew were extracted in a maneuver similar to our arrival—racing across the landing strip lugging our heavy equipment, scrambling aboard a hovering helicopter, and lifting off swiftly before the surrounding Communist troops could aim mortar or artillery rounds at us. The battle for Khe Sanh lasted more than three months before reinforced American units, supported by air strikes, finally drove away the Communists.

General Creighton Abrams, deputy U.S. military commander in Vietnam at the time, has said he believes the Communists had hoped to turn Khe Sanh into another Dien Bien Phu, the battle that convinced the French to surrender in the First Indochina War. From a military point of view, the Tet offensive was a horrendous defeat for the North Vietnamese and Vietcong. They lost thousands of troops, and they were not able to hold on to any territory. But from a psychological and public relations point of view, Tet was a great victory for the Communists. They had demonstrated that after years of American military involvement, the North Vietnamese and Vietcong were still capable of mounting a large and aggressive offensive across a large section of South Vietnam.

After Tet, Lyndon Johnson lost whatever public support remained for the war. And he lost his stomach for continuing the fight. Tet was the beginning of the end of the American commitment.

Some of the nastiest fighting I covered in Vietnam was not between American and Communist troops. It was between South Vietnamese Catholics and South Vietnamese Buddhists. Violent Buddhist protests against the Saigon government had been going on at least since 1963. One particularly grisly form of protest was self-immolation. A number of Buddhist monks in their saffron robes sat down on Saigon's streets, crossed their legs in the lotus position, poured gasoline over themselves, and set themselves on fire.

In the spring of 1966, a new round of sectarian violence was ignited when South Vietnam's Catholic premier Nguyen Cao Ky fired one of the army's few Buddhist generals, Nguyen Chanh Thi. The war-within-a-war broke out initially in Da Nang, a center of Buddhist activism. Buddhists virtually shut down the city with a general strike. And they burned down the U.S. Information Services library in nearby Hue. Government troops struck back by shooting, tear-gassing, and beating protesters and smashing Buddhist religious symbols.

When the Buddhist protests erupted, my camera crew and I were in Da Nang, working on another story. We were diverted to cover the Buddhist uprising. A message was delivered to the marine press compound one day: all reporters and cameramen should come immediately to the Buddhist temple about a mile away for an important development. The temple was a massive white building, enclosing an enormous statue of Buddha.

As soon as the press contingent rushed into the temple, we realized that we had been duped. The building was surrounded by Vietnamese government troops. We were now hostages, human shields for the Buddhists against a government assault. This stalemate lasted all day. As darkness began to fall, I and the other newsmen in the temple—including my rival Dan Rather—began to suspect that the government troops were awaiting nightfall to attack under cover of darkness. We journalists would be in grave danger.

So we decided to leave the temple and try to get behind the government troops before the assault started. The cameramen turned on their camera lights and shone them on our group. Some of us took off our white undershirts and waved them. When we were in the no-man's-land between the temple and the soldiers, the Buddhists opened fire, and the government troops fired back. We were pinned down in between. The marines somehow heard about our plight and came to rescue us. Three reporters were wounded in the encounter.

II

"I Don't Want to Die"

Like most reporters in Vietnam, I had a set of rules I followed to try to stay alive while covering the war. My rules included

- Don't do anything just for kicks. There was enough danger without taking additional risks for the thrill of it.
- Don't stay in a dangerous area overnight. We couldn't film in the dark anyhow, and it was a favorite time for Communist attacks.
- Don't go out with a small unit. A skirmish involving a few American troops was rarely newsworthy, and the risk of being overrun by the Vietcong was high.

In the summer of 1966, I violated that last rule, and I paid a high price for it. I and my camera crew hooked up with a small patrol of Charlie Company, of the 101st Airborne Brigade, in the Central Highlands near the town of Dak To. It was the first anniversary of the brigade's arrival in Vietnam. The 101st was one of the few American units fighting like the enemy guerrillas—small patrols, carrying plenty of ammunition and food so they didn't have to be resupplied by helicopter, taking the war to the enemy.

I might not have chosen to accompany the 101st if I had known that two other reporters traveling with that unit had been wounded recently. But I did accompany them. The troops hid along a red dirt trail, hoping to ambush a Vietcong unit they believed was using the trail. But no Vietcong appeared, and after several hours the U.S. troops gave up their ambush plans. They trekked down to the bottom of the trail to refill their canteens from a stream. First, though, they performed a maneuver called "recon by fire," which meant everyone in the patrol simultaneously fired his gun into the dense jungle on the other side of the stream for sixty seconds—called "the mad minute"—in case any Vietcong guerrillas were hiding there. The noise of the "mad minute" was so cacophonous it made me grin.

Then I suddenly noticed that the jungle vegetation on the other side of the stream was flipping back in our direction. Somebody *was* hiding in there, shooting at us! I started to duck down. Just then, I felt a thump on the left side of my chest. I looked down. A bloodstain was spreading across the front of my shirt. I began to feel woozy. I was spitting up blood. I was having trouble breathing. I lay down on my back on the ground. Everything began to get dark. There was no medic with us. One of the soldiers radioed for a helicopter to evacuate me. But between eight-foot-high elephant grass and thick jungle, there was no way a helicopter could land. If the troops tried to carry me to a place where a medic was stationed, it was unlikely that I would survive the trip.

"I don't want to die," I whispered to a soldier trying to comfort me.

"You're not going to die," he reassured me, not very convincingly.

Meanwhile, my cameraman, Peter Boultwood, and my sound technician, Tony Mitchell, good journalists that they were, continued to film the scene. Boultwood recorded a narration for the *Huntley-Brinkley Report*. I watched his story later. Peter obviously thought I was going to die. In his script, he spoke of me in the past tense. It was like watching my own obit!

A 101st Airborne colonel, David Hackworth, who had briefed me on the mission that morning, heard about my plight in a radio message from the patrol. He flew to the scene in his helicopter, hovered overhead so the wind from the rotor blades beat down the elephant grass, and gradually dropped lower and lower until the troops were able to lift me up and toss me into the chopper. I was only dimly conscious. The chopper airlifted me to a medical field station in a tent near the battlefield. I was in shock. The medics jabbed an intravenous tube into my arm and began pumping fluids and medications into my bloodstream. That immediately brought me out of shock. In fact, it produced a kind of "high."

"Let's see you top this one, Morley Safer," I crowed. I have regretted that ill-considered taunt ever since.

An X-ray showed that a grenade fragment was lodged in my left lung, and the lung was filled with blood. The medics produced a stainless steel tube with a sharp point on one end. They jabbed the point through my skin, between my ribs and into the lung. I watched the blood drain out of my lung into a basin. The medics could not give me any painkillers or anesthesia because they did not want to suppress my breathing. It was worst pain I had ever felt.

Later I learned that the fragment may have been from an *American* grenade. A 101st trooper may have tried to lob a grenade over the trees into what he believed were Vietcong hiding on the other side. However, the grenade apparently hit the trees, bounced back onto our side of the stream, and exploded.

After my condition stabilized somewhat, I was taken by helicopter from the field station to the Eighty-fifth Evacuation Hospital in Qui Nhon on the seacoast. I was placed in a bed in a long, narrow ward. Beds holding wounded troops lined both sides of the ward. Late one night, a hospital staffer came to my bedside and asked if I wanted anything. Obviously feeling better, I responded, "I'd love a martini." In a few minutes, he returned with a paper cup of gin!

Some of my NBC colleagues cabled me humorous get-well wishes to boost my spirits. Sander Vanocur's message from Washington read: "Switchboard here swamped with female callers anxious to know exact whereabouts your wound. Audible sighs of relief from all over nation when ladies learn it's upper part of your anatomy which [was] damaged." And John Rich cabled from Tokyo: "Sorry hearing about your injury. Hope fast recovery. Japanese sake firms waiting your visit." I guess my colleagues knew some of my favorite habits!

Meanwhile, my mother was complaining to NBC and to the Pentagon that I was not getting adequate care, that the doctors were not good, that she wasn't being told the truth about my wound, that she wanted to be allowed to visit me. I fired off a cable to her, declaring, "I am deeply ashamed and embarrassed, and am now spending a good deal of my time getting apologies through to the people you have offended. . . . Please please please leave alone the Pentagon and NBC who have done so much for me." Still an overly protective mother after all those years.

After I had spent a week or so in the Eighty-fifth Evacuation Hospital, the military doctors decided I should be transferred to Walter Reed Army Medical Center in Washington, D.C., where better physical therapy facilities were available.

There was no way Cindy could quickly get the necessary visa and other documents she needed to enter the United States. On the morning I was to leave Saigon for Washington, Cindy came to the hospital to say good-bye. It was a tearful and emotional farewell. As my ambulance pulled away from the hospital on the way to the airport, I watched Cindy through the rear window, standing in the street waving and weeping, receding into the distance. It was like a scene from a bad war movie.

After a few weeks of physical therapy at Walter Reed, I was judged by the army doctors to be sufficiently recovered from my wound and its af-tereffects, and I was discharged. It was a little more than one year after my initial arrival in Saigon.

NBC News directed me to come to New York, where I was to be the anchor of a new half-hour program called *Vietnam Weekly Review*, devoted to news and analysis of the war. During my stint as anchor of that pro-gram, I learned a great journalistic lesson from my mentor, Reuven Frank. It happened at the end of 1966, when we broadcast a clip of Pope Paul's annual Christmas message, in which he prayed for peace in Vietnam. Still in my insufferably self-important phase, I inanely proclaimed on the air, "And I think we can all agree with the pope on the need for peace."

Immediately after the program, Reuven came up to me in the studio and in his very soft voice said, "Ron, nobody cares what you think." It was a great lesson from a great mentor, a lesson that most of today's TV and cable correspondents and anchors don't seem to have learned.

Meanwhile, I was contacting State Department officials, trying to per-suade them to grant Cindy a visa to come to America. I had decided that our affair in Saigon was more than a passing wartime romance. I cared for her. I had bought her an engagement ring in Hong Kong during a vacation we took together. I worried about what would happen to Cindy if I *didn't* help her get to the United States. Would she wander for years through Asia singing at second-rate nightclubs until she grew too old? And then would she have to take on some menial job to support herself and her family?

I finally succeeded in persuading the State Department to grant her a visa, and Cindy flew to New York. Our reunion took place when she emerged from the customs and immigration checkpoints at JFK Airport. We rushed into each other's arms. We hugged and kissed passionately, ignoring the throngs of passengers and greeters surging around us. I was so happy to be reunited with Cindy after months apart and the uncertainty of whether the U.S. authorities would allow her to come to America. Indeed, absence had made my heart grow fonder. My concerns about how Cindy would fit into the sophisticated world of Manhattan had evaporated. During my time as a bachelor in New York City, I had not been tempted to date other women. At last I seemed ready to settle into a faithful relationship.

I had sublet a furnished apartment on the East Side from another NBC correspondent, who had been assigned to Africa. Once the cab from the airport had dropped us off at the apartment, Cindy and I fell into each other's arms and resumed our passionate romance. Within days it was obvious that we loved each other deeply. I proposed that we get married, and she accepted. We were married shortly afterward in a ceremony attended by a few friends and colleagues. I did not invite—or even tell—my parents about the marriage. They had made clear their strong opposition to my marrying a Korean woman.

Later, I pulled more strings at the State Department to get visas for Cindy's mother, her college-age brother, and a married brother, his wife, and their three children. They all moved to America.

After my marriage to Cindy, I went back to Vietnam four more times for reporting tours. My last trip was to cover a so-called cease-fire ending America's involvement.

12

The Cease-Fire That Wasn't

In January 1973, Secretary of State Henry Kissinger and leaders of North and South Vietnam signed a peace agreement in Paris. The agreement called for a cease-fire to allow America to withdraw its remaining 23,700 troops and to entrust to the Vietnamese the task of resolving their own fate. In a nationally televised speech that night, President Richard Nixon announced what he called the "honorable" agreement, which was intended to "end the war and bring peace with honor to Vietnam and in Southeast Asia." It didn't.

The cease-fire ending the Vietnam War was supposed to go into effect at 8 a.m. Sunday January 28, 1973 (Saigon time). It was a historic moment, like 11 a.m. November 11, 1918, when the Armistice ended World War I, or noon August 15, 1945, when the emperor announced Japan's surrender, ending World War II.

I wanted to cover the moment when the Vietnam cease-fire took effect somewhere close to Saigon so I could get back quickly to ship my film and file my story for radio. With my camera crew, I drove to a village west of Saigon. It was a few moments before 8 a.m. when we arrived. We found a ferocious firefight under way. American and South Vietnamese troops in a ditch on one side of the road were exchanging heavy fire with Communist troops dug in on the other side of the road. Our driver pulled the car over. He refused to drive any closer. I and my crew jumped out, ran up the road, and dove into the ditch.

I looked around to see who else was in the ditch. It was like a reunion of Vietnam War correspondents. Many of the reporters I had covered the war with over the past eight years had come back to report on the cease-fire. And somehow a lot of them had ended up in the same ditch in the same little town. The moment for the cease-fire to take effect had arrived.

But the firing did not cease there or elsewhere in the country. It continued for days before gradually tapering off.

Over the months and years after the cease-fire and the American withdrawal, the North Vietnamese slaughtered as many as one million South Vietnamese and imprisoned tens of thousands more in "reeducation camps." Hundreds of thousands of South Vietnamese fled their country and its conquerors by sea—the so-called "boat people."

One of the provisions of the cease-fire agreement was for a Communist delegation to come to Saigon to negotiate with the South Vietnamese government the details of their future relations. A heavily guarded compound was set up for the North Vietnamese and Vietcong delegation at Tan Son Nhut Airport. Virtually no Western reporters had ever seen a live North Vietnamese or Vietcong up close, much less interviewed one. So I headed for the airport to try to interview the Communist delegation.

I found the compound housing the delegation surrounded by armed South Vietnamese troops. I told them I and my camera crew wanted to interview the Communists. The South Vietnamese soldiers blocked our way. When I asserted our right to interview the delegation, the soldiers put their gun barrels against our chests, shoved my cameraman, and confiscated some of our film. We backed off.

The next day, a South Vietnamese military spokesman warned that the troops had orders to shoot anyone who attempted to enter the compound where the North Vietnamese were staying. The spokesman said I and my crew were lucky we had not been shot. A day or so later, South Vietnam's president, Nguyen Van Thieu, was taking part in a public ceremony of some kind. I and my NBC crew approached him, camera running. I shouted, "Mr. President, did you order your troops to shoot American news correspondents trying to interview the North Vietnamese delegation?" With a laugh, he replied that if he had issued such an order, "You all would have been shot already."

Shortly afterward, a letter arrived at the NBC News office in Saigon, signed by the director of the government's public affairs center, informing the network that the government was taking "punitive measures" against me—canceling my visa and kicking me out of the country—because I had "distorted" the South Vietnamese prohibition on interviews with the Communist delegation. Another Vietnamese official, speaking more informally, told me I was being expelled for displaying "impertinence" toward President Thieu.

The State Department filed a protest on my behalf. NBC News appealed my expulsion. I wrote a letter to the Vietnamese ambassador in Washington offering "my sincere apologies" if I had violated his government's press regulations. To no avail. The government would not rescind my expulsion. I packed up my belongings at the Caravelle Hotel, bid farewell to my friends, colleagues, and competitors, and departed Saigon for the last time.

Twenty-six months later, I stood at the podium in the White House Press Room and announced the end of the war.

The common wisdom is that the United States "lost" the Vietnam War. I believe the common wisdom on this and other matters almost always turns out to be wrong in the long run. Certainly these many decades later, Vietnam, north and south, is ruled by a rigid Communist government. But Vietnam has a booming, largely free economy, with American Express–recommended restaurants, five-star hotels, high-rise condos on China Beach, vacation resorts in the highlands, a Nike shoe factory, and KFC and Pizza Hut fast-food outlets.

Thirty years after the war ended, Henry Kissinger told me in a conversation that the late Vietnamese revolutionary leader Ho Chi Minh "would probably be horrified" by how his country's economy has boomed. According to Kissinger, Vietnam "turned out better than anyone could have expected." Maybe we won the war after all. Or at least maybe we helped the Vietnamese people to achieve a better lifestyle than they would have had otherwise.

During my five reporting tours in Vietnam, my heart and mind and soul had been shaken by witnessing many horrors. I had looked down at a pile of charcoal on a roadside and been told it was the remains of two Vietnamese children burned to death in the Tet offensive. Only because of a soldier's bad aim and my fast running did I avoid being shot to death on the bridge across the moat at the Citadel in Hue. I had escaped from the Buddhist temple in Da Nang just moments before it was attacked by government troops. I had jumped out of a helicopter at the Khe Sanh Special Forces camp and made it safely into a ditch with mortar rounds exploding all around me. I had camped out with and kept up with the toughest soldiers in the world in some of the roughest terrain in the world. I had watched a Buddhist monk burn himself to death on a Saigon street. I had seen human beings literally blown apart. I had seen the brains of victims of a Communist bomb on the street in Cholon. I had flown away from one battlefield in a helicopter sitting on a pile of plastic body bags containing the remains of dead American soldiers.

And I had almost bled to death myself after a fragment of a hand grenade penetrated my lung.

I was changed forever by what I saw and what I experienced in Vietnam— human beings acting inhuman. I will never forget it. I will never get over it.

13

Around the World in Eighty Stories

Sometimes the danger I faced covering stories for NBC News came not from enemy bullets but from high winds, crashing waves, and flying debris. I was assigned to cover two hurricanes as they smashed ashore in the United States—Hurricane Dora in August 1964 and the monster storm Hurricane Camille in August 1969.

Dora slammed into Florida at St. Augustine on the Atlantic coast with winds of 125 miles per hour shortly after midnight, then spun up the St. Johns River to Jacksonville. I was broadcasting from a balcony on the second floor of the NBC affiliate station in Jacksonville, WFGA-TV, which was located on the banks of the river. I had my script taped to a clipboard so it wouldn't blow away, and my microphone was wrapped in plastic so it wouldn't get soaked by the rain. A man was posted off-camera to grab me in case the wind blew me over. Because of the wind and rain, I and the WFGA-TV staff were unable to leave the station for three days. We napped on cots and dined on ham and eggs from the station's cafeteria.

As soon as Dora blew past Jacksonville, I got new orders from NBC—hurry to Montgomery, Alabama, the next major city where the storm was expected to hit. I had just checked into a motel in Montgomery, sent my wet clothes to the laundry, and grabbed my first real meal in days, when I received *new* orders—Get back to Jacksonville as fast as you can. President Johnson was coming to inspect the hurricane damage. My camera crew and I chartered a twin-engine Beechcraft to fly back to Jacksonville. We got a firsthand look at Dora—our plane was buffeted as we flew through the fringes of the storm.

Once the storm had passed and the president had returned to Washington, after I had filed my final stories from the WFGA-TV studios, I walked outside into the now calm, warm Florida air, eager to have my first shower and decent meal in days. But we couldn't go anywhere. The streets were jammed. Traffic wasn't moving. There was a Beatles concert at the Gator Bowl stadium two blocks from the station!

Five years later, NBC waited until the last minute to send me and a camera crew to New Orleans to cover a huge storm, Hurricane Camille, then approaching the Louisiana coast with 190-mile-an-hour winds, one of the most powerful hurricanes of the twentieth century. By the time NBC dispatched us, the New Orleans airport was closed in anticipation of the storm. The closest airport still open was in Jackson, Mississippi. We flew there, rented a car, and drove south to New Orleans, about four hours away.

Ours was one of the very few cars heading in that direction, into the storm. On the other side of the road, heading north, was a solid line of vehicles carrying people escaping Camille. The farther south we drove, the more intense the winds and rain became. I and my crew arrived in New Orleans after dark, at the height of the storm. We made our way to the French Quarter, where the NBC affiliate station WDSU-TV was located. We found a hotel open and checked in. It was too dark, windy, and wet to film.

The cameraman, soundman, and I got up at first light and headed east along the Gulf Coast of Louisiana and Mississippi, where the center of the storm had slammed into the towns of Bay St. Louis, Pass Christian, Long Beach, and Gulfport during the night. We filmed destroyed businesses and churches, flattened homes, piles of debris, knots of stunned survivors. Camille's winds had created a storm surge twenty-four-feet high in the Gulf of Mexico. More than ten inches of rain pounded down. Damage totaled nearly a billion and a half dollars. More than five thousand homes and businesses were destroyed. The hurricane killed more than 250 people.

Many residents of the Gulf Coast had fled inland as the storm approached. But about two dozen tenants of a beachfront apartment building called the Richelieu Manor in Pass Christian decided to ride out the storm. In fact, they held a "hurricane party." The Richelieu collapsed in the high winds. Eight tenants died. After filming the destruction and interviewing survivors at the Richelieu and elsewhere, my crew and I headed back toward WDSU-TV in New Orleans to process and edit our dramatic footage and prepare our story for that evening's *Huntley-Brinkley Report*.

Then we learned that our carefully planned timetable was not going to work. A bridge across one of the branches of Lake Pontchartrain, which we needed to cross on our drive back to New Orleans, had been washed out. We had to detour north to the next bridge, cross it, then turn south again toward New Orleans. By the time we got to WDSU-TV, with the evening newscast fast approaching, we had time to process only one four-hundred-foot magazine of film, just ten minutes of the thousands of feet of spectacular footage we had shot.

I spent a week doing stories on the aftermath of Camille, interviewing survivors about their harrowing experiences, about their efforts to put their lives back together, about their sorrow over friends and family members killed. Perhaps the most heartrending footage we shot showed people who had lost their homes and all their belongings picking through donated clothing in a churchyard.

My final Camille story, on a Sunday, a week after the hurricane struck, was filmed outside a church whose side wall had been ripped off by the storm. While I recounted the events of the week, the camera showed the parishioners and their pastor behind me praying and giving thanks for their survival.

Covering Camille, especially in the first hours, I tried to follow another journalistic lesson I learned from my NBC mentor Reuven Frank: "The bigger the story, the less you have to say. Shut up and let the pictures tell the story."

In 1967, while based in Mexico City as NBC's Latin American correspondent, I was dispatched to Punta del Este, Uruguay, to report on a Western Hemisphere economic summit meeting, at which Lyndon Johnson and the leaders of Central and South American nations launched the ten-year, $20 billion Alliance for Progress program to encourage development, promote democratic governance, and eliminate poverty on the continent. In Punta del Este, a part-time NBC correspondent based in Buenos Aires told me about rumors that Che Guevara—a close associate of Fidel Castro—and a band of like-minded revolutionaries were in southern Bolivia fomenting a Communist overthrow of the government. The part-timer was not considered very reliable, and I dismissed the rumors.

But a short time later, one of Che Guevara's close associates, French Communist Régis Debray, was captured in southern Bolivia and was to be put on trial in a small town called Camiri. That probably meant that Guevara and other revolutionaries were in the area, too. NBC News sent me and a camera crew to Camiri to cover the trial and the Bolivian army's search for Guevara.

Camiri had unpaved streets, board sidewalks, horses and mules tied to hitching posts. It might have been 1867 instead of 1967. I and my camera crew checked into the only hotel in town, the Oriente. It was a converted stable. The rooms had dirt floors and unpainted, rough wood walls. There was one common bathroom. The room rate was one dollar per night. Fortunately, there was one decent restaurant in Camiri, run by an Italian immigrant couple. Why they decided to open a restaurant there, I have no idea. But I and my crew were. glad they did. We took almost all our meals at their restaurant.

Then came bad news. Debray's trial was postponed. NBC News in New York, communicating with me in that tiny, remote town through an old-fashioned telex machine, directed that while I and my camera crew were waiting for the trial to open, we should cover the Bolivian army's hunt for Guevara and his band. Every day we accompanied the Bolivian troops as they searched for Che Guevara. And every night we returned to our stable/hotel without finding him.

Meanwhile, the Debray trial was postponed again and again. Finally I sent a telex message to NBC News headquarters in New York: I had a long-planned vacation scheduled to start soon, I didn't think Che Guevara was really around Camiri, and I wanted to come home. An NBC executive cabled back: come home.

The network executives sent another correspondent, Dick Valeriani, to Camiri as my replacement. Valeriani had the same experience I did: the Debray trial was repeatedly postponed, and the Bolivian army troops looking for Guevara in the hills and valleys of southern Bolivia couldn't find him. So Valeriani eventually telexed NBC News headquarters, saying he, too, doubted that Guevara was around Cimiri and requesting permission to return to the United States so he could depart on *his* vacation. Permission granted.

A few days day later, newspapers all over the world ran the now-famous picture of the dead Che Guevara, lying on his back on a cement slab, his glassy eyes open. He had been in southern Bolivia after all. He had been captured by the Bolivian army, then shot and killed. I had missed it.

Late in 1966, when I was anchoring the *Vietnam Weekly Review* program on NBC, I was dispatched to Israel to interview Moshe Dayan, a hero of the 1948 Arab-Israeli War and later chief of staff of the Israeli armed forces. I was sent to talk to him about the recent trip he had made to Vietnam at the behest of the U.S. government, which sought his suggestions for American commanders mired in an unconventional war. During our interview at his home in Tel Aviv, Dayan's advice to the United States was: U.S. troops should take over military operations against the Vietcong and North Vietnamese and let the South Vietnamese forces devote themselves entirely to meeting the needs of the people.

But Dayan, an amateur archaeologist, was much more interested in talking to me about his hobby—collecting antiquities from the Middle East, a cradle of civilization. He led me to his garage and showed me stacks of pots, statues, weapons, and other centuries-old objects he had "liberated" during various Israeli military forays in the region.

On July 24, 1969, I was among the reporters aboard the aircraft carrier USS *Hornet* in the Pacific Ocean about twelve hundred miles south of Hawaii, awaiting the splashdown of the *Columbia* space capsule returning Apollo 11 astronauts Neil Armstrong, Buzz Aldrin, and Michael Collins from their historic first landing on the moon. TV and radio coverage of the splashdown was transmitted from the ship to a satellite 22,300 miles overhead, relayed to a receiving station in California, and then distributed to the networks via land lines. It was one of the earliest uses of a satellite to broadcast live pictures of a news event.

With an estimated five hundred million television viewers watching in forty-nine countries, and President Richard Nixon watching from the bridge of the *Hornet*, the astronauts reentered earth's atmosphere in the *Columbia* capsule and drifted down under a gigantic parachute into the calm Pacific Ocean. In bright sunshine, I described navy frogmen dropping from the *Hornet*'s helicopters, swimming to the spacecraft, and attaching a floatation collar to prevent it from sinking. The TV cameras showed the astronauts crawling out of their capsule and into orange rubber rafts manned by the frogmen.

Space agency officials, having no prior experience with humans visiting an extraterrestrial locale, were worried that during their time on the lunar surface, the astronauts might have picked up "moon germs"—microscopic organic particles that could spread unknown diseases or cause other catastrophic effects if brought back to earth on the capsule or the astronauts' spacesuits. So, before being hoisted aboard the helicopters, the astronauts were scrubbed down with disinfectant. After being decontaminated, the astronauts donned special biological isolation suits as further protection against spreading any "moon germs."

Then the spacemen were flown to the *Hornet* by helicopter. The astronauts entered a special Airstream trailer lashed down to the carrier's hangar deck. Air pressure inside the trailer—a "mobile quarantine facility," or MQF in space agency jargon—was maintained at a lower level than outside the trailer so no "moon germs" could escape and infect President Nixon, the sailors, or the reporters. The astronauts remained in isolation in the trailer for three weeks. There was no evidence that they had brought back germs from the moon.

In addition to my five tours in Vietnam, I covered wars in Africa, Latin America, Bangladesh, and Borneo during my twelve years with the network. Often the move from one story to the next was head-snapping. Once, in 1968, I was in Biafra covering a tribal uprising on Friday, in my home base of London on Saturday, and in Miami Beach to cover the Republican National Convention on Monday.

The very first week of my assignment to the NBC News London bureau, early in 1968, should have put me on notice that being based in London didn't mean I would actually spend much time in London. Cindy and I devoted our first few days in London to looking for a furnished flat. We found a nice one in the Kensington section, just up the street from Harrod's department store, close to Princess Margaret's house. We moved in at 11 a.m. on our first Saturday in London. At 3:30 that afternoon I was on a plane to South Africa to interview the first successful recipient of a transplanted heart.

A few months earlier, a young South African doctor, Christian Barnard, had performed the first human heart transplant operation—removing the healthy heart from an auto accident victim and installing it in the chest of a recipient whose own heart was failing. The recipient died eighteen days later.

NBC decided to pay Barnard for the exclusive rights to conduct the first postoperative interview with his next transplant patient. That patient was Philip Blaiberg, a fifty-nine-year-old dentist whose own heart was giving out after a series of heart attacks. A few days after Barnard performed a successful transplant operation, Blaiberg had recovered enough to answer my questions on camera.

Because he was taking autoimmune drugs to prevent his body from rejecting the new heart, Blaiberg was very susceptible to infection and was confined in a germ-free glass enclosure. Our microphone was sanitized and slipped under the door into the glass enclosure. The opening between the door and the floor was taped. Blaiberg's doctors had advised that after open-heart surgery—which involved stopping the patient's heart, pumping his blood out of the body, circulating it through a cleansing machine, and then pumping it back into the body—the patient could undergo a personality change, at least temporarily.

In Blaiberg's case, the operation made him childlike for a time. With our cameras rolling, Blaiberg in his germ-free glass enclosure began to recite nursery rhymes and to sing songs from his childhood. Blaiberg lived nineteen months with his new heart.

The interview with Blaiberg was probably the most benign story I covered in Africa. Most of my assignments there involved wars, revolutions, assassinations, and uprisings. One of my first African reporting trips was to the Congo. In July 1967, the latest in a series of internal wars between various factions broke out in the former Belgian colony. I and my camera crew flew to the Congolese capital of Kinshasa—known as Leopoldville before independence. We checked into an inn run by an old Belgian woman. We ate our meals at various restaurants and bars crowded with aging Belgian expatriates and their Congolese girlfriends.

Other reporters advised me that in the Congo a well-timed gratuity would make my job easier. The first time I went to the post and telegraph office to file a radio report to NBC News in New York, I gave a bribe to the attendant. Not yet fully understanding the currency exchange rate in the

Congo, I accidentally gave him ten times the usual bribe. He got my line through to New York so fast I hadn't finished writing my report when he waved me into the studio.

Most of the fighting in the Congolese civil war was going on in the country's far north, around the city of Kisangani, or Stanleyville, as it was called during the Belgian colonial period. Hundreds of Catholic nuns, missionaries, and other civilians were trapped in Kisangani by the fighting. Several U.S. Air Force planes were dispatched to rescue the nuns. I and my camera crew hitched a ride on one of the planes. It flew low over the Congo River. I looked down at the brown water, at the muddy banks, at the jungle, at a scene that hadn't changed for hundreds or thousands or millions of years. There were no signs at all of civilization.

By the time the story had played out and it was time to leave the Congo, all commercial air traffic out of Kinshasa had been suspended. But I and my camera crew managed to get aboard a commercial jetliner that had been chartered by the U.S. government to evacuate Americans and others trapped in the fighting. The pilot invited me to come up to the cockpit to watch the takeoff. He taxied to the end of the runway and awaited clearance from the regional air control center, which was located on the other side of the Congo River in a former French colony also called the Congo. We waited and waited. No clearance to take off was given.

The government of the former French Congo leaned strongly toward communism, and we suspected that was why its air traffic controllers refused to give our American refugee flight permission to take off.

Finally, the pilot ordered, "Hold tight!" He revved the engines, released the brakes, screamed down the runway, and lifted off without permission from across the river. Once off the ground, he pulled back hard on the controls, sending the plane screaming upward at a very sharp angle, in case the hostile neighbors across the river decided to fire on the unauthorized flight. But they didn't, and our planeload of grateful evacuees relaxed. We had escaped.

Another scary place I was dispatched to in the 1960s was the island of Borneo, in the South China Sea south of Vietnam. In Indonesia's West Kalimantan section of Borneo, a group of Dayak tribal members had launched a grisly, primitive war against the prosperous Chinese who dominated the economy. The young driver of the car I had hired to get me and my crew around West Kalimantan was a Dayak. One day, grinning, he reached into his shirt pocket and pulled out a prized possession: a brown hunk of leather several inches long.

"What's that?" I asked. He explained it was part of the liver of a Chinese killed in the fighting. The Dayaks believed that if you cut out your enemy's liver, it would make you stronger. And if you *ate* your enemy's liver, it would make you even stronger.

Yet another ugly story I covered during that period took place in one of the most beautiful cities I've visited—Dhaka (sometimes spelled "Dacca"), the capital of Bangladesh. When Great Britain granted independence to its colony India after World War II, that country was split into two independent nations: Hindu India and Muslim Pakistan. In turn, Pakistan consisted of two separate territories: East Pakistan and West Pakistan, separated by a thousand miles of Indian territory. While both halves of Pakistan were Muslim, West Pakistan dominated the culture, economy, and politics.

Finally, in 1971, East Pakistan declared its independence from West Pakistan and renamed itself Bangladesh. Pakistan fought to retain the territory, but with the help of Indian troops, Bangladesh preserved its independent status.

The legendary Bangladesh independence leader Sheikh Mujibur Rahman, who had lived in exile in London for years, announced he was returning to his homeland to lead its newly independent government. I was dispatched to Dhaka by NBC News to cover his arrival. Looking out the taxi window on the way from the airport to the hotel, I was bombarded by contrasts: the worst filth, hunger, homelessness, despair, and poverty I had ever seen, and then the stunningly contemporary Parliament building designed by famed architect Louis Kahn.

My crew and I checked into the luxurious Intercontinental Hotel, a beautiful white modern structure symbolically located on a hill looking down at the city. Somehow amid the poverty and the war, the hotel's Scottish chef managed to present an appealing and appetizing buffet lunch every day.

One of the unsettling aspects of staying at the Intercontinental was that young Bangladeshi independence fighters, some only twelve or thirteen years old, armed with AK-47 rifles, would ride up and down on the hotel's elevators. Many of the boys were from rural villages and had never seen a building more than one story tall. They also would knock on the doors of our hotel rooms and demand to inspect our luggage, in case we were secret agents from Pakistan. I did not argue with twelve- and thirteen-year-old boys carrying AK-47s.

Aside from my NBC team, there were only seven other television news organizations in the Bangladesh capital to cover Mujibur Rahman's return. Four million jubilant Bangladeshis were expected to jam Dhaka's streets to welcome home their leader. In that throng, it would be impossible for the TV news crews to move from place to place. So we decided to pool our film. That is, each crew would be assigned to film at one place along Mujibur Rahman's triumphal route from the airport into the heart of the city. Then each news organization would deliver its film to a designated place at the Dhaka airport, where it would be handed to a British pilot who owned the only private charter plane in Dhaka, a tiny propeller-driven aircraft. We paid him to fly the film to Bangkok for processing and distribution. All the participants in the pool would have access to all the film. Given the size and hysteria of the crowds and the complexity of the arrangements, the plan worked amazingly well. Only one of the news organizations failed to get its film to the airport in time.

The only slight hitch occurred when the pilot was flying over Burma. Burmese air traffic control radioed the pilot, demanding to know whether he had permission to fly over Burma. In his Cockney accent, the quick-witted Brit assured them on the radio that he did. (He didn't.) He urged them to rummage around on their desks; surely they would find the proper papers. By the time the Burmese had searched for the nonexistent permits, the pilot was out of Burmese airspace, over Thailand.

I had covered wars, revolutions, tribal uprisings, riots, executions, hurricanes, and the murders of civil rights workers. About the only man-made or natural tragedy I had not covered was an earthquake. That missing experience was finally added to my résumé two days before Christmas in 1972, when a powerful earthquake devastated Nicaragua. I and a camera crew were dispatched to cover it. What I remember most vividly was not the quarter of a million homes destroyed or the five thousand people killed or the water and electric service being cut off or the tall hotels and office buildings and hospitals crumbling or the Nicaraguan troops patrolling against looters or the general incompetence of the authorities.

What I remember most vividly was the ground under my feet quivering with aftershocks of the 6.2 magnitude quake. The earth trembled almost continuously for days, rising and falling. Walking or standing still, I felt unsteady. I felt something like seasickness. And, at the end of a horrendous week, I had to cover one last horror: Hispanic baseball star Roberto Clemente flew to Nicaragua aboard a plane full of relief supplies he had collected. The plane crashed on New Year's Eve, and Clemente was killed.

During that period, when I seemed to travel the world nonstop, covering wars, disasters, and death, I somehow managed to get an entire month off in the summer of 1968 when my ex-wife Sandy allowed our daughter Caren to visit me for several weeks at my London base. Caren was twelve years old. I had not seen her in two years.

We spent the first week sightseeing in London. By a stroke of good luck, Queen Elizabeth took part in a public parade that week, riding up a broad avenue on a black horse, escorted by brightly uniformed guards and preceded by military bands and by bagpipe-playing, kilt-wearing marchers. So my daughter got to see Her Royal Highness. And, perhaps more important, Caren got to visit Carnaby Street, ground zero of 1960s hippiedom. She bought some go-go wristbands, a hippie ring, and a hippie poster.

We then rented a car and drove to Windsor Castle, then Oxford, then Stratford-upon-Avon, Shakespeare's home, where we saw one of his plays performed. From there, we visited Shrewsbury and North Wales, then took a car ferry across the Irish Sea to Dublin. After five days relaxing at a seaside resort, we drove down the coast of Ireland to Wexford, the ancestral home of the Kennedy family, fished for an afternoon, then took another ferry back to England. En route back to London, we spent a night in a charming English inn at Salisbury and visited Stonehenge.

We had been gone for ten days. The sun shone all but one day—highly unusual for rainy, foggy England—a symbol of our happy time together.

Not having seen Caren for so long, and remembering my last, strained vacation with her in Hawaii, I did not know how she would react to spending time with me. But unlike the tense child I had taken on that trip just before I departed for Vietnam, Caren seemed to relax and enjoy herself as we toured England and Ireland. For the first time in a long time I felt like I was being a good and loving father.

14

"Nattering Nabobs of Negativism"

In the early 1970s, NBC News reassigned me again, this time back to the Washington bureau. For some time, Cindy and I had been trying, unsuccessfully, to conceive a child. Having lost my son Steve to cancer, and having lost my daughter Caren for years in a nasty divorce, I yearned for one more chance to be a good father. Cindy finally became pregnant and, after long and difficult labor, gave birth to a son on March 17, 1973. We named him Edward Song Nessen—Edward for my late father, Fredrick Edward Nessen, and Song for Cindy's family name.

Cindy, Edward, and I settled into a contented family life in the Maryland suburbs of Washington. And I undertook a string of interesting and challenging assignments at NBC News. One of those assignments began when I was awakened about six o'clock one morning in August 1973 by a phone call from the NBC news desk.

The editor informed me of a stunning revelation in that morning's *Wall Street Journal*: federal prosecutors were conducting a criminal investigation into allegations that Richard Nixon's vice president, Spiro Agnew, when he was governor of Maryland, had extorted bribes from construction firms, engineers, and architects in return for awarding them state contracts. Agnew also was alleged to have committed tax fraud. The article made the even more stunning revelation that the prosecutors were trying to determine if Agnew continued to collect bribes after he became vice president. The story indicated that the investigators were preparing to present their case to a grand jury in Baltimore.

The NBC News editor instructed me to get up, get dressed, and meet an NBC camera crew outside Agnew's home in the exclusive Kenwood neighborhood, only about three blocks from my much more modest house. (There was no official VP residence in those days, as there is now.) When

Agnew stepped out of his home that morning to enter the waiting White House limousine that would drive him to his office, he was greeted by a media throng shouting questions at him about the bribery charges. The vice president waved, smiled, and climbed into the limo without responding.

Agnew detested the press, and the feeling was mutual. He happily took on the role of Nixon's "hatchet man." In speech after speech, he attacked the news media, often using alliteration. He most famously labeled reporters "nattering nabobs of negativism." He also referred to them as "pusillanimous pussyfooters" and "hopeless hysterical hypochondriacs of history." I spent the next two months digging into Agnew's activities as governor and vice president, crisscrossing Maryland, interviewing sources in and out of the state and federal governments, producing story after story about Agnew's dealings and about the investigation.

In early October, as I and other reporters dug deeper and deeper into Agnew's misdeeds, the vice president struck back. He filed a legal action demanding that I and eight other reporters—thereafter known as the "Agnew Nine"—reveal the names of our sources. The other eight defendants were Fred Graham of CBS, Richard Cohen of the *Washington Post*, Nicholas Cage of the *New York Times*, William Sherman of the *New York Daily News*, Ronald Sarro and Robert Walters of the *Washington Star-News*, Stephen Lesher of *Newsweek*, and Sandy Smith of *Time*.

I and the other eight reporters received subpoenas from the U.S. District Court in Baltimore, ordering us to appear in court and to bring with us "all writings and other forms of record, including drafts and transcripts of all broadcasts . . . reflecting or related to direct or indirect communications between you and anyone on your behalf or associated with you and (i) any officer or employee of the United States Government, or (ii) any other person who has asserted that he was, or whom you have reason to believe was, in direct contact with an officer or employee of the United State Government" concerning the Agnew investigation.

In plain English: "Come to court and name the sources of your Agnew stories." If we refused, we could be found in contempt of court and sent to jail. Washington's NBC bureau chief Frank J. Jordan, in his response to the subpoena, told the court in an affidavit: "This subpoena will effectively deter the news media in the performance of their functions. It will intimidate, if not silence, sources of information available only on assurances of confidentiality. As such sources dry up, we will be reduced to broadcasting only official statements of government." NBC hired the famed First Amendment lawyer Floyd Abrams to defend me.

On October 10, 1973, the day before our court hearing, Agnew dropped a bombshell. He announced that he had submitted his letter of resignation as vice president. The next day, in accord with the subpoena, I and my colleagues in the "Agnew Nine" and our lawyers were sitting in a courtroom in the U.S. Federal Court House in Baltimore, awaiting the arrival of District Court Judge Walter E. Hoffman, who would hear our lawyers' arguments for dismissing the vice president's demand that we reveal our sources.

I was sitting in the back row of the courtroom. Out of the corner of my eye I caught sight of someone entering the courtroom and starting down the aisle. I turned to see who it was. It was Spiro Agnew. All conversation stopped. It was dead quiet. Why was he there? He was not scheduled to appear in the courtroom until later for oral arguments on his motion to halt the federal criminal investigation of his alleged misdeeds. Agnew approached the bench and announced that he wished to plead nolo contendere—essentially "I offer no defense"—to charges of bribery, extortion, and tax fraud.

Every reporter in the courtroom wanted to jump up and run to the nearest phone. But Judge Hoffman had one more bit of business. He dismissed all charges against the "Agnew Nine," pounded his gavel, and adjourned the hearing.

Subsequently, Agnew was fined $10,000 for his crimes, required to pay $160,000 in back taxes, put on three years' probation, and disbarred from practicing law. The Agnew case and other stories of financial or sexual misconduct by public officials always made me wonder why people destroy their careers for relatively paltry amounts of illicit money or fleeting moments of illicit sex. These officials didn't follow the old Washington rule: "Never do anything or say anything that you don't want to see on the front page of the *Washington Post*."

Invoking the provisions of the Twenty-fifth Amendment to the Constitution for the first time to fill a vacancy in the vice presidency, Nixon selected Congressman Gerald R. Ford of Michigan to replace Agnew. Ford was not totally surprised by his selection. Various politicians, including some in the White House, as well as reporters, were publicly mentioning Ford as a possible successor to Agnew. The night of Agnew's resignation, Ford received a phone call from Melvin Laird, an old friend and former House Republican Conference chairman.

"Jerry, if you were asked, would you accept the vice-presidential nomination?" Laird inquired.

Ford wrote later that he knew Laird was asking him that question at the behest of someone else, presumably Nixon. Ford asked Laird for time to think it over.

As a congressman, Ford had traveled endlessly on behalf of the Republican Party and in his own campaigns, essentially leaving his wife, Betty, to manage their home and raise their four children. Ford had recently promised his wife that he would retire after one more term in Congress to spend more time with her and their children at their homes in the Washington suburbs and in Vail, Colorado.

Ford had never aspired to higher office as so many politicians do in ways that distort their judgment and personalities. And now he was being asked if he was willing to become vice president, which would mean postponing his retirement plans and his commitment to spend more time with Betty and their children. Ford discussed the prospect with his wife for more than an hour, weighing the pros and cons. She told him, "If the opportunity comes, I don't see how you can say no."

Ford called Laird back and said that if he were asked, he would accept the VP nomination. A few nights later, the phone rang in Ford's modest 1950s two-story redbrick-and-white-frame home at 514 Crown View Drive in the Clover subdivision of Alexandria, Virginia, across the Potomac River from Washington. It was Nixon. He instructed Ford to have Betty pick up an extension so she could participate in the conversation. But no other phones in the Fords' house could access the line Nixon was calling on. Ford asked the president, "Can you hang up and call back on the other line?" Nixon did, and told Ford that he was to be the new vice president.

Nixon officially announced the nomination on October 12, 1973. The Senate and House began hearings almost immediately. The hearings were televised, giving the American people their first extended exposure to Ford. They liked what they saw. In contrast to the combative, paranoid, secretive Nixon and the small-time crooked politician Agnew, Ford came across as candid, likable, and honest. The House and Senate approved Ford's nomination to be vice president by wide margins. With Betty holding the family Bible, he was sworn in by Chief Justice Warren Burger on December 6, 1973, in the Capitol. In his speech to the legislators and to the American people, Ford said, "I promise my fellow citizens only this, to do the very best I can for America."

The common wisdom was that Nixon, already embroiled in the expanding Watergate scandal, appointed Ford because the twelve-term congressman and Republican leader of the House of Representatives was popular with both his GOP and Democratic colleagues on Capitol Hill. He was probably the only nominee the president could be sure would be confirmed by Congress. Nixon also may have calculated that Ford's portrayal in some media reports as a plodding workhouse without a first-rate intellect, and therefore not up to the demands of the presidency, would be an insurance policy against the president's being forced from office. If that was Nixon's belief, he badly miscalculated. Ford's long experience in Congress and the support and respect he enjoyed from members of both political parties made him a plausible replacement for Nixon, and thus increased the demands that the president resign or face impeachment.

As William Greider of the *Washington Post* wrote during that period, "The more Americans thought *about* Jerry Ford, the more they thought *of* him."

In January 1974, NBC broadcast its annual TV news panel at which correspondents offered their predictions of what to expect in the new year. I forecast that Agnew's resignation made a Nixon resignation more likely because it reinforced the image of widespread corruption in the administration and because it demonstrated that the political system could survive the resignation of a senior official.

"What about the new vice president, Jerry Ford?" the moderator asked me.

"There's a Ford in your future," I predicted.

And in my future, too.

NBC decided that since I had covered the former vice president, I should now cover the new vice president.

15

"Our Long National Nightmare Is Over"

Having been one of the "Agnew Nine," I now became one of the "Ford Five"—the five reporters who traveled 130,000 miles with Ford as he criss-crossed the country during his eight months as vice president. My press corps traveling companions were Phil Jones of CBS, Tom DeFrank of *Newsweek*, Marjorie Hunter of the *New York Times*, and David Hume Kennerly, then a photographer for *Time*. (Occasionally, Bill Zimmerman of ABC and Bob Leonard of the Voice of America would join us.)

As new details of the Watergate scandal—and of Nixon's role in it—were being revealed almost daily by the *Washington Post* and other news outlets, impeachment of the president was being mentioned openly. Nixon had become so unpopular and controversial that no Republican candidates wanted him to campaign for them in the months before the 1974 congressional elections. That task fell to Ford.

The Nixon White House staff, in their usual disdainful manner, decided that instead of traveling the country in one of the modern Air Force 707 jetliners in the presidential fleet, Ford and his press corps would fly in an ancient Air Force Convair 580, a two-engine, propeller-driven airplane with a top speed of only 330 miles per hour. The official name was Air Force Two. But since the tail of the shabby aircraft was emblazoned with the unofficial insignia of the Air Force unit to which it belonged—a raccoon with its tail raised—those of us who had to fly on the plane dubbed it Coonass Airlines.

Ford and his news media companions visited forty-one states in that decrepit plane. A typical travel day began at dawn at Andrews Air Force Base and ended back at Andrews Air Force Base early the next day. In one twelve-day period in late May of 1974, Ford campaigned in Washington State, New York (three times), Delaware, Michigan, Boston, Connecticut,

New Hampshire, Charlotte, North Carolina, and Birmingham, Alabama. During one nineteen-hour day, the vice president logged five receptions, three speeches, and two press conferences. No event was too small to attract the vice president. He took part in the dedication of a container ship wharf in New Orleans, a Saint Patrick's Day Parade in Charleston, South Carolina, a lunch with seventh graders in Honolulu.

A joke aboard Coonass Airlines was that if you were holding a banquet and couldn't get the local police chief as the speaker, invite Ford. The vice president did not lack stamina, although the "Ford Five" sometimes did.

Ford had a small, spartan compartment in the back of the Convair 580, while I and the other reporters sat in airline-style seats near the front. Frequently the vice president would wander up the aisle to chat with us. Traveling together all those long days, sharing those early starts and late returns, staying nights in the same Holiday Inns, the five of us and the vice president developed close relationships. We played practical jokes on each other. We drank together. Ford told jokes on himself, then let loose one of his loud, high-pitched horselaughs.

As he traveled those endless miles, attended those countless dinners and lunches and breakfasts and receptions and rallies, as he conducted fifty-two news conferences and gave eighty-five interviews, Ford delivered mixed messages. Sometimes he stoutly defended the embattled president and attacked Nixon's critics as "extreme partisans" who were waging a "massive propaganda campaign" to oust the chief executive. Some of those speeches were written by Nixon's White House staff. After a long meeting with Nixon, Ford told a news conference, "The president had no prior knowledge of Watergate, had no part in the cover-up, and has not been party to any of these allegations made by some."

But on other occasions Ford proclaimed, "I am my own man," praised journalists for pursuing the Watergate story, and criticized Nixon for not being more forthcoming in responding to the allegations and for not seeking a compromise on the demand by congressional committees that he turn over secretly recorded tapes of White House meetings.

A *New York Times* editorial declared, "Mr. Ford zigs and zags." During a campaign stop in North Carolina, Ford—the former football player—joked to me and the other reporters, "A zigzagger makes touchdowns."

Finally, Ford decided he needed to explain his position more clearly. He

As a child

With my parents in front of their store

My first job in radio—while still in
high school—co-host of a weekly
program of school news and talent

High school graduation

As a young radio reporter for
WARL, Arlington, Virginia

Asking South Vietnamese president Nguyen Van Thieu an "impertinent" question, for which I was expelled from the country

Trying to stay out of the line of fire, with my NBC News camera crew, in Vietnam

Recovering at Walter Reed Army Medical Center from a wound received covering a battle in Vietnam. *Photo: Wm. Berkeley Payne, Cameramen, Inc.*

Reporting from an aircraft carrier in the Pacific on the safe return of the astronauts from their moon landing (they are in the trailer)

With press colleagues aboard an aircraft carrier after covering a safe return of the astronauts from a spaceflight

Covering one of LBJ's walking news conferences around the South Lawn of the White House. *Photo: Abbie Rowe, National Park Service*

Lunch in the White House, where there was no time to go out. *Photo: Frank Johnston/Getty Images*

During the 1972 election campaign, helping Eunice Kennedy Shriver, wife of the Democratic VP candidate, carry a bucket of ice to a party for the press. *Photo: Tommy Noonan & Camera*

Conferring with Ford aboard Air Force One

One of the perks of being press secretary—dancing with the president's daughter

Trying on the bulletproof vest given to me by friends at the Justice Department to protect against attacks by the press

With Henry
Kissinger,
whom I
admired but
also clashed
with

Another hard day

Walter Cronkite
(center, back turned),
who said he just
wanted to shake the
president's hand . . .
but really wanted an
interview

chose to deliver this important speech at the commencement ceremony at Utah State University. "Why do I uphold the president one day and the next day side with the Congress, which is deliberating impeachment?" Ford asked rhetorically in the packed auditorium. "Well, I have not seen a controversy in which one side was all wrong and the other one hundred percent right, nor have I seen a human being who is totally good or altogether bad. . . . I consider it my duty to try to head off deadlock and seek a reasonable and prompt solution to the nagging Watergate issue."

But as the days and weeks of that 1974 spring and summer passed, as new details of the Watergate scandal emerged, and as Nixon's survivability became questionable, Ford more and more abandoned his role as defender of the president. Although he never said so publicly, he knew by then that Nixon probably would be forced from office, and that he would succeed to the White House.

He began to hedge his defense of Nixon. In a speech in Boston during that period, he said, "I don't happen to believe *on the basis of evidence I'm familiar with* . . . that the president was in any way connected with Watergate *per se*, and I don't believe that he had any part in the cover-up. *But only time will tell.*" (Emphasis mine.)

Only years later, in his autobiography, did Ford reveal his true assessment of Nixon's conduct in the Watergate scandal: "His pride and personal contempt for weakness had overcome his ability to tell the difference between right and wrong. What some journalists called the 'dark side' of his personality had prevailed over his judgment, which was normally sound. And once the course had been set, there was no turning back."

An insightful joke made the rounds in Washington as Nixon's presidency collapsed: "If the president had made the football team at Whittier College, Watergate never would have happened." In other words, Nixon would have had more self-confidence, wouldn't have felt the compulsion to prove himself, to go after supposed enemies. On the other hand, Ford *had* made the football team at the University of Michigan, been named to the collegiate All-Star team, been admitted to Yale Law School, married the woman he loved, never lost an election. Perhaps that was why he was comfortable and confident with who he was.

In April, during Ford's annual Easter break with Betty in Palm Springs, California, reporter Tom DeFrank of *Newsweek* commented to him during a private meeting that Nixon was on his way out. "It's over," the reporter recalls saying. "He can't survive, and you're going to be president." The reporter was stunned when Ford replied, "You're right." Instantly the vice president realized his mistake. If his comment appeared in print, the reaction would be horrendous.

"You didn't hear that," Ford told DeFrank. "But I did," DeFrank replied. "Tom, you did *not* hear that," Ford persisted. The vice president reached over and grabbed the reporter's necktie. "Tom, you are not leaving this room until we have an understanding," Ford declared. "Write it when I'm dead." Intimidated, the twenty-eight-year-old neophyte reporter agreed. Before, during, and after his presidency, Ford held many private conversations with DeFrank, with the understanding that the reporter would write about them only "when I'm dead." After Ford's death, DeFrank wrote a book about those candid talks. It is less-morbidly titled, *Write It When I'm Gone.*

During his 1974 Easter vacation in Palm Springs, Ford stuck to his daily holiday routine of playing eighteen holes of golf, a game he loved and pursued with varying levels of skill. Each day, I and the other reporters gathered beside the first tee in the morning and shouted questions at him about the unfolding Watergate scandal as he prepared to tee off. He smiled and waved and said nothing. We gathered again beside the eighteenth green as he took his final putts and shouted more questions at him. He smiled and waved and said nothing.

The stresses on Ford during this period were enormous, and their effects sometimes showed. He suffered mood swings. He lost his temper. In speeches, his references to Nixon were now extremely guarded. As time passed, I and the other reporters noticed that his defense of Nixon lessened and his positions became more independent of the White House.

Finally, on the morning of August 1, 1974—a rare day when the vice president was not traveling—Ford received a phone call from White House chief of staff Alexander Haig. Haig told Ford: "Mr. Vice President, it's urgent that I see you as soon as possible. I want to alert you that things are deteriorating. The whole ball game may be over. You'd better start thinking about a change in your life."

Haig came to Ford's vice-presidential office and explained that new White House tapes were about to be released that would show Nixon knew about and participated in the cover-up of the Watergate burglars' break-in at Democratic National Committee headquarters despite his previous denials to the public, the press, and congressional investigators. It was, Haig said, the "smoking gun" that would that would bring down Nixon.

Later that August afternoon, Haig called Ford again and asked for a second meeting immediately. The White House chief of staff came to Ford's Capitol office and told him that after listening to more Watergate tapes and reading more transcripts of Oval Office conversations, he had no doubt that Nixon would be forced from office when this new evidence of his involvement became public.

"Are you ready, Mr. Vice President, to assume the presidency in a short period of time?" Haig asked. "If it happens, Al, I'm prepared," Ford replied. Of course, I and the rest of the press corps had no hint of these conversations at the time.

In his autobiography, Ford recalled that Haig raised the possibility that Nixon might issue pardons for himself and others involved in Watergate, either before or after a congressional vote to impeach him. According to Ford's recollections, Haig also explained that some members of Nixon's staff believed the president would resign *if* his successor—Ford—promised to pardon him. Ford gave no immediate answer to Haig. He asked for time to think about the options the chief of staff had presented, and to talk them over with Betty and with longtime, trusted staff members Robert Hartmann and Jack Marsh.

A few days later Ford took off on his next speaking trip, to Hattiesburg, Mississippi, and New Orleans. As the likelihood of a Nixon resignation and a Ford ascendancy to the Oval Office grew, the size of the vice president's traveling press corps increased. The original "Ford Five" aboard Coonass Airlines became the "Ford Sixteen." Ford made no mention of Watergate in his speeches in Hattiesburg or New Orleans. I and other reporters in his entourage asked him about this omission at a news conference. "I don't want anyone to get the wrong impression," Ford answered, disingenuously. "My views today are just as strong as they were two days ago. I believe the president is innocent of any impeachable offense, and I haven't changed my mind."

Flying back to Washington from the Hattiesburg–New Orleans trip, Ford received a phone call aboard Air Force Two from Jack Marsh advising him that the White House was going to make an announcement later in the day that would be harmful to Nixon's chances of remaining in office. Even though we were only a few feet away from Ford, I and the other reporters on the vice president's plane had no knowledge of Marsh's call or that it meant Nixon's final days in the White House were at hand.

In the bombshell announcement that Marsh had alerted Ford was coming, Nixon acknowledged that he had tried to use the Central Intelligence Agency to stop an FBI investigation of his reelection committee's role in the break-in at the Democratic National Committee offices in the Watergate office building. Ford issued his own statement, announcing that he would no longer repeat his previous arguments that Nixon was not guilty of an impeachable offense, and would not involve himself in the impeachment debate.

But privately, unbeknownst to me and the rest of the press corps, Ford began a series of meetings with old and trusted friends and staff members to prepare for assuming the presidency. He instructed Hartmann to start drafting an acceptance speech.

At 11 a.m. on August 8, 1974, one week after Haig had advised the vice president to prepare to ascend to the presidency, Ford met in the Oval office with Nixon. The president explained that he would make a televised address to the nation that night announcing his resignation. The next morning, Nixon would hold a farewell meeting with his White House aides and their families in the East Room. Then he and his wife, Pat, would fly into exile in San Clemente, California. And Ford would be sworn in as the new president.

"Jerry, I know you'll do a good job," Ford recalled Nixon telling him.

Ford and his wife watched Nixon's resignation announcement on television at their home in Virginia. I was in the considerable mob of reporters, camera crews, and neighbors waiting in a drizzling rain outside the house. The scene was illuminated by harsh television lights. After the speech, Ford came out of the house and made a short statement: "I pledge to you tonight, as I will pledge tomorrow and in the future, my best efforts and cooperation, leadership and dedication that is good for America and good for the world."

The next morning, I and other reporters, as well as presidential staff members, were restrained behind a rope barrier on the South Lawn of the White House as Nixon and his wife walked out of the Executive Mansion for the last time, accompanied by Jerry and Betty Ford. The Nixons traversed a red carpet and boarded an army helicopter that would take them to Andrews Air Force Base, where they would board a plane to California. Pat Nixon's face was a frozen mask of anguish and pain.

At the top of the short stairway leading into the helicopter, Nixon turned around, gave "V" signs with the fingers of both hands, waved both arms in an exaggerated farewell gesture, and ducked into the chopper. I'll never forget that farewell wave. It was filled with resentment and anger and defiance. Ever since that historic moment, I have thought of it as the "Fuck you!" wave.

Once the Nixons' helicopter had departed, Ford and his wife, the staff people, and the reporters and cameramen tramped into the East Room of the White House, where Ford placed his hand on a Bible held by a somber-looking Betty and took his oath as president of the United States from Chief Justice Warren Burger. I watched and made notes in my seat in the very last row of the packed room. The television networks transmitted the historic moment.

"I am acutely aware that you have not elected me as your president by your ballots, and so I ask you to confirm me as your president with your prayers," Ford told the nation. "My fellow Americans, our long national nightmare is over. Our Constitution works. Our great Republic is a government of laws and not of men. Here the people rule."

Almost immediately after his swearing in, Ford came to the White House Press Room, stood behind the podium, and spoke to the reporters packed in the room. He said he hoped to continue the "kind of rapport and friendship" he had enjoyed with the press in the past, and he promised to have an open and candid administration. "I can't change my nature after sixty-one years," Ford declared.

Ford didn't know it then, but his honeymoon with the White House press corps would last just four weeks.

Nixon's White House press secretary, Ron Ziegler, departed with his boss. Ford selected as his press secretary Gerald F. terHorst, Washington bureau chief for the *Detroit News*, a friend from Michigan dating back to Ford's first campaign for Congress.

And, since I had covered Ford as vice president, NBC News assigned me to join Tom Brokaw on the White House beat.

16

The President Next Door

It took a few days for the White House staff to collect the Nixons' belongings, pack them, and ship them to the former president in San Clemente. And it took a few more days for the staff to tidy up and do some needed painting in the First Family's residential quarters on the second and third floors of the White House. During that ten-day period, now-President Ford and now–First Lady Betty Ford continued to live in their modest suburban house in Virginia. He was the president next door. I thought it was symbolic of Ford's down-to-earth, unpretentious, neighborly personality. He often described himself self-deprecatingly this way: "I'm a Ford, not a Lincoln."

Another symbol: On his first full day as chief executive, when Ford entered the White House through a lower-level doorway in the West Wing, the marine guard on duty snapped to attention and smartly saluted his new commander in chief. Ford stuck out his hand to shake and said to the marine, "Hi, my name is Jerry Ford. I'm going to be living here. What's yours?" More proof that the imperial presidency was dead: Soon after Ford became president, his dog Liberty had an accident on the rug in the Oval Office. A navy steward, who normally provided meals and other routine services in the White House, rushed to remove the dog's droppings. Ford waved him away and collected the mess himself.

"No man should have to clean up after another man's dog," the president said.

During Ford's first ten days as president, a White House motorcade formed up in front of 514 Crown View Drive early each morning—the president's White House limousine, vehicles for the Secret Service, vehicles for the press contingent, and a police motorcycle escort. Ford's neighbors came out to wave hello and to wish him good luck. Of course, I and the other reporters would shout questions at the president as he climbed into the presidential limousine.

One morning, as the president was walking between his front door and his ride, I shouted, "Mr. President, are you going to pardon Nixon?" He smiled, waved, and got into his car without responding. The limousine moved a few feet ahead, then stopped. Ford lowered his window, stuck out his head, and called "Nice try, Ron!"

In addition to deciding whether to pardon Nixon, Ford faced another important choice during his first days as president. Under terms of the Twenty-fifth Amendment to the Constitution, he had to nominate someone to fill the now-vacant job of vice president. He chose former New York governor Nelson Rockefeller, a moderate, who would balance Ford's conservative reputation and appeal to independents and middle-of-the-road Republicans.

At Ford's first televised news conference as president, about two and a half weeks after he took office, eleven out of twenty-nine questions focused on Nixon and Watergate, rather than on a number of pressing economic, foreign policy, or Vietnam issues. The very first question, from Helen Thomas of the UPI, set the tone: "Would you use your pardon authority if necessary" to prevent the prosecution of Nixon? Ford replied evasively, "There has been no action by the court; there has been no action by any jury, and until any legal process has been undertaken, I think it's unwise and untimely for me to make a commitment."

Ford's aides used this first news conference to send several symbolic messages that Ford was different from Nixon in large ways and small ways. When he faced the press, Nixon had stood in front of a blue velvet backdrop along the East Room's windowless long wall. Ford's podium was set up on the opposite side of the room, in front of an open doorway, perhaps symbolizing Ford's openness. Unlike the pallid Nixon, the ruddy Ford wore no television makeup.

But the changed atmosphere in the White House was not just about symbolism. Jerry and Betty Ford genuinely enjoyed socializing with old friends, including reporters. The Nixons had been stiff and uptight. The Fords were relaxed and convivial. This new atmosphere in the White House was clearly on display at a state dinner for the visiting king and queen of Jordan just a week after Ford was sworn in. I and some of the other Ford Five were invited to attend as guests.

Ford wrote later: "During the Nixon years, those occasions had been formal and rather dull." There was nothing formal or dull about the Fords' dinner for King Hussein and Queen Alia. After dinner, the Fords stayed, mingled with the guests, and danced to the band. At one point, Ford spun my wife Cindy around the dance floor to the very upbeat song "Bad, Bad Leroy Brown." Finally, at 1 a.m., the Fords said goodnight to their guests and retired to their residence.

I invited Ford to attend a poolside barbecue / reunion party of the Ford Five at my house in suburban Maryland two weeks after he became president. I never expected him to accept. But he did. In an open-necked shirt and a loud sport jacket, the president sat in a lawn chair, sipping a cool drink, joking and reminiscing with the reporters and their families. The Ford Five serenaded the president by singing "Thanks for the Memories." Ford described the outing this way: "We talked a little, we drank a little, and we had a helluva good time."

Did dancing with the president of the United States make up to Cindy for all the days when my travel schedule, as a reporter and then as press secretary, left her to cope with raising our baby by herself? Did having the president of the United States relaxing in her backyard make up to Cindy for all the days when I departed our home before dawn and returned after midnight? Did being invited to White House dinners make up for having a husband who was distracted, exhausted, and testy from the demands of his job? Probably not. Those demands and pressures took a heavy toll on our marriage. And I was not sensitive enough to prevent or minimize the damage.

Once they moved into the White House, the Fords followed the custom of their predecessors dating back to James and Dolly Madison by attending Sunday morning services at the white-pillared St. John's Episcopal Church directly across Lafayette Square from the White House. I and a small group of reporters accompanied them, sitting in the back row. Normally, after Sunday services, the White House Press Office would advise reporters that no more news was expected until the next day. But after the Fords returned to the White House from services at St. John's on Sunday, September 8, 1974, the Press Office suggested that I and the handful of other reporters who had accompanied the First Family to church stick around. The Press Office phoned other reporters at home and advised them to come to the White House. The president was going to make an announcement, the Press Office disclosed.

His statement was a bombshell:

I, Gerald R. Ford, President of the United States, pursuant to the pardon power conferred upon me by Article II, Section 2, of the Constitution, have granted and by these presents do grant a full, free, and absolute pardon unto Richard Nixon for all the offenses against the United States which he, Richard Nixon, has committed or may have committed or taken part in during the period from January 20, 1969, through August 9, 1974.

Ford added, "I do believe, with all my heart and mind and spirit, that I—not as President but as a humble servant of God—will receive justice without mercy if I fail to show mercy." He then signed the pardon document.

I and the other correspondents raced to our cameras and phones to report this stunning development. On an NBC News television special that night, I was asked about the rumors of a deal: had Nixon agreed to resign, making Ford president, in return for Ford's promising to pardon him? My answer was that many people suspected there was such a deal, but there was no proof. And during almost two and a half years in the White House as Ford's press secretary, I never heard anything or saw anything that led me to believe there had been a deal. Nor has any evidence of a deal surfaced in the decades since then.

During Ford's first month in office, he and his senior staff members had been spending 25 percent of their time on leftover Nixon matters—including legal and congressional efforts to obtain White House documents and tapes relating to Watergate. Nixon aides in San Clemente were transmitting to the White House hints that Nixon was so mentally agitated that he might take his own life if forced to face a criminal trial.

Ford explained that he issued the pardon, in part, so he could devote 100 percent of his time to pressing policy issues, including the lingering Vietnam War, a troubled economy, and tense relations with the Soviet Union. The president wrote in his autobiography that he believed putting Nixon on trial would have resulted in a prolonged period of vituperation and recrimination that would be disastrous for a nation facing serious economic and foreign policy problems. "America needed recovery, not revenge," Ford wrote. "The hate had to be drained and the healing begun."

It was revealed later that in the days and weeks leading up to the resignation and pardon, operatives for Ford and Nixon had secretly been trying to reach agreement on the wording of a statement in which the former president would acknowledge wrongdoing and show repentance, and thereby provide some justification for what was certain to be an unpopular pardon. Nixon refused to go any further than this: "One thing I can see clearly now is that I was wrong in not acting more decisively and more forthrightly in dealing with Watergate, particularly when it reached the state of judicial proceedings and grew from a political scandal into a national tragedy."

Ford described Nixon's statement as "inadequate." But he granted the pardon anyhow, setting off a firestorm of outrage. Ford's popularity and nice-guy reputation with the public, the news media, and both Republican and Democratic politicians evaporated. And speculation about a deal with Nixon exploded.

Many decades later, the Kennedy family presented its annual John F. Kennedy Profile in Courage Award to Ford for his pardon of Nixon. Senator Ted Kennedy said on the occasion, "I was one of those who spoke out against his action then. But time has a way of clarifying past events, and now we see that President Ford was right."

One other consequence of the pardon was that Jerry terHorst resigned as Ford's press secretary because he disagreed with the president's action.

In his resignation letter, terHorst wrote—somewhat self-importantly in my opinion—"I cannot in good conscience support your decision. . . . As your spokesman I do not know how I could credibly defend that action in the absence of a like decision to grant absolute pardons to the young men who evaded Vietnam military service as a matter of conscience."

Some more cynical members of the press corps speculated that at least part of terHorst's motive for resigning was that he was overwhelmed by the long hours, the demands of managing fifty-five people in the Press Office, and the never-ending pressures of the job.

17

Changing Sides

When terHorst resigned, I wanted to be chosen as the new press secretary.

One reason I wanted the job was that I was ready for a new challenge. After almost two decades as an observer at events, I had the itch to be a participant for once. I also wanted the job so I could see what really went on behind the scenes in the White House. As an NBC News correspondent covering the Lyndon Johnson White House and the first month of the Gerald Ford White House, I suspected that what I and other correspondents were allowed to see and know was perhaps 10 percent of what was really going on.

Recalling my early doubts about my manhood, implanted by my overprotective mother, I saw the high-visibility White House job as yet another test of my ability to handle challenging tasks. After reporting on wars, revolutions, tribal uprisings, political battles, racial confrontations, and natural disasters for NBC News, I was sure I was capable and ready to take on new and bigger responsibilities in the White House. Initially, I did not consider that I might not have the right temperament to handle the demands of the job.

One morning, about a week after terHorst quit, I received a phone call at home from a White House personnel recruiter. He asked me if I was interested in the press secretary's job. I relied, "Yes, I'm interested, under certain conditions." Later that afternoon, I received another phone call from a White House staff member, asking for my full name. I assumed he was going to submit it for an FBI background check.

The following Sunday, while I was enjoying a sunny afternoon sitting on my patio watching a Washington Redskins football game on television, I received a phone call from Robert Hartmann, a key aide during Ford's years in Congress and as vice president, and newly appointed to the job of chief White House speechwriter. Hartmann, a gruff and assertive man, was my neighbor in Bethesda, Maryland. Often, when we arrived back at Andrews Air Force base after one of Vice President Ford's long days of campaigning, Hartmann had offered me a ride home in his chauffeur-driven White House car. A friendship had developed.

In his Sunday phone call, Hartmann advised me that I was on a list of candidates for the press secretary's job. Hartmann did not ask me if I wanted the press secretary's job. He did say, "I wouldn't want anybody to turn down the president to his face." When I didn't say I would turn down the job if offered, he assumed I would say yes. Two days later, Hartmann phoned me again. This time he was more direct. He asked me if I was interested in being Ford's press secretary. I said yes. He asked me to come to the White House that afternoon to meet with the president.

In those days, it wasn't unusual for a journalist to change sides and become the White House press secretary. Franklin Roosevelt's spokesman, Stephen Early, had been an editor and reporter with the UPI and AP. Press secretaries for Presidents Truman, Eisenhower, Kennedy, and Johnson had been journalists before joining the White House staff. More recently, White House press secretaries have tended to have a background in public relations or as career government public affairs officers.

When Hartmann escorted me into the Oval Office to accept Ford's invitation to be his press secretary, the president stood up, shook hands, and invited us to sit down in the two chairs facing his desk. Behind him, through the large windows, the White House Rose Garden and South Lawn were visible. Ford looked very much at home in the Oval Office. After some small talk about a speech he had made the previous evening at the National Press Club, Ford got to the business at hand. He said he badly needed a press secretary and was surprised to hear that I was interested in the job. For one thing, he thought it would be a big pay cut for me. I said I had no idea what the press secretary earned. He said the salary was $42,500—which was, indeed, a pay cut from my network correspondent's salary. I said the pay was not the major consideration for me.

Ford openly expressed his anger at terHorst for resigning. He complained that terHorst had never really severed his loyalties to the press corps and transferred his loyalties to the president. After that pronouncement, Ford paused, waiting for me to say something. What I said was: I understood that he would be my boss and that if I took the job, I would be totally loyal to him. Later in the conversation, I told Ford I disagreed with ter Horst's view that he couldn't serve as White House spokesman if he disagreed with a presidential decision. The press secretary's job, in my view, was to accurately convey what the *president* thought, what the *president* did, and why the *president* did it. I told Ford I believed it was irrelevant whether the press secretary agreed with the president or not.

I also told Ford that as a reporter, I had seen good press secretaries and not-so-good press secretaries. The good ones, I said, got their information firsthand, talking directly with the president daily and attending most of the White House meetings and discussions. I mentioned Pierre Salinger, John Kennedy's press secretary, and Bill Moyers, one of Lyndon Johnson's press secretaries, as being particularly good at their jobs because they were allowed to witness or were kept informed about everything going on in the White House. Ford assured me he wanted that kind of press secretary. He promised that I would have direct access to all his advisers, and that I could attend all White House meetings except private talks with individuals and meetings involving highly sensitive national security matters.

I told Ford that I didn't feel comfortable being a "salesman" for his decisions. I said I would announce the decisions and explain how and why he had reached those decisions. But I said I didn't think the press secretary should be a promoter, working to drum up support for his programs.

"If I can't sell the program, then the press secretary can't sell the program," he replied.

Our conversation was very relaxed. Finally, the president said he would like me to accept the job as his press secretary. He asked me if I wanted to think it over. I responded that I had suspected for a few days that the offer was in the wind, that I had thought it over and discussed it with Cindy. "There's no need to think it over further," I told him. "My answer is yes."

I didn't anticipate having a problem serving as the spokesman for a moderately conservative Republican president. While most of my colleagues in the press corps leaned toward the left in their personal political views, I was less liberal than I had been in my younger days. I thought of one of my favorite maxims: "If you are under thirty and a conservative, you have no heart. If you are over thirty and a liberal, you have no brain." I was forty years old.

Ford said he would announce the appointment himself the next day. But at the moment, he was late for his next meeting. I asked the president one last question: Would I be one of his senior advisers?

"Of course," Ford replied.

But then Hartmann spoke up, "You'd better tell him, Mr. President, that I have a lot of experience in the [press relations] field and that I'm going to be looking over his shoulder a lot." Relating the incident in his autobiography, Ford wrote, "I didn't think that was any way to welcome Ron to the staff." At the meeting, Ford put down Hartmann by telling me, "Bob's had a lot of experience *writing my speeches.*"

Hartmann's threat to involve himself in Press Office matters was a foretaste of the many personal rivalries I would soon encounter among the senior members of Ford's White House staff. I suspect Hartmann recommended me to the president for the press secretary's job because he thought I would be his ally in the warfare that was developing among Ford's senior staff members. If so, I disappointed him.

My hunch about staff rivalries in the White House was almost immediately confirmed in a long conversation with Jack Hushen, the competent and well-liked assistant press secretary, a carryover from Ziegler's staff. After outlining my new duties and responsibilities and describing the Press Office operation, Hushen gave me a disturbing briefing on the atmosphere in the Ford White House: Some senior staff members were leaking negative stories about other senior staff members to settle personal vendettas; there was ongoing jostling for power and access to the president; Hartmann was "knifing" White House Chief of Staff Alexander Haig in anonymous conversations with reporters; Ford friend and adviser Melvin Laird was leaking negative stories about Henry Kissinger.

By the time my meetings with Ford, Hartmann, and Hushen were over, it was 6 p.m. I had not yet told NBC News that I was resigning and that my new job as press secretary would be officially announced the next morning. But somehow the word was already spreading. As I exited the White House through the West Wing lobby, some reporters waiting outside asked me if I was going to be the new press secretary. It was my first press query as the president's spokesman-to-be, and I blew it.

"Not that I know of," I blurted, misleadingly. At the White House gate I ran into my NBC News colleague Tom Brokaw. He asked me the same question, and I gave him the same inaccurate answer.

When I got to the NBC News offices, about a half-hour drive from the White House, Hushen called and advised me I had given "the wrong answer." Not a good way to start my new duties. Hushen suggested I phone all the reporters to whom I had given the misleading answer and tell them that, in fact, I had been interviewed for the job, I was under consideration, and any announcement would have to come from the White House. I followed his recommendation.

I reached the last reporter and corrected my denial shortly before midnight. Some of the reporters I phoned seemed pleased with my anticipated selection and told me the news would go over well among the White House press corps. Someone told me that veteran White House reporter Helen Thomas "giggled like a schoolgirl" when she heard the news. "Isn't that exciting," she had proclaimed.

The next morning, the president came to the White House Press Room to announce my appointment. He recalled that he had gotten to know me when I had covered him as vice president. "I admired his skill and objectivity as a reporter," Ford said. "I enjoyed his company."

In my response, I promised that I would never knowingly mislead or lie to the White House press corps. With the Watergate scandal and the pardon of Nixon so fresh in everyone's mind, I said it was probably too late for a "honeymoon" between the press corps and the press secretary. But perhaps, I suggested, we could have "a trial reconciliation." And echoing Ford's frequent description of himself as "a Ford, not a Lincoln," I declared, "I am a Ron, but not a Ziegler."

Ford presided over my swearing-in ceremony in the Oval Office. Cindy held our son Edward in one arm and the Bible in her other hand. Although other journalists before me had crossed the line to become White House press secretaries, I soon found out that some of my former colleagues in the press considered me a traitor for changing sides. Additionally, after Richard Nixon, Watergate, and Ron Ziegler, reporters automatically assumed the White House, particularly the official spokesman, was lying and/or covering up negative news.

Time magazine wrote that I had stepped into a "thankless job." And

John Osborne of the *New Republic* observed: "The atmosphere in the White House Press Room is the meanest I've ever seen. After you've been on a diet of blood for 18 months to two years [as the Watergate scandal unfolded], it's hard to kick it."

After one particularly hostile briefing, I fantasized about writing a magazine article or giving a speech in which I would declare, "In Washington there's a dirty little secret . . . that about forty or fifty grown men and women—including some who are quite well known and get paid quite a lot of money—get together in a room every day and beat up the press secretary . . . beat him up verbally." Part of this hostility and suspicion on the part of White House reporters stemmed from a feeling of anger and frustration because they had never gotten a whiff of the Watergate scandal even though they worked every day about fifty feet from the Oval Office. The Watergate scandal was exposed by two young reporters at the *Washington Post*, Bob Woodward and Carl Bernstein, who never went inside the White House gates.

I confronted one other factor in assuming the press secretary's position: I was supposed to both live down Ziegler's reputation for mendacity and evasion, and live up to terHorst's reputation for resigning as a matter of principle when he disagreed with a presidential decision. Beginning the day Ford announced my appointment, I was frequently asked at my daily press briefings whether I agreed with this or that decision made by Ford. My answer was always the same: "Who gives a damn?" The press secretary is not a policy maker or a decision maker. In my concept, the press secretary was, literally, the president's *spokesman*, he spoke *for* the president, he reflected the *president's* views. The press secretary's role, in my view, was to explain White House decisions and to answer reporters' questions as the president himself would if he were at the podium.

I initially thought of myself as still a kind of reporter whose job it was to relay to the other reporters attending my daily briefing what I had seen and heard *inside* the White House. I quickly realized that was a naive belief. I had changed sides. I worked for and spoke for the president. The best I could do was maintain a delicate balance that would enable me to fulfill my responsibilities to the president and my responsibilities to the press corps, and to remain true to my own principles of never telling a lie, of representing Ford's interests to the reporters, and representing the reporters' interests behind the scenes in the White House.

My relationship with the White House press corps was also complicated by another naive belief on my part—or at least an outmoded belief—about what kind of information reporters wanted and needed. My early journalistic mentors at the UPI had taught me that every well-written news story contained the "five Ws and an H"—Who, What, Where, Why, When, and How. As press secretary, I assumed that if I provided those basic facts about presidential actions, I would be fulfilling my obligation and the reporters' needs. But by the time I changed sides, journalists wanted to know way more than the who, what, where, why, when, and how of what was going on in the White House. They wanted to know what secret deals had been made, what ulterior motives the president was pursuing, what political objectives were behind Ford's decisions, what pressures were being applied and on whom and by whom, and what *wasn't* being announced. The demands from reporters to provide that kind of information were relentless.

But in one way my challenges as press secretary may actually have been a bit easier than what my successors faced. In the mid-1970s, there were no all-news cable channels, no Internet, no blogs. The White House press corps in those days mostly represented morning newspapers and evening television news programs. The deadline for both was around 6 p.m. So, unless there was late-breaking news, one late-morning White House briefing provided them with all the information they needed for their stories. Now, in the age of twenty-four-hour-a-day all-news cable channels and the Internet, reporters face a deadline every minute. Consequently, they look to the White House for fresh news and instantaneous reactions around the clock.

I began my career as a journalist in an era when reporters asked questions to get factual answers from which to write objective stories. Personal viewpoints were strictly excluded from journalists' questions and from their stories. And if any crept into the copy, editors were there to delete them. I often thought of the admonition from Reuven Frank: "Ron, nobody cares what you think."

By the time I became press secretary, that rule had changed. The viewpoints and attitudes of reporters were often obvious in their stories, as well as in their questions at my daily briefings and at presidential news conferences. The questions were sometimes accusatory or critical. And I bristled and got testy when reporters asked questions that began, "Ron, doesn't the president realize that he's making a mistake by . . ." or "Ron, how can the president expect anyone to support his decision to . . ."

I liked Ford as a person. I considered him a friend. And so I became protective and defensive when reporters asked hostile questions. It became obvious to me in my first days as press secretary that my personality might not be suited to the job. I did not suffer fools easily, and I thought that a number of my former colleagues in the White House press corps sometimes acted like fools. Maybe that judgment said more about my attitude than it did about the reporters. I had a short temper. And I had a healthy ego, or what I euphemistically referred to as "a high level of self-esteem," which had been inflated still more by my selection to be the White House press secretary.

Perhaps these testy, hypersensitive characteristics explain the code name the Secret Service assigned to me—"Sunburn."

18

The First Days

Almost immediately after Ford announced my appointment, I attended my first substantive Oval Office meeting, a session between the president and his economic advisers to discuss what to do about the country's high inflation rate. This economic crisis was partly caused by an embargo on oil shipments imposed by Middle East petroleum-producing countries as a protest against American aid to Israel after the so-called Yom Kippur Arab-Israeli War. Gasoline was in short supply in the United States. Gas prices soared. Frustrated drivers waited in long lines at gas stations for their share of the limited supplies.

The Oval Office meeting was supposed to focus on what steps the president should take to solve the economic crisis. But it quickly degenerated into haggling over the date and place for a proposed major economic speech by Ford and into a debate over the political implications of the economic crisis. It was my first experience with the kind of staff disputes that I would soon discover went on constantly in the Ford White House. The president sat behind his desk listening, asking questions, making suggestions and decisions, puffing on his ever-present pipe.

I left that meeting thinking how quickly I had been accepted by Ford and his senior advisers as a member of the team, a trusted "insider," when only the day before I had been looked upon warily as an "outsider," a prying reporter trying to sniff out secrets and scandals. I also was a bit dazzled by the prospect of being part of the inner circle of the president of the United States every day for at least the next twenty-eight months. I felt calm and confident in my abilities to master this new high-visibility challenge.

After the Oval Office economic meeting, I went to my new office and spent the rest of the day meeting other presidential staffers, discovering what daily life in the White House entailed, and acquainting myself with my new staff. Fifty people worked in the Press Office and the companion Communications Office. The largest group I had ever supervised until then had been a three-person NBC News camera crew. One of my first decisions was to retain most of the Press Office staff I had inherited, at least until I could judge their strengths and weaknesses, and assess my needs.

I called a meeting and told the staff that I wanted everyone to work together for the president's benefit. I almost immediately discovered that "working together" was going to be difficult to achieve. Some of my staff members were quarrelsome, dissatisfied, argumentative, and jealous of others on the staff. One woman said she couldn't get along with her colleagues and wanted to transfer to Mrs. Ford's press operation. One of the assistant press secretaries had no office, just a desk jammed behind a filing cabinet. A stream of Press Office staffers came to my office griping about other staff members, wanting a pay raise and/or shorter hours, asking for a better title.

Among my first decisions were to retain Jack Hushen, Ziegler's assistant in the Nixon Press Office; to assign a solid staffer, Tom DeCaire, to manage the day-to-day administrative work of the office; and to name another likable carryover, John Carlson, as my deputy, focusing primarily on domestic issues. I also asked two other carryovers, Bill Roberts and Larry Speakes, to remain. Additionally, I decided to keep Gerald Warren, a gentlemanly, wise, and competent member of the Nixon Press Office team. He took on the task of running the Communications Office, which provided information about Ford's activities to newspapers and broadcasters outside the Washington area and compiled briefing books for the president before media interviews.

Initially, I brought in only one new person for a senior position in the Press Office—James Shuman—an old friend, dating back to when we worked together at the UPI. More recently, he had worked as a writer for the *Reader's Digest*. I enlisted him to prepare the president's daily news summary, calculating that his experience at the *Digest* would enable him to boil down the day's news into a manageable and useful synopsis for Ford.

Because of her efficiency and long experience in the White House as personal secretary to a number of press secretaries, I kept Connie Gerrard in her same capacity. My first day on the job, she dumped a pile of material on my desk for me to absorb and deal with, including my daily intelligence briefing paper, my packed schedule, background material on policy issues and pending decisions, and a list of requests from reporters for interviews with Ford, with a place for me to check "yes" or "no."

I fell into a frenetic daily routine. Each morning I spent considerable time with my staff anticipating what questions reporters would ask at my briefing and making sure I knew the answers. For some of the anticipated questions, only the president could provide the answers, so I put them on my list of items to discuss with Ford at my daily Oval Office meeting, which usually began at 10 a.m. and lasted about thirty minutes. Additionally, there were press releases to write, edit, circulate for approval, and distribute. There were presidential trips for which my office had to organize transportation, communications, press rooms, and filing facilities for the correspondents. There were briefing books to assemble, to prepare the president for interviews and news conferences.

And there were phone calls and meetings with reporters seeking information. One of the ways Ziegler antagonized reporters was by rarely returning their phone calls. I had experienced his cavalier treatment as a journalist. I made a commitment that I would return every reporter's phone call every day, no matter how long that took. Sometimes it took until 9 or 10 p.m. In my first hours as press secretary, I placed phone calls seeking advice from two of my predecessors, Jerry terHorst and Bill Moyers. In spare moments I also returned calls from friends and former colleagues who had phoned to congratulate me—or express condolences.

After I had been on the job a short time, William Castleman, one of the White House lawyers, said the advice I was giving to Ford and the way I was handling the press corps suggested to him that my "attitude sure has changed in a hurry since you changed sides." In fact, I did worry that I was trying too hard to be a White House team player and thereby was losing the respect and confidence of reporters. I wondered whether I should step up my behind-the-scenes advocacy for putting out more information.

As one of the nine senior members of Ford's staff, I was entitled to have a White House car drive me to the office in the morning and take me home at the end of the day. On the way home after my first day on the job, I wanted to turn on the light in the back seat and start on some of the paperwork I was taking home. But the driver was chatty. He told me he was familiar with the neighborhood where I lived because he had frequently driven Dwight Chapin, Richard Nixon's White House appointments secretary, who lived across the street from my house. Before Watergate, I was friendly with Chapin. When he and his wife had a baby, Cindy and I lent them the crib our son had used. After the *Washington Post* broke the first story about the Watergate scandal and Chapin's role in it, I never saw him in the neighborhood again.

On my first day as press secretary, I got home about 9 p.m. My son Edward, a year and a half old, was not asleep yet, so I had a chance to play with him. For the rest of my tenure, I almost never got home that early. I sometimes woke up Edward when I arrived. It was the only way I could spend time with him. After Edward fell asleep that first night, I gobbled down a fast dinner and then tackled the paperwork I had brought home. Finally, I made up my "to do" list for Day Two, turned out the light, and fell asleep. It was after midnight.

I arrived at the White House the next morning, a Saturday, at 9:15 and learned that my daily meeting with the president was scheduled for 9 a.m. But fortunately (for me), Ford was running behind schedule—a not uncommon occurrence—so my tardiness wasn't noticed. At my meeting, I asked the president if he was interested in holding out-of-town news conferences for local reporters when he traveled. He pointed out that he was scheduled to speak to a meeting of UPI editors in San Francisco in the near future and probably would answer questions afterward. Oops! I should have known that. But he didn't make an issue of my gaffe.

I also went over with Ford various international, economic, and domestic issues that I was likely to be asked about, to make sure I understood his views and had my facts straight. And then there were the less momentous matters in the folder of issues my staff had prepared for me to discuss with the president. For instance, there was a note to tell Ford that the entertainer Sammy Davis Jr. had called and would like the president to contact him. Ford said he knew Davis and liked him and would get back to him sometime over the weekend.

The next day, Sunday, I got to the White House Press Office at 9 a.m. I was the first one there. And I didn't know how to turn on the lights! The main item on the Press Office agenda that day was to duplicate and distribute to news organizations copies of a major speech on the energy crisis that Ford was scheduled to deliver the next day in Detroit. Hartmann, the chief speechwriter, said he was waiting for Ford to sign off on the latest draft. I went to the Oval Office to find out if Ford had approved the speech, and found that the president had left the building to play a round of golf at the Burning Tree Country Club in Maryland, one of his favorite pastimes. When he returned, he approved the speech.

In a symbolic gesture, I had my staff remove the enormous bulletproof podium behind which former press secretaries had briefed. They replaced it with a simple music stand to hold my notes. Beside the music stand was a small table to hold a glass of water, an ashtray, and my cigarettes. In a further effort to emphasize the new informality and openness of the Ford White House, I announced that news photographers, TV cameramen, and radio reporters would be allowed to record my daily briefing. This had not been allowed in the past. I also tried using humor to keep the mood light. And on a warm and sunny October day early in his presidency, I arranged for Ford to hold a news conference outdoors on the South Lawn of the White House. I also changed the rules of presidential news conferences by allowing reporters to ask follow-up questions if they didn't think Ford had fully answered their initial question.

I heard complaints from a few reporters after my first briefings that I was taking up too much time looking through my notes to find the answers to their questions. I wasn't doing it deliberately to slow the pace of the briefing, but upon reflection I did think the slower pace had a calming effect. As I settled into the press secretary's role, I had the feeling that I was not going to have many problems seeing and talking to Ford when I needed to, or getting information I needed from the senior staff. I sensed that most of them were bending over backward to avoid another terHorst episode, and so they were keeping me informed and giving me access. Still, I realized my new job was going to be hard . . . really, really hard.

- The hours were long.
- The stresses were great.
- The press corps was disbelieving.
- The White House and Press Office staffs were mired in strife.
- I had to read and absorb huge amounts of information.

But I felt there was a compensating factor, namely that for the next couple of years I would have a front-row seat . . . indeed, a major role . . .

as President Ford made his decisions, reacted to crises, ran the country, and confronted a world full of problems.

On the way home that first Sunday night, I asked the White House driver to stop at the NBC News offices, not far from my house, so I could clean out my office there and pick up my personal belongings. It took me only ten minutes to pack all my stuff in three cardboard boxes. As I walked out the door, it struck me as odd that I could pack and walk away from a twelve-year career in ten minutes.

The Ghost Who Wouldn't Go Away

I learned very quickly that Richard Nixon was the ghost who continued to haunt the Ford White House. On many occasions, I was prepared to provide information on important issues and to make real news at my daily briefing, if only I had been asked the right questions. For instance, after a Ford speech warning Middle East nations about the consequences of their oil embargo, I was prepared at my briefing to elaborate on his threat. But most of the questions at my briefings were about Nixon matters. I even tried reading a passage from the Bible at one briefing: "Let all the bitterness and wrath and anger and clamor and slander be put away from you with all malice . . ." If I thought the Bible was going to persuade the bitter, wrathful, angry, and clamorous White House reporters to refocus their attention from Nixon to Ford, I was mistaken.

At the beginning of my first full week as press secretary, Mrs. Ford flew to Chicago, accompanied by her own press contingent. She was asked by a reporter during that trip if she or the president had been in touch with Nixon or the Nixon family recently. She answered, "Yes." She was asked when, and replied, "Last week." It didn't take long for the phone lines in the White House Press Office to light up with inquiries from reporters requesting elaboration. Who originated the call? How long did they talk? What did they talk about?

Ford himself helped keep the news media's focus on Nixon. The president told Hugh Sidey of *Time* magazine, in a late-afternoon Oval Office conversation, that Nixon had phoned him, expressed regret for all the trouble he had caused, and said he wouldn't care if Ford withdrew the pardon. Once Sidey's column appeared in *Time*, I was bombarded with more media questions. After checking with the president, I told reporters that Nixon's remark was an offhand courtesy, not a formal, legal offer to return the pardon.

My temper flared after one of my first briefings because I had prepared myself with information to answer queries on a wide range of issues, but almost all the questions during the forty-five-minute session were about Nixon. As I stepped off the podium after the briefing, a reporter came up and asked me about a substantive matter. I told him brusquely that he should have asked that question at my briefing, instead of dwelling on Nixon issues. Then I stormed back to my office.

After I cooled down, I explored with my staff ways to encourage reporters to focus more on substantive issues. One idea we kicked around was that the next time reporters at my morning briefing primarily asked about Nixon matters, I would read this statement: "Ladies and gentlemen, I have an announcement to make before you go. When I took this job, I promised that my goal would be to get out the most information possible about the Ford White House. I have found myself unable to live up to that goal [at this briefing] because of your focus on Nixon matters. And therefore, we'll have another briefing at four o'clock." And if the 4 p.m. briefing still produced mostly questions about Nixon, I would announce another briefing for 8 p.m. Talking about that idea helped me let off steam. But we didn't actually implement it.

On a day when I announced that Ford had decided to hold a series of meetings to discuss large cuts in the federal budget, most of the questions at my briefing and most of the resulting news stories focused on a revelation that the Ford White House was continuing to send Nixon daily classified briefing material. When I suggested at another briefing that Ford might impose a limit on oil imports, the *Washington Post* and the *New York Times* ignored that story entirely, but continued their intense coverage of Nixon in exile. A Gallup poll taken during that period showed that 86 percent of Americans thought inflation was the most important issue confronting the nation, while only 3 percent thought the aftermath of Watergate or the Nixon pardon was the most important issue. The results would have been a lot different if the poll had been taken among the White House press corps. Even months after Nixon's resignation, reporters at my briefings continued to ask questions about the former president.

Nixon didn't help efforts by the Ford White House to shift media and public attention from the former president to the new president. Not long after flying into exile in California, Nixon underwent emergency surgery to remove blood clots in his legs caused by phlebitis. When Ford visited California shortly afterward to campaign for Republican candidates in the 1974 congressional elections, Nixon's doctors thought a visit from the president would brighten Nixon's spirits and help his recovery. Ford agreed to see Nixon.

I went with the president and his Secret Service agents to Nixon's room on the seventh floor of the hospital. In order to gather details to pass on to the press corps, I stood outside the hospital room listening to the brief conversation between Ford and Nixon. Holding the hand of his ailing predecessor, Ford asked Nixon how he was feeling. Speaking in a low, hoarse whisper, his hair grayer than I remembered it, his face ashen, the former president replied, "I'm not feeling too well, but I'm going to make it." Ford asked Nixon if he had had a good night. Nixon answered, "None of the nights are good."

Before the California trip, I had argued against Ford visiting Nixon. I suggested a phone conversation instead. I thought a visit would only feed the news media's continuing obsession with Nixon and Watergate and would further link Ford with his discredited predecessor. Ford did not agree. Aboard Air Force One, leaving California, I again expressed to the president my concerns about the harm he was suffering from maintaining a public relationship with Nixon.

"If compassion and mercy are not compatible with politics, something is the matter with politics" was his reply.

Another reason the president continued to be haunted by the ghost of Richard Nixon was that Ford retained Nixon's White House chief of staff, Alexander Haig. Ford initially resisted strong pressure from longtime friends and advisers—particularly Hartmann—to replace Haig. These friends and advisers told Ford that while Haig and many other Nixon staffers remained in their jobs, the president could never erase the taint of Watergate and put his own imprint on the White House.

Urging Ford to dump the Nixon carryovers, Hartmann told the president in his usual blunt and profane manner, "You don't suspect ill motives of anyone until you're kicked in the balls three times." But even the bombastic Hartmann reluctantly agreed that Ford needed to keep Haig around for at least a brief period until the new president's staff had learned how to run the place. Haig was "the only one who knows how to fly the plane," Hartmann grumbled. "We're not going to shoot him in the cockpit before we learn how to fly the plane, or design a new plane."

Haig was exhausted from the long hours and incredible pressures he had endured, particularly while working out the details of Nixon's resignation and Ford's ascension to the presidency. Additionally, Haig had kept the day-to-day operation of the White House functioning throughout the Watergate scandal. Some thought he was almost an acting president during Nixon's final, chaotic months. Finally, Ford gave in to the urging of friends and advisers, and reassigned Haig—a former general and army vice chief of staff—to serve as NATO military commander.

My first weekend in the White House was Haig's last weekend in the White House. I spent more than an hour with him, absorbing his insights, wisdom, and advice. It was one of the most important meetings I attended in my two and a half years in the White House. For one thing, it confirmed my feeling that reporters only knew about 10 percent of what was really going on behind the scenes.

At the outset, Haig volunteered the candid assessment that Nixon was a man "really going to pieces" during his last days as president. Haig told me he liked Ford, thought highly of him. But based on the way Ford was organizing his White House staff, Haig said he had doubts about whether the White House could function effectively under the new president. Ford had announced he was bringing Donald Rumsfeld home from Brussels, where he was serving as American ambassador to NATO, to take on the chief of staff's duties, although initially without the chief of staff title. Rumsfeld, a former congressman from Illinois, former head of the Office of Economic Opportunity, and former head of the Economic Stabilization Program, was a longtime friend of Ford's and an experienced administrator.

In his new job, Rumsfeld would coordinate White House activities under what was known as the "spokes of the wheel" system of organization, which Ford had installed. The president was the hub of the wheel, the nine senior staff members—national security adviser, press secretary, congressional liaison, economic adviser, legal counsel, personnel director, and so forth—were the spokes. All nine had direct access to the president whenever they thought they needed to meet with him.

Haig told me he didn't think the "spokes of the wheel" system was a practical way to organize the White House and manage the president's time. Haig favored a strong chief of staff with authority to supervise the White House staff, manage the president's schedule, and determine who got into the Oval Office, for how long, and on what issues.

I mentioned to Haig that even before becoming press secretary, I had been aware of the Ford loyalists fighting with the leftover Nixon people, particularly Kissinger. Haig said that wasn't the real problem. He said the real problem was Ford loyalists fighting with other Ford loyalists. Haig specifically complained to me that Hartmann was competing with him and trying to undermine his authority.

Eventually, the infighting among staff members became even more complex and divisive, with Rumsfeld's coterie, the Hartmann faction, and the Kissinger team engaging in a daily struggle for influence. Believing that my primary role was to inform the press of the president's views and decisions, I tried to stay out of the never-ending staff feuds. But that was not possible. Even though Hartmann had been responsible for my getting the White House job, I usually allied myself with Rumsfeld.

Kissinger blamed me for leaking stories to the press critical of his actions and statements. And I blamed Kissinger and his staff for leaking stories to the press critical of my performance as press secretary. The *Washington Star* ran a front-page story during this period claiming that Rumsfeld was the leader and I was the front man for an effort to unseat Kissinger. Kissinger assured me that he did not believe the stories. I admired Kissinger for his diplomatic skills, his strategic and tactical policy moves, and especially his long view of history. But he often made my life difficult by doling out information on foreign policy and national security issues in ways that enhanced his own power and advanced his policy objectives.

At one point, Ford lost his temper over the anti-Kissinger leaks. At an Oval Office meeting his ire boiled over. Pounding the desk with his fist, the president said he was enraged over staff members fighting, bickering, sniping, and leaking. He demanded that it stop. He warned that any staff member who violated his dictum on this point would suffer dire consequences. "God damn it, I don't want this anymore!" he shouted. As he delivered this outburst, he swiveled his head back and forth, staring at each staff member in turn. I thought he stared at me the longest.

During my instructive final meeting with Haig, Haig had some complaints about my performance as press secretary, even though I had been on the job less than two days. He said I should not have promised the White House press corps that I would never knowingly lie or cover up the truth. I should have let reporters discover for themselves that I was honest, he advised, and then they would write stories about their conclusion. By proclaiming that I would always tell the truth, Haig said, I gave reporters an incentive to catch me in a lie.

Haig suggested that I meet twice a day with Ford to make sure I kept current on his views of various issues and on decisions he was pondering. But Haig also advised me to meet frequently with other members of the senior staff to make sure I knew everything that was going on. The implication was that Ford would not necessarily immerse himself in all the details of every issue.

Finally, Haig gave me an insight that stuck with me for the rest of my time in the White House. He said the three most important people in the White House were the president, the chief of staff, and the press secretary. He pointed to his head and said they were three "computers" who needed to know everything that was going on, had to absorb it, had to make sense of it.

If I was one of the White House "computers," I was already suffering from data input overload. On my desk were two thick briefing books, one on foreign policy issues and one on domestic policy issues. I also was trying to read a large folder of background information for an energy speech the president was making the following week. Additionally, I needed to read and master a tabbed notebook outlining the administration's position on dozens of issues. I soon learned that in order to do my job I needed to read virtually everything the president read.

Haig had warned me that one of the prime requirements for working in the White House was sheer physical stamina.

Ford inherited a sick economy from Nixon. Inflation was increasing prices by a stunning annual rate of more than 12 percent. Wholesale prices had shot up by more than 20 percent in the year before Ford took office. At the same time, 5.5 million unemployed Americans were looking for work. And as with so many other problems, Ford's chief advisers could not agree on a solution. Alan Greenspan, Arthur Burns, William Simon,

James T. Lynn, John Dunlop, William Seidman, and others were spending more time fighting among themselves than they were crafting policy proposals.

During one Oval Office meeting to draft a major speech Ford was scheduled to deliver to a "summit meeting" of representatives from various elements of the economy, I made a note to myself that it was almost impossible to write the speech "because nobody could agree on anything." Ford seemed to be "walking through a sea of molasses," I jotted down. The president kept urging his advisers to recommend a course of action to fix the economy, but they just kept arguing among themselves. By the night before the speech, no text had been written. Hartmann, the chief speechwriter, and White House economist Bill Seidman, an old Ford friend from the president's hometown, Grand Rapids, Michigan, went out to dinner and began outlining the speech. Since the economists couldn't agree on what steps should be taken, the Hartmann-Seidman outline consisted mostly of generalities and inspiration. Hartmann stayed up all night composing the speech. The concluding paragraph was slipped into Ford's text in the holding room minutes before he was to deliver the address.

In his first days as de facto White House chief of staff, Rumsfeld came to my office for our first detailed conversation. He was referred to as "Rummy" by most of his friends and colleagues, but I could never bring myself to call him that. He told me he planned to return to NATO headquarters in Brussels briefly to wrap up matters there. The official announcement of his White House appointment would be made in a few days, and he would be sworn in shortly afterward. I asked him if he wanted me to book him on the network TV Sunday news interview shows the following weekend. He said yes, that he wanted to do a lot of interviews at the outset, and then adopt a lower profile. Rumsfeld also advised me that he had "a few friends" of his own among reporters, and so he wouldn't be relying entirely on the White House Press Office to manage his media contacts.

Having almost no management experience before coming to the White House, I had learned a lot from Haig. Now I was about to learn a lot from Rumsfeld. He had formalized his management techniques in a set of "Rumsfeld's Rules," which I tried to follow. His "rules" included: "Don't think you're the president"; "Don't say 'The White House wants.' Buildings don't want"; "Don't divide the world into them and us"; and "It's easier to get into something than to get out of it." I thought the most important "Rumsfeld Rule" was: "For every problem there is a solution which is easy, obvious, and wrong."

When he was a member of Congress, Rumsfeld recruited a bright young intern named Richard Cheney for his staff. For the next few years, Dick Cheney followed Rumsfeld from job to job as his assistant. And when Rumsfeld came to the White House chief of staff's office, he brought Cheney with him.

Decades later, I didn't recognize the Cheney caricatured by the news media during his eight years as George W. Bush's vice president and afterward—a dark, hulking Darth Vader–like evil monster pulling the strings of a compliant puppet-president, personally plunging the United States into an unnecessary war, supervising torture of captured terrorists, plotting revenge against critical reporters. The Cheney I knew always had a lopsided smile on his face. He was relaxed around reporters, trading jokes and gossip with them. He was close friends with a number of journalists.

As de facto chief of staff, Rumsfeld issued several initial orders: Everyone on the White House staff had to report to one of the nine senior staffers. There would be no more "floaters," as there were in the Nixon White House—lower-level aides who dealt directly with the president without any other supervision. Rumsfeld assigned each of the Nixon floaters to one of Ford's nine senior staff members. If we wanted to keep them, fine. If we didn't want to keep them, we had to take the responsibility of firing them. Two of the "floaters" were assigned to me—Nixon speechwriter John McLaughlin, a former Jesuit priest, and Deputy Communications Director Kenneth Clawson, a former *Washington Post* reporter who had been involved in the Nixon reelection campaign's "dirty tricks" activities. I did not want to keep either one of them on my White House staff. So, following Rumsfeld's directive, I called each of them into my office to give them the news.

McLaughlin's reaction was that he worked for Ford and wouldn't leave unless he was told to do so directly by the president. I told McLaughlin that I was going to announce his departure at my briefing the next morning whether I had his letter of resignation or not. He gave me his resignation letter one hour before my briefing.

Clawson's dismissal went easier, but his response was more poignant. He asked me, "But how am I going to pay my mortgage?"

During this period, when I was spending a huge amount of time dealing with these and many other issues left over from the Nixon presidency, Rumsfeld came into my office one evening while I was meeting with my assistants and asked, "What are you doing here so late?" I replied, "We each have a little shovel and brush, and we're going around cleaning up other people's messes."

After a couple of weeks as press secretary, I felt I had turned a corner. I was no longer overwhelmed by the demands of the job. I thought I was finally doing pretty well—absorbing huge amounts of information, running a large and complex operation, fitting into a competitive and contentious team, and dealing with my suspicious and aggressive former colleagues in the press corps.

As I left the Press Office one night to head home, I commented, "Another day without the roof falling in."

A Press Office staffer replied, "Ah, you have practical objectives."

20

The First Lady

One evening not long after I became press secretary, I received a phone call asking me to meet the White House doctor, William Lukash, in his office at eight o'clock the next morning. At the meeting, Lukash—a navy rear admiral—informed me that Betty Ford was going to enter Bethesda Naval Hospital just outside Washington that evening. She would undergo surgery to determine whether a lump discovered in her breast during a routine checkup was malignant. If it was found to be cancerous, Lukash told me, she would immediately undergo a mastectomy. Mrs. Ford indicated she wanted me to delay announcing her surgery until she was already in the hospital so she would not be besieged by cameras and reporters shouting questions at her as she entered.

In the hours before she entered the hospital, Mrs. Ford stuck to her normally crowded schedule—dedicating a Lyndon B. Johnson memorial park along the Potomac River, entertaining Lady Bird Johnson at a tea, and dropping by a Salvation Army luncheon. I accompanied the president later that evening when he visited Mrs. Ford at the hospital. I followed the Ford entourage into the dining room of the presidential suite.

We found Mrs. Ford, dressed in a pink bathrobe, having a dinner of steak and french fries with her daughter Susan; one of her aides, Nancy Howe; Dr. Lukash; and a nurse. I started backing out of the dining room, not wanting to intrude on a private family occasion. But the president instructed me, "Sit down, join us."

During the meal, I kept up a whispered conversation with the president about the plans I was formulating for press coverage of Mrs. Ford's hospital stay. The First Lady kept looking over at us. Finally, I told him, "You'd better spend some time with your wife." After dinner, Ford asked everyone to leave the dining room so he could have some private moments

with Betty. Finally, I saw him kiss her good-bye. Riding down on the elevator, the president indicated he would stop and talk to the throng of reporters and TV correspondents waiting outside. But he didn't take time to
compose himself after his emotional visit with his wife. Answering the
press questions, he was close to tears.

Betty's operation began at eight the next morning. Within fifteen minutes, the lump in Mrs. Ford's breast had been removed, biopsied, and
found to be cancerous. A full mastectomy was performed. Lukash delivered the news to Ford by telephone while the president was meeting in
the Oval Office with Hartmann about an upcoming speech. After the doctor's call, Ford excused himself from the meeting, stepped into an adjoining bathroom, and tried to get his emotions under control. Jerry and Betty
Ford had been a close and loving couple for a quarter of a century. The
possibility of losing his life partner hit Ford hard. When the president returned to his desk, Hartmann could see how upset he was. "Go ahead and
cry," Hartmann urged the president. "Do cry." And the two old friends sat
in the Oval Office and wept.

Meanwhile, I had drafted a two-paragraph statement to distribute to reporters, saying that the biopsy results were unfavorable and that Mrs. Ford
was undergoing a mastectomy. The president approved the statement,
and we handed it out to the press. We issued that statement while Mrs. Ford
was still on the operating table, which may have set a new standard for
candor and openness by a White House in providing information on a
sensitive personal issue.

Later that afternoon, Ford decided to visit his wife in the hospital. It was
raining hard in Washington, marginally acceptable for travel by helicopter.
Taking off from the South Lawn of the White House in the storm, the
chopper veered frighteningly close to the Washington Monument. The
president was accompanied by his oldest son, Michael, a seminary student.
I watched as Michael knelt in the aisle of the chopper, holding a Bible and
praying with his father for Betty's recovery. Mrs. Ford was still in the recovery room when the president reached the hospital. She was not yet fully
awake from the anesthesia. But she squeezed his hand and gave him a smile.

Meanwhile, the rainstorm had worsened. The weather was too bad for
helicopter travel, so Ford returned to the White House by car. During the
drive, the president wrote out in longhand on a piece of paper a personal

statement about Betty, which he read at the beginning of a speech he delivered later that afternoon at an economic conference: "One personal note, if I may. I just returned from the hospital where I saw Betty as she came out of the operating room. Dr. Lukash has assured me that she came through the operation all right. It has been a difficult thirty-six hours. Our faith will sustain us, and Betty would expect me to be here." Ford was near tears, his voice shaking with emotion when he read the statement to the conference attendees.

Some reporters seemed to think they were better at diagnosing and determining the proper treatment for Mrs. Ford's cancer than the doctors were. I was asked why the First Lady's doctors had performed a radical mastectomy, removing the entire breast and the tissue around it, when less-invasive surgery might have been sufficient. But over the next few days, when Ford stopped on his way in or out of the hospital to chat with reporters, the journalists were uncharacteristically humane in their questions. They asked him if his faith was helping him get through those difficult days. They asked him how he was holding up. They asked him if he was getting much sleep.

The First Lady's highly publicized experience persuaded thousands of women all over the country that they should undergo examinations for breast cancer. Many discovered they had the disease. One of those was Happy Rockefeller, the wife of Vice President Nelson Rockefeller. Another woman who decided to have a breast examination as a result of the news stories about Betty Ford's experience was my mother. She found she also had cancer. Since I had never gotten over the pain of losing a young son to cancer, and since my mother had been such a huge influence on my life, I was very upset at the prospect of losing her. She underwent a mastectomy and subsequent radiation treatments. She died in 2010 at the age of ninety-nine.

Despite the positive effect Mrs. Ford's openness about her breast cancer had on other women, she did not want to be the figurehead for a breast cancer awareness program. Shortly after her mastectomy, she phoned me at home on a Sunday to tell me that. I got the impression that she did not want to play any role in a breast cancer program because she wanted to forget about her experience. In that phone call, she told me the two issues she *did* want to work on were cultural affairs and help for developmentally challenged children.

To celebrate Betty's successful operation, and to provide her with a diversion during her recovery, the president and their children bought her a gift: a copper-colored six-month-old female golden retriever. The family named the dog Liberty.

In addition to her breast cancer, Betty Ford experienced another health problem while she lived in the White House. And the very public way in which she and the president and their children dealt with that problem also helped many Americans who were struggling with the same problem. For many years, Mrs. Ford had suffered from arthritis and a pinched nerve in her neck. In addition, she carried the primary responsibility for raising the four Ford children while her husband, as House Republican leader and later vice president, worked long hours at the Capitol and traveled endlessly.

Because of these stresses, Mrs. Ford sometimes was depressed. To relieve the emotional stresses of her life and the physical pain of her ailments, Mrs. Ford became dependent on painkillers, tranquilizers, and alcohol. Often during the White House years, Mrs. Ford seemed drowsy, her speech slow and slurred. For once, reporters did not make a public issue of her personal problem. More than a year after leaving the White House, Mrs. Ford checked herself into a drug and alcoholism rehabilitation program, which cured her of the addictions. She later founded her own addiction clinic, the Betty Ford Center, in Southern California.

One good thing about living in the White House was that Mrs. Ford got to spend more time with her husband than she had in previous years. The president sometimes joked that he lived upstairs over the office. The Fords broke a White House tradition—most presidents and First Ladies had separate bedrooms in the Executive Mansion. The Fords shared a bedroom and a bed.

Mrs. Ford was always good for a colorful quote. In an interview on the CBS program *60 Minutes*, correspondent Morley Safer asked her what she would do if her teenage daughter Susan came to her and said, "Mother, I'm having an affair." Betty responded: "Well, I wouldn't be surprised. I think she's a perfectly normal human being like all young girls." Safer then asked the First Lady what she thought of the Supreme Court ruling legalizing abortions. Mrs. Ford called it a "great, great decision . . . the best thing in the world." The First Lady's answers set off a firestorm of protest from conservative voters, conservative editorial writers, and conservative columnists. The White House was flooded with letters, telegrams, and phone calls from the public about the Safer interview, most of them critical of Mrs. Ford's comments.

Betty's openness and honesty drew more criticism from conservatives when she told an interviewer from *McCall's* magazine, "The only thing that reporters haven't asked me was how often I slept with my husband."

"Well, I'm asking you," the interviewer said.

"I sleep with him as often as I can," she replied.

While Mrs. Ford's candor sometimes caused discomfort to the president, his conservative supporters, and the White House Press Office, it made her enormously popular, even beloved, among millions of ordinary citizens—especially women—who greatly admired her determination to be an independent voice, not just a smiling First Lady standing silently by her husband's side.

She was certainly not a silent, smiling First Lady when she thought another woman was getting too friendly with her husband. When Vicki Carr, an attractive Mexican American singer, was selected to be the entertainer at one White House state dinner, she flirted with the president, and he flirted back. At the end of the evening, as Ford was escorting Carr out of the White House, the singer asked the president, "What's your favorite Mexican dish?"

"You are," Ford responded. Mrs. Ford overheard the president's comment and snapped, "That woman will never get into the White House again."

Betty Ford was not a traditional presidential wife who avoided controversial causes and never spoke her mind in public. She was no Pat Nixon. Ensconced in an office in the East Wing of the White House, with her own press secretary, Betty seemed to blossom as an outgoing woman with strong and independent views. Sometimes those views were in conflict with her husband's positions on policy issues. At a time when the movement for equality for women was gaining strength, Mrs. Ford became a leading advocate of the Equal Rights Amendment for women, and she favored more-liberal abortion laws. She was a role model for modern political wives, demonstrating that they could have strong opinions and causes of their own and still be loyal, loving, and supportive of their husbands.

21

"WIN" and Other Economic Disasters

The economy—specifically roaring inflation—was the most pressing issue Ford had to deal with during his first months in the Oval Office. Yet nearly every speech-writing session ended with staff members fighting with each other about what the president should say to Congress and the nation. I told both Rumsfeld and Hartmann that if the president would decide on a policy first, the speeches would virtually write themselves. The fights, I told them, were the result of the writers not having a clear idea of what Ford's anti-inflation proposals were, and therefore they could not outline a policy in the president's speeches. Rumsfeld and Hartmann listened to my argument and relayed it to the president. He agreed. Ford settled on a number of steps to deal with the high inflation rate.

In a speech to a joint session of Congress about two months after becoming president, Ford announced those anti-inflation moves, including holding the federal budget to $300 billion. (A billion dollars was a lot of money in those days.) Ford's anti-inflation program also included imposing a 5 percent surtax on corporations and high-paid executives to soak up cash in the economy; encouraging farmers to grow more; providing stimulus to the housing industry; and launching the WIN program, standing for "Whip Inflation Now."

Ford wore a red and white WIN badge on his lapel for the speech to Congress. Initially, before they were mass-produced and distributed to the public, only two handmade red and white cardboard WIN badges were crafted. They were loaned out to the president and staff members to wear whenever they were delivering a speech or being interviewed on television. I still have one of those handmade WIN buttons.

The WIN idea was that ordinary citizens could play a role in stifling inflation by such steps as cutting back on their spending, planting gardens to grow their own food, riding bicycles to work to drive down the cost of gasoline, cutting back on use of electricity, and so forth. Whatever effect the voluntary WIN program may have had on curbing inflation, it became rich fodder for comedians, cartoonists, and political opponents. I'm not sure who dreamed up the WIN program. Nobody claimed credit.

Ford undertook a series of speeches around the country to generate public support for his anti-inflation campaign. His WIN speech in Kansas City to a Future Farmers of America meeting touched off a confrontation with the television networks. Ford wanted the speech to be broadcast live by the networks so he could reach a large national audience with his proposals to curb inflation. But none of the networks planned to carry it. When I reported this to the president, he instructed, "Well, do what you have to do." I telephoned executives at NBC, CBS, and ABC and told them the president thought his Kansas City speech was important enough for them to broadcast live. They all said no. Hoping to persuade them of the newsworthiness of the speech, I sent each network an advance copy of Ford's remarks. They still declined.

I was asked at my press briefing what the White House intended to do about the networks' refusal. I was tempted to give a tongue-in-cheek response, "We never talk about future military operations." But given the sour and hostile mood of the White House press corps, I decided not to make that joke. Some of the correspondents probably would report my humorous reply as a serious threat.

The only option left for the White House was to make a formal request for the networks to broadcast Ford's speech. Traditionally, when the White House made such a request, the networks complied. So I again phoned the network executives, and this time I made a formal request for airtime on the president's behalf. The three television networks agreed to broadcast the speech, but under protest.

To show its displeasure, CBS canceled an interview of the president by *Evening News* anchor Walter Cronkite. I was astounded. I had never heard of a news organization turning down an exclusive interview with a president, in this case Ford's first TV interview since becoming chief executive. Since it would look like favoritism for the president to give his first TV interview to NBC, my former employer, by default it went to ABC. Ford met with that network's evening news anchor, Harry Reasoner, at Camp David on a beautiful warm autumn Saturday in late October.

The first part of the interview consisted of Ford and Reasoner talking as they strolled about the grounds of Camp David amid falling gold and red leaves. Then, after a lunch break, the real face-to-face interview took place. Ford did not make big news, but he came across as friendly, knowledgeable, and capable of meeting the challenges he faced. He also kept his cool in the face of Reasoner's patronizing attitude. At one point in the interviewer, the TV anchorman asked Ford: "Do you think you're up to the job? A lot of people say you don't know enough." Ford explained patiently but firmly: "Look, I served on the Appropriations Committee. I was on the Defense Appropriations Subcommittee and the CIA Subcommittee. And I've been dealing with these kinds of figures and proposals and this kind of information for many, many years in Congress. That experience helps me as president."

Following the interview, the president invited me to sit around his Camp David swimming pool for a while. Mrs. Ford was napping and reading beside the pool. The president was standing knee-deep in water in the shallow end of the pool, dressed in slacks and a blue sports shirt, trying to persuade his dog, Liberty, to join him in the pool. And David Kennerly was snapping photos of the scene. I grabbed Liberty's collar and dragged him to the edge of the pool so Ford could pull him into the water. And the next thing I knew, Mrs. Ford's assistant, Nancy Howe, had pushed me into the pool fully dressed in a corduroy jacket, cashmere turtleneck, and Hush Puppies. I retaliated by climbing out of the pool, picking up Nancy Howe, and throwing her in.

The president and Mrs. Ford seemed to enjoy watching their aides acting like children. I still have one of the photos Kennerly snapped that day, showing me falling into the pool, with the president in the water trying to catch me. Ford autographed the picture with this inscription: "To Ron Nessen, who knew the job would be tough but not this bad. Liberty and G.R.F. tried to save you." It was a hilarious episode. I thought to myself that it was like something the Kennedys might have done. It was a side of Ford that I hadn't seen before and that the press hadn't seen before— putting aside the burdens of the presidency for a while and relaxing with his wife and friends.

But the burdens didn't go away. They got worse. One idea Ford initially adopted for fighting inflation was to reduce government spending. I attended one meeting during this period at which Ford and his budget and economic advisers went through 144 proposals for cutting the federal budget. Some of the proposed cuts were certain to be unpopular, such as reducing the school lunch program, cutting veterans benefits, and trimming the space program. Many of these budget cuts would be so unpopular with the public that Ford decided they should not be announced until after the November 1974 congressional elections.

Not long after Ford launched the WIN program and decided on these more substantive steps to combat the high inflation plaguing the country, he was suddenly confronted with an entirely different and unexpected economic threat—recession. Unemployment was rising, the gross domestic product was declining, automobile sales were falling, factories were laying off workers. This combination of high inflation and a declining economy was referred to as "stagflation." Initially, Ford was reluctant to publicly acknowledge the signs of recession, fearful that such an acknowledgment would frighten Americans into cutting back on their spending, which would deepen the recession. Finally, the president's economic advisers convinced him that it would be worse if he refused to publicly recognize what millions of Americans were experiencing in their daily lives.

So, in mid-November, the president called me to the Oval Office and instructed me to issue this statement to the press: "When the statistics come in for November and are analyzed, it will probably appear that this month we are moving into a recession." Alan Greenspan, then the chairman of the president's Council of Economic Advisers, made a disquieting forecast to me and other presidential staff members at a private meeting: "We think this is going to be a rather deep but short recession, but we could fall off the cliff."

In fact, the economy did fall off the cliff. It plunged into the deepest recession since the 1930s. Ford scrapped the WIN program and other anti-inflation measures launched only a short time before. Many of the policies he had instituted in the first days of his presidency had to be reversed in the face of the economic downturn. For instance, instead of tax increases, the president now asked for tax cuts so that consumers and corporations would have more money to spend. WIN buttons went into desk drawers, never to reemerge.

During that period when Ford was forced to map out a drastic shift in the government's economic policies, a reporter asked me at my briefing if the president's new anti-recession program would be a 180-degree shift from his anti-inflation program. No, I joked, it would be only a 179-degree shift.

Partly as a consequence of the nation's economic problems, partly as a rejection of the political party that gave the nation Richard Nixon, and partly as a show of displeasure at the Republican president who pardoned Nixon, the GOP suffered major losses in the November 1974 congressional elections. I watched the returns on television in the Oval Office with Ford, Betty, and a few invited friends and political allies. Surprisingly, despite the bad news for Republicans, there was a party mood.

The next morning, I commented to Ford that if we had such a good party on a night when Republicans were losing, what was the celebration going to be like when we won? Although I was not a registered Republican and in fact had tilted toward liberalism during my reporting days, I found myself routinely using the term "we" when referring to the Republican administration or the Republican Party.

I also realized that I had taken on responsibilities beyond the normal duties of a press secretary. I was helping to write speeches, passing messages to the president from staff members, passing instructions from Ford to staff members, offering ideas in areas beyond media relations, and calling to Ford's attention situations that needed his attention.

22

Too Much Vodka, Too Much Nicole

Ford set aside his efforts to deal with the country's economic and energy problems in late 1974 to travel halfway around the world to visit Japan, South Korea, and the Soviet Union. Nixon had been planning to make this diplomatic journey when Watergate destroyed his presidency. Ford believed it was important for him to go through with the trip. One purpose was to assure Japan and South Korea that America's withdrawal from Vietnam did not mean we would abandon them. And the purpose of Ford's stop in Vladivostok, in the bleak far eastern corner of the Soviet Union, was to size up the Soviet leader Leonid Brezhnev.

But before Ford could undertake his diplomatic negotiations, I had to conduct my own difficult negotiations with the Soviets. The Russians decreed that Ford could bring only forty reporters with him to Vladivostok, and they all had to hold American passports. More than one hundred and fifty reporters had signed up for the trip, including forty-one non-American citizens representing foreign publications and broadcast outlets that normally cover the White House. After I implored Soviet embassy officials in Washington to allow more reporters on the trip, they grudgingly agreed to admit an additional ten.

I asked Henry Kissinger to help me with this battle. Kissinger surprised me by asking if I wanted "a fight or an excuse"—in other words, did I really want more reporters on the trip, or did I just want reporters to think I had gone to bat for them. I responded that I wanted both. At Kissinger's urging, the Russians agreed to admit seventy reporters, only Americans. That would allow each newspaper and magazine that had signed up to cover the president's journey to have at least one reporter in Ford's press contingent. Each of the TV networks was allowed five correspondents and cameramen, plus producers and a lighting technician, and the wire services were each allowed four correspondents. The wire services thought the networks got too many places, and vice versa. But, generally, everyone ended up happy with the final arrangements.

After flying through turbulent weather over the Pacific Ocean, Air Force One landed at Tokyo's Haneda International Airport. Ford was taken by helicopter to the Akasaka guesthouse near Emperor Hirohito's Imperial Palace. The Akasaka was an ornate replica of Versailles, decorated and furnished in the style of Louis XVI. Ford's suite featured a pink canopied bed, and all four formal dinners in Tokyo consisted of French cuisine.

The day after Ford's arrival in Japan, the president and his entourage lined up for the official welcoming ceremony with the emperor. Ford and the rest of us were required to wear formal attire—swallow-tailed morning coats, black and gray striped trousers, gray vests, wing-collared shirts, and black and gray ascot ties. Never willing to pass up an opportunity to focus on trivia rather than substance, the press corps played up the fact that the pants of Ford's rented formal outfit appeared to be too short, showing his ankles.

The pool reporters—those selected to cover the ceremony and report back to their colleagues who couldn't be accommodated at the palace— wrote: "Mr. Ford then reviewed the guard, with his long strides emphasizing that his trousers were considerably shorter than those of the others who were wearing formal dress." This was the first visit ever by a sitting American president to Japan, an important nation economically and strategically in the western Pacific. And the reporters thought the length of Ford's trousers was more newsworthy than the significance of the trip and of the issues being discussed.

At the end of the first full day in Tokyo, Ford and his entourage attended a formal state dinner at the Imperial Palace hosted by the emperor and empress. The attire was even more formal—white tie and tails. This time the president's pants reached to his shoe tops, perhaps disappointing the press corps. During the dinner, I noticed Ford and the emperor carrying on a lively conversation, speaking to each other through an interpreter. I found out later that during their conversation the emperor and the president discovered they had a shared interest—a love for baseball.

The next stop on the Far East trip was Seoul, South Korea. The crowds on the streets of the capital to welcome Ford were huge, estimated at two million. My wife Cindy was Korean. Her mother was visiting Korea at the time of the president's trip and was in the official greeting area when Ford arrived. Before the Far East trip, the president's deputy national security adviser, Brent Scowcroft, had shown me an intelligence cable warning that the Korean intelligence agency was collecting data about me and my wife, our backgrounds, and our associates in hopes of finding information that might be used to influence me to advance Korean interests within the White House. I assured Scowcroft that on the day I became press secretary, I had told Cindy not to have any dealings with Koreans if she had not been friendly with them in the past, or if she did not know exactly whom they represented. I also decided that neither Cindy nor I should give interviews to Korean journalists.

Since my first days in the White House, I had been alert for possible efforts by Korean officials to gain information or to influence American policy through me and my Korean wife. I had been on guard ever since attending a Washington reception in honor of a visiting Korean Cabinet minister. At the reception, I made small talk with the minister, mostly about his son, who was attending American University in Washington, where I had been a student. Shortly after the reception, I received a letter from the minister, stating, "It was a pleasure for me to exchange information with you which will be beneficial to both your country and mine, and will further enhance mutual cooperation and friendship." I immediately took the letter to Scowcroft, who dictated a reply in which I told the minister I didn't know what "information" he was talking about, since our conversation had consisted entirely of polite pleasantries.

From Korea, Ford flew on to Vladivostok for meetings with Brezhnev. Getting from the airport where Air Force One landed to the meeting site, a health resort for government officials and trade union members, required a ninety-minute train ride aboard an ornate green and gold train. During the trip, Ford and Brezhnev sat across from each other, getting acquainted.

Arriving at the meeting site, the two leaders continued their discussions in a meeting room overlooking a glass-enclosed garden. The two delegations sat across from each other at a long table, talking through translators, nibbling from dishes of refreshments, and drinking bottled mineral water. Brezhnev chain smoked cigarettes while Ford puffed on his pipe, clouding the room with smoke. The two men—both big, both exhibiting a sense of humor, both with a hearty laugh—seemed to hit it off. The Soviet leader, who had played soccer when he was younger, and the American president, who had played football, used sports analogies to make points about their approach to the negotiations.

"I played the left side," Brezhnev explained.

"I wasn't very fast, but I could hold the line," Ford countered.

The substantive focus of the summit negotiations was on the enormously complex and divisive issue of limiting the American and Russian arsenals of strategic nuclear weapons. The agreement Ford and Brezhnev were trying to reach was called SALT II—standing for Strategic Arms Limitation Treaty. Each side had different advantages in the nuclear arms race. Neither country wanted to give up its advantages. The Soviets had missiles capable of carrying larger warheads than American missiles. The United States had missiles with more-accurate guidance systems. The Soviets intended to build more missiles than the United States. The United States had long-range bomber planes and unmanned robot planes to offset any Soviet numerical advantage in missiles. The United States had more missile-firing submarines in its fleet, but Russia was catching up fast.

With these daunting and competing agendas, it was no wonder that the first Ford-Brezhnev negotiating session, which was supposed to last ninety minutes, continued for six and a half hours, ending at twelve thirty in the morning. A planned dinner was canceled. After that initial meeting, Ford invited Kissinger, Rumsfeld, me, and several other aides to his cottage—or *dacha* in Russian—for a post-midnight snack. We walked along a dark road, our breath turning to steam in the subzero air. The Russian staff at Ford's dacha quickly put together a meal for the president and the rest of us—thick soup, black bread, caviar, cheese, salami, Russian beer and vodka, and ice cream for dessert.

It was long after midnight when we finished eating, but our day still wasn't over. Kissinger and I were driven to the press hotel about a mile away for a briefing on the first day's discussions. In the car, Kissinger told me that Ford was a better negotiator than Nixon. He said Ford was more personable and seemed to get along well with the outgoing Brezhnev. Kissinger also told me that while Nixon liked to follow a prepared script, Ford was comfortable with a genuine give and take. Kissinger said that for some reason Nixon couldn't look foreign leaders in the eye.

Once we reached the press briefing, Kissinger chose his words carefully. He needed to indicate that some progress had been made, so if an agreement was reached on the second and final day of negotiations it would not seem like a last-minute PR gesture. But he did not want to be overly optimistic, so that if the two leaders failed to reach agreement it would not seem like a last-minute collapse. Kissinger was a master at walking that fine line.

The second day of the Ford-Brezhnev negotiations was scheduled to last from 10 a.m. to 2 p.m., to be followed by a lunch to replace the previous night's canceled dinner. But, again, the talks ran two hours longer than scheduled. Near the end of the negotiations, Ford called me in and instructed me to make arrangements for announcing that the two leaders had reached a historic agreement on arms limitations. Each country committed to possessing no more than 2,400 missiles and bombers capable of carrying nuclear warheads. And they agreed that no more than 1,320 of each country's missiles could be equipped with multiple warheads. It was one of the rare times in history when adversaries had mutually agreed to limit their arsenals. While Ford and Brezhnev and members of their delegations sat down to a late lunch of bear meat and venison, Kissinger and I drove again to the press hotel to announce the momentous agreement. At his briefing, Kissinger explained that lower-ranked officials of the two countries would begin technical negotiations almost immediately to establish procedures for verifying compliance with the agreement.

"The negotiations could be difficult and will have many technical complexities, but we believe that the target is achievable," Kissinger told the reporters. After his press briefing, Kissinger and I rushed back to the meeting site for the official signing ceremony and champagne toasts to the successful conclusion. As Ford said good-bye to Brezhnev, the president impulsively took off the gray wolf fur parka given to him by a fan in Alaska when Air Force One landed there to refuel, and presented it to Brezhnev to seal the relationship they had established and the treaty they had negotiated.

On the train ride back to the Vladivostok airport, Ford and his staff gathered in the dining car to celebrate and unwind. I kept downing vodka, and the more I drank, the more outspoken I became in hailing the president's triumph. Back on Air Force One, flying home, I babbled to the reporters that the arms limitation treaty signed by Ford and Brezhnev at Vladivostok was "one of the most significant agreements since World War II."

And, I foolishly proclaimed, "Richard Nixon could not achieve this in five years. President Ford achieved it in three months." With that, I staggered to the VIP lounge on Air Force One, stripped to my underwear, stretched out on a couch, covered myself with a blue air force blanket, and fell asleep. Drunk on vodka, exhausted from tension and lack of sleep, I did not wake up for nine and a half hours.

Ford and his entourage arrived back in Washington on a Sunday night, in time to watch the 11 p.m. news. My gratuitous comment about Ford achieving in three months what Nixon could not achieve in five years was the lead item. I knew instantly that I had made a dumb mistake. By Monday morning, I was in the middle of a full-scale controversy. The *Wall Street Journal* ran a boxed article that morning saying I had emerged during the trip as an outspoken advocate for the president. The *New York Daily News* described my praise for Ford's negotiating ability as "gushing." The *Boston Globe* referred to my "puffery." The *Chicago Daily News* said I was "an inexperienced flack." And *Time* magazine quoted a reporter as calling my performance on the Far East trip a "disaster."

I told Ford several times that I was sorry I had caused such a flap about his Vladivostok achievement. And each time he brushed aside my apologies, saying he thought my statements to the press had been correct. Nevertheless, I decided that I needed to express to the reporters the contrition I felt. I invited about fifteen correspondents to my White House office and tried to repair my relationship. I explained that the Far East trip was my first overseas jaunt since becoming press secretary. I confessed that I didn't have the necessary experience, that my short temper had flared, that I had been petulant. And I had not been available to the reporters while I attended official functions. I asked for the reporters to be understanding and to give me more time to improve the White House Press Office operation.

We talked for two hours. The reporters expressed their specific complaints about my performance. Helen Thomas insisted, "The president's pants being too short was a big story, and you can't expect us not to write about it." By the end of the meeting, the reporters had softened their criticism somewhat and seemed to be willing to give me time to grow in the job. But my honeymoon with the White House press corps, such as it was, had ended.

About a month after returning from the Far East, the president undertook another overseas trip to meet a foreign leader, this time to the island of Martinique in the Caribbean to confer with French president Valéry Giscard d'Estaing. I wondered how the aristocratic Frenchman and the down-to-earth American would get along. Ford expressed this same concern. But as the *New York Times* wrote, they got along "swimmingly." That was a little joke. At one point during the two days of talks, Ford, Kissinger, Giscard d'Estaing, and French foreign minister Jean Sauvagnargues donned bathing suits and went for a dip in the swimming pool of the resort hotel where they were meeting. I will never forget the sight of the chubby Kissinger in blue swimming trunks.

On the substantive side, the issues on the agenda were serious and complex—the high price of petroleum, worldwide economic problems, relations with the Soviet Union, and arms controls.

And then there was the Nicole issue. Almost as soon as we arrived at the conference site on Martinique, I noticed a very attractive redheaded woman named Nicole hanging around. When she came to me and asked whether Kissinger would be willing to meet with five or six French reporters, I assumed she was part of the French press office staff. Given my proclivities, I flirted with her. Nicole was hovering about during a press photo session with the two leaders. To my amazement, Kissinger introduced her to Ford and told him, "We're going to trade Nessen for her." And then to my even greater amazement, Ford took her to Giscard d'Estaing and said, "We're going to trade my press secretary for your press secretary." The French president looked irritated and told Ford she wasn't his press secretary, she merely worked in the press office.

I found out afterward that Nicole didn't actually work in the French press office. She was a model and TV actress, and the mistress of the French president's press secretary. The president told me later that when he got back to Washington, Mrs. Ford pretended to be mad at him after she saw a front page picture in the *New York Times* of Ford, Giscard d'Estaing, and Nicole.

23

Slippery Slopes

As 1974 waned, Rumsfeld, Cheney, Greenspan, Marsh, and I frequently gathered in Rumsfeld's office at the end of the day to drink beer, talk about the economy and other problems confronting the president, and discuss steps Ford should take to deal with those issues. At one of those sessions, Rumsfeld said Ford was tottering on the brink. I thought he meant tottering on the brink of making some major decisions. But what he meant was that the president was tottering on the brink of a long slide downward during which he would steadily lose influence with Congress and popularity with the public. Rumsfeld predicted that Ford had three months to announce concrete solutions to the nation's problems.

"At the end of three months, the Ford administration will either have the smell of life or the smell of death," Rumsfeld predicted. "If it's the smell of death, this White House is going to be torn to pieces by the press, by the Democrats, even by other Republicans who will challenge the president for the nomination in 1976."

A few days before the Fords and their children departed the White House for their traditional Christmas and New Year's ski vacation in Vail, Colorado, the president held a long Saturday meeting with his economic advisers to discuss what to do next about the stagflation problem. The mood at the meeting was gloomy. Everyone looked somber. Earlier, the advisers had told Ford the economic downturn would bottom out in the spring and start improving by mid-1975. Now they said they weren't sure the economy would recover that fast. Previously, they had told the president the unemployment rate would peak at 7 percent. A little later they raised that to 7 ½ percent. Now they predicted 8 percent.

Alan Greenspan, the president's chief economic adviser, explained that until a few weeks ago the recession appeared to be following a normal course for an economic downturn. But then, he said, businessmen and consumers alike suddenly seemed to lose all faith in a rapid recovery. The economy was dropping fast, Greenspan said, and, frankly, he didn't know when it would hit bottom. The other bad news delivered at the session was that the federal budget was climbing rapidly, which was likely to feed inflation. Looking grim, Ford took in all the bad news. When the president asked Roy Ash, the director of the Office of Management and Budget, to report on any good news concerning the economy, Ash joked, "That'll take about four seconds."

At the end of the meeting, in a manner that I thought seemed surprisingly casual, given the stakes involved, the president checked off his decisions on an option paper handed to him, marking his approval for Option A or Option B or Option C for each proposal. His major decision was to combat the recession by proposing a $20 billion tax cut. He would announce this in his State of the Union speech to Congress in January.

And with that done, the Ford family prepared to depart for the Colorado ski slopes. The day before the year-end trip, I received a phone call from Mrs. Ford. She said she was angry at having to pay the equivalent of first-class airfare when she flew aboard Air Force One for personal trips, such as the vacation flight to Vail. She threatened to fly to Colorado on a commercial airliner, coach class. In the end, she was talked out of that idea.

A number of ski magazines had contacted me, eager to take pictures and write articles about the president on the slopes. I turned them down. I wanted to de-emphasize Ford's skiing and emphasize his work on policy issues while in Vail. I told Ford I thought I had made a mistake by describing his Vail trip as a "working vacation," because reporters then kept demanding to know what work the president was doing when he was not on the ski slopes. I should have announced that he was putting aside work for a few days to take a vacation with his family. Then, when reporters learned that he was dealing with policy matters for part of each day, they would write that the demands of his office had cut into Ford's vacation plans.

Like most skiers, the president sometimes fell on difficult runs. The networks stationed their cameras along the slopes, hoping to catch him taking a tumble. This would support their frequent story line that he was clumsy, even though he was a former All-Star college football player who had been courted to play professional football and was an avid and competent skier, tennis player, golfer, and swimmer. One night, when I was having a predinner drink with him at his rented trailside house in Vail, the president complained about the news media's preoccupation with his supposed clumsiness. "Those reporters get their exercise mostly sitting on bar stools," he grumped.

The caricature perpetuated by many in the press corps, by Johnny Carson in his late-night TV monologue, and by other comedians—especially Chevy Chase on *Saturday Night Live*—was that Ford was not only physically ungainly, but that he also was not very bright. The portrayal of Ford as klutzy and dumb was not limited to comedy skits. Perhaps the most outrageous example was a cover of the mainstream *New York* magazine in which a doctored photo appeared to show Ford getting off of Air Force One dressed as Bozo the Clown. The cover was to promote a critical article in that issue by Richard Reeves, the reporter who most unrelentingly demeaned Ford as clumsy and not bright. In a critical book he wrote about the president, Reeves approvingly quoted Lyndon Johnson as saying, "Jerry Ford is so dumb he can't fart and chew gum at the same time."

In his own book about the White House years, Ford labeled Reeves's articles as "poppycock."

Even serious, generally professional journalists couldn't resist pursuing the "Ford's too dumb" smear. In a live interview on NBC, Tom Brokaw informed the president, "It has been speculated on in print not only in Washington but elsewhere, and it crops up in conversation from time to time in this town, the question of whether or not you are intellectually up to the job of being president of the United States." Showing amazing forbearance, Ford earnestly explained to Brokaw his academic record and the knowledge he had attained during twenty-five years in Congress and the White House.

Harry Reasoner of ABC told Ford in an interview that many in the public did not believe he had the "magnitude" to handle the presidency. "Can you grow in this job?" Reasoner asked condescendingly.

In more subtle ways, the mainstream media questioned the president's intelligence. *Time* magazine described a dinner the president held at the White House with historian Daniel Boorstin, the Librarian of Congress; Harvard professor James Q. Wilson; and other scholars in terms that suggested the event was part of a cram course to educate the president. UPI credited the successful meeting with Giscard d'Estaing at Martinique not to Ford, but rather described it as a "triumph for Henry Kissinger." And *Newsweek* magazine referred to Ford attending a "seminar" at which Henry Kissinger and others were trying to "teach" him about foreign policy and national security issues. After one such story appeared, I phoned the reporter and informed him that as far back as 1958, then-Congressman Ford had lectured on defense issues to then-professor Kissinger's classes at Harvard.

Kissinger often did not follow the old White House rule for staff members: "You credit the president when there is a success, and you take the blame when there is a failure."

Reporters and comedians suggested that Ford's college football career was responsible for his supposed mental inadequacies. One popular put-down was that he was slow-witted because he had played too many football games without wearing a helmet. This, despite the fact that he was near the top of his Yale Law School class, had dealt with complex issues for twenty-five years as a congressman, including service on the appropriations and intelligence committees, was the elected leader of Republicans in the House of Representatives for a decade, and served as a member of the Warren Commission, which investigated the assassination of John F. Kennedy.

During this period, both Hartmann and Rumsfeld suggested to me that I might be unintentionally contributing to the news media's portrayal of Ford as a dullard struggling to understand the complex issues facing the country, particularly the economic and energy problems. Hartmann thought I might be encouraging that portrayal by frequently describing Ford as sitting behind his desk listening, while a circle of advisers told him what was going on and suggesting what action he should take. Rumsfeld took issue with my quoting Ford as commenting at one meeting on energy issues, "This is complex as the devil." Rumsfeld thought that suggested the president was just discovering how complex the issues were. He and Hartmann had a point. After that, I was careful to describe Ford as an active and knowledgeable participant in those meetings, and a confident decision maker, which was an accurate portrayal.

On the flight to Vail for the Ford family's 1974 Christmas ski holiday, the president spotted a front-page article in that morning's *New York Times* by investigative reporter Seymour Hersh, alleging that the CIA had conducted an extensive program of spying on Americans in the United States during the 1950s and 1960s, at the height of the Cold War with the Soviet Union. According to Hersh's story, the intelligence agency tapped the phones of Americans, read their mail, kept them under surveillance, and broke into their homes and offices.

The pool reporters aboard Air Force One asked me what was Ford's reaction to the article. I walked forward to the president's compartment and told him about the query. Ford decided to give the reporters his thoughts about the domestic spying allegations in person. The president told the correspondents aboard his plane that CIA director William Colby had assured him no domestic spying on Americans was currently being conducted. Ford declared forcefully, "I told him that under no circumstances would I tolerate any such activities under this administration." The president informed the reporters he had reminded Colby that the CIA was prohibited by its charter from conducting operations within the United States. And he had ordered Colby to compile and send him a written report responding to the *New York Times* allegations.

But, as Ford wrote later, "The problem didn't die away. Sniffing a potential Watergate, reporters bore down hard on the story." The CIA domestic spying allegations dominated my daily news briefings in Vail. When I announced that Ford had given Colby instructions to prepare a written report on the Hersh allegations and send it to him within a few days, the White House press corps was skeptical that the report would be truthful. I was worried that Ford did not take the Hersh allegations and their possible consequences seriously enough, especially in the post-Watergate environment. I shared my concerns with Rumsfeld. He showed me a memo he was writing by hand on a yellow legal pad saying Ford should learn the lessons of Watergate and should not make the same mistake of failing to act strongly and quickly on allegations of misconduct by the CIA.

I told Rumsfeld I was concerned that Ford may have known about CIA assassination plots or domestic spying when he was in the House of Representatives or as vice president or president. Rumsfeld said he had asked the president that question directly, and Ford had insisted he had never known about the CIA's misdeeds, even though at one point he had been a member of the House CIA Oversight Committee. Rumsfeld asked me how big a story I thought the allegations of CIA misdeeds would be. I replied that it would be one of the biggest stories of 1975.

The report Ford ordered from CIA director Colby arrived at Vail by courier in a few days. The CIA director confirmed some of Hersh's allegations but denied that they amounted to a massive domestic spy operation. Colby's memo contained a revelation of its own—the existence of the "Family Jewels"—a series of documents compiled several years earlier by then-CIA director James Schlesinger listing previous agency activities that might have been improper, including plotting in the 1950s and 1960s to assassinate foreign leaders who were considered enemies of the United States.

On New Year's Eve, Ford gave a party at his rented house in Vail for friends and staff. Wearing a bright red blazer, he was in good spirits, even though some reporters had written stories critical of the president for taking a vacation at a time when the nation was confronting so many problems. CBS correspondent Phil Jones complained in one of his stories that Ford's energy advisers had burned fourteen thousand gallons of jet fuel flying to a meeting in Colorado to discuss ways to reduce energy use. At midnight, I shook hands with the president and wished him a happy New Year. I told him I hoped 1975 would be a good year. He replied in a strong voice, "It *will* be a good year."

On the day Ford returned to Washington from his holiday in Vail, Colby presented to him details contained in the "Family Jewels." The president realized that he needed to be open about past abuses or else he would face charges of covering up wrongdoing. But he also knew that he needed to deal with the revelations in a way that would not cripple the CIA's effectiveness and undermine the morale of its staff. Ford's immediate response to Colby's revelations was to appoint a special commission to investigate CIA activities, determine whether they were illegal, and make recommendations on how to prevent future misdeeds by the spy agency. Ford appointed Vice President Rockefeller to be chairman of the commission. And the president named seven commission members, some of them with previous connections to intelligence activities. These appointments set off a flood of criticism by reporters, who suggested that the commission was a vehicle to whitewash illegal activities by the CIA. Some in the press corps portrayed it as another Watergate cover-up.

24

The CIA Did WHAT?!

As the commission began its investigation, veteran CBS correspondent Daniel Schorr declared in a news report, "It would be unfair to suggest that the Rockefeller blue-ribbon panel on the CIA is a stall. It would not be unfair to suggest that blue-ribbon panels have as one of their purposes the postponement of issues until the excitement has abated." Schorr did all he could to make certain the excitement would not abate. In February 1975, on Walter Cronkite's *CBS Evening News* program, Schorr reported that investigations of intelligence operations in the 1950s and 1960s would reveal at least three assassinations in which the CIA was involved.

Unwittingly, Ford was probably the original source for Schorr's scoop. Before Christmas 1974, Ford held an off-the-record lunch at the White House for a number of top executives and correspondents from the *New York Times*. It was one of a series of meetings we were organizing to help Ford and the Washington media establishment get to know each other better. The *Times* executives were interested in pursuing the Hersh story on domestic spying. Ford, puffing on his pipe, insisted that the conversation be kept off the record. Then, sounding appalled, the president told the *Times* executives they wouldn't believe the horror stories revealed by the "Family Jewels." "Like what?" the executives asked. "Like assassinating foreign leaders," the president replied.

I joked later to Brent Scowcroft of the National Security Council that if Ford were not the president, his security clearance would be revoked for his indiscreet revelation of classified information. I had no sooner returned to my office after Ford's lunch with the *New York Times* team than I had a phone call from the *Times* bureau, asking me to put the exchange about assassinating foreign leaders on the record. I said I couldn't change the ground rules after the fact. And, to its credit, the *Times* lived up to the off-the-record ground rules and never printed Ford's revelation that the CIA had been involved in assassinations.

But six weeks later, Dan Schorr did broadcast that revelation. I've always believed that someone in the *Times* delegation had shared Ford's private disclosures with Schorr, who was not bound by the off-the-record ground rules at the lunch. The day after Schorr's broadcast, I knew I would be bombarded at my briefing by questions from reporters about CIA assassination plots. I consulted with Scowcroft and Rumsfeld's deputy Dick Cheney. The problem we faced in crafting answers to the anticipated media questions was that we did not know what the CIA had done in the 1950s and 1960s, and we were not going to find out until the Rockefeller Commission completed its investigation and submitted its report. That was probably six months away. So it was decided I would tell reporters at my briefing that I would not respond to queries on the topic before the Rockefeller Commission had completed its work.

After my briefing, I got a phone call from Schorr. He said he wanted to compliment me. "For what?" I asked. "You didn't lie about the assassinations," Schorr said. "I warned CBS that you were probably going to lie and flatly deny my story. But you didn't. You just said you weren't going to talk about it. I was pleasantly surprised. That's an amazing improvement over Ziegler."

For a year after the Hersh and Schorr stories, the news media produced a nonstop flood of allegations about past CIA misdeeds, almost always attributed to unnamed sources. Questions about the spy agency dominated my daily press briefing. Some days I spent an hour or more with Ford, pumping him for information to answer the press queries. Rumsfeld encouraged me to continue bringing the media questions to the president's attention as a way of pressuring Ford to take some concrete action to deal with the flood of allegations about CIA misdeeds.

There was the story that the CIA had plotted to assassinate "Papa Doc" Duvalier of Haiti, Rafael Trujillo of the Dominican Republic, Prince Norodom Sihanouk of Cambodia, and Patrice Lumumba of the Congo. *Time* magazine reported that the CIA once recruited Mafia bosses Sam Giancana and John Roselli to help assassinate Cuba's Fidel Castro. And some stories speculated that Castro had recruited Lee Harvey Oswald to assassinate John F. Kennedy in retaliation for several CIA attempts to kill the

Cuban leader. One day at the height of the Oswald-CIA speculation, anticipating questions at my briefing because Ford had served on the Warren Commission, which investigated Kennedy's assassination, I sought guidance from the president. I expected him to brush off any Castro connection with Oswald. I was surprised when instead he told me that in writing its conclusions, the Warren Commission had carefully avoided saying there was "no evidence" of a conspiracy to assassinate Kennedy. Ford got up from his desk, walked to his adjoining study, and returned with a copy of the Warren Commission's final report.

He opened it to a well-worn page and read to me a sentence declaring that the commission had *found* no evidence that Oswald was part of a conspiracy, domestic or foreign, to assassinate Kennedy. Ford emphasized the word "found," suggesting that there might be evidence the commission did not know about. Ford told me he personally doubted that the CIA had told the Warren Commission everything it knew about Oswald. Then he really shocked me by saying he was thinking about reopening the investigation of Kennedy's assassination, focusing primarily on any connection between CIA efforts to kill Castro and the murder of JFK.

Congress launched two investigations of the CIA's past activities, one in the Senate conducted by Frank Church of Idaho and the other in the House of Representatives conducted by Congressman Otis Pike of New York. Ford considered Senator Church's investigation "sensational and irresponsible," designed primarily to boost Church's presidential ambitions.

The president believed that some members of Congress wanted to dismantle the CIA, or at least to restrict its operations to such an extent that the agency would not be able to fulfill its mission. Ford was informed that valuable employees were leaving the spy agency because they were afraid the Church investigation would destroy their reputations. Others had become extremely cautious in carrying out their duties.

Allegations of CIA assassinations weren't the only intelligence controversy Ford faced. In mid-March 1975 the investigative columnist Jack Anderson alleged on his radio program that the CIA had paid $250 million to eccentric aviator-industrialist-philanthropist-film producer Howard Hughes to build a deep-sea salvage ship called the *Glomar Explorer*. According to the Anderson account, the CIA had dispatched the ship to retrieve the wreckage of a Soviet submarine that had sunk in the Pacific Ocean near

Hawaii. The columnist claimed that the *Glomar Explorer* had located the submarine's wreckage resting on the seabed three miles below the surface. Anderson said the submarine had been lifted to the surface, only to split in two and drop back into the sea. The columnist claimed that three nuclear missiles, two nuclear torpedoes, and code books were recovered from the Soviet vessel.

I was instructed to answer no press questions about the episode. Ford himself replied bluntly "no comment" when reporters questioned him. I learned later that, on his second day as president, Ford had been informed that the *Glomar Explorer* was on its way to the site of the sunken Soviet submarine. One of his first acts as chief executive was to give the order for the ship to try to find and retrieve the wreckage. The matter was kept secret out of fear that the Soviet Union would be humiliated by any public revelation of the *Glomar Explorer* incident and would feel the need to retaliate. When rumors of the episode began circulating, CIA director Colby personally visited news organizations in Washington, imploring them not to print or broadcast the story for fear of provoking a Soviet reaction. All agreed, except Anderson. Until five minutes before Anderson broadcast the revelations, Colby was on the phone, pleading with him not to run the story. Colby explained that the Russians would likely feel the need to retaliate if the *Glomar Explorer*'s search for the submarine wreckage was publicized. Anderson rejected the pleas and used the story. As a result, instructions were radioed to the *Glomar Explorer*'s captain to abandon efforts to retrieve the Soviet submarine.

In the summer of 1975, the Rockefeller Commission completed most of its report on spying by the CIA within the United States. Ford was in Europe at the time, meeting with foreign leaders. He returned to the White House at one o'clock one morning and had to leave less than eight hours later to deliver the commencement speech at the U.S. Military Academy at West Point. Vice President Rockefeller had led reporters to believe that they would receive the text of the commission's report that day, even though Ford had not read it. Rockefeller had also indicated to reporters that the report would contain a section on allegations of CIA assassinations, even though the commission's investigation of those allegations was not complete. When the White House found out that the news media's anticipation had been falsely raised on both counts, Rockefeller's office was ordered to issue a statement announcing that the report would not be issued until after Ford had read it, and that the report would not contain any findings on the assassination issue.

The press corps went ballistic. Reporters thought they detected another Watergate-style cover-up. At my next press briefing, I tried to explain why publication of the report was delayed and why there were no findings on assassinations. It was one of the nastiest briefings I ever faced. It lasted for an hour, and all the questions were about the Rockefeller Commission report. Some reporters wrote that the briefing was reminiscent of Ziegler's confrontations with the press. One reporter said I was trying to cover up the Rockefeller Commission's findings. Another reporter asked whether I had telephoned Nixon to get his advice on how to run a cover-up. One reporter shouted that I was a liar.

That word hit me hard, and not just because I was trying to keep my promise to never lie or cover up. Being called a liar in public hurt deeply because I had tried all my life to live up to my mother's admonitions when I was a boy to never lie, to always tell the truth, to never do anything wrong, to never break the rules, to always do what was right. That was why I was thrown off balance when a reporter publicly called me a liar. I retreated to my office to recover my composure.

Three days later, after Ford had read the Rockefeller Commission report and after members of the Senate and House had read it, we released it to the press and public. The report found that over a period of twenty-eight years, the CIA had engaged in some activities that were "plainly unlawful and constituted improper invasions upon the rights of Americans." However, most of the agency's activities were judged to be legal. Some of the illegal activities were found to have been undertaken after receiving orders "directly or indirectly" from the president in office at the time. I was irritated because there were no follow-up stories saying that the White House had put out the report as promised, that there had been no cover-up after all, that I did not lie, that Ford had been completely open and candid throughout the process, that he had not been involved in any way in the CIA activities.

More than a year after Seymour Hersh's original *Times* article triggered the great intelligence controversy, and after studying thick notebooks containing information about the CIA, its shortcomings, and the internal

conflicts of the American spy system going back to the Kennedy administration, Ford proposed a sweeping reorganization and reform of U.S. intelligence activities. The president's proposals included prohibitions against
spying on Americans within the United States or infiltrating dissident
groups, a commitment to work with Congress to draft legislation against
electronic surveillance of Americans, creation of an oversight board to
monitor all intelligence programs, a suggestion that Congress set up a joint
Senate-House committee to monitor intelligence activities, and a promise
to support legislation prohibiting intelligence agencies from assassinating
foreign leaders.

"As Americans, we must not and will not tolerate actions by our government which abridge the rights of our citizens," Ford declared in announcing his reforms. "At the same time, we must maintain a strong and
effective intelligence capability. . . . I will not be a party to the dismantling
of the CIA and other intelligence agencies."

To further restore public confidence, Ford dismissed Colby as director
of the CIA and replaced him with George H. W. Bush, then the U.S. envoy
to China, previously congressman from Texas and chairman of the Republican National Committee.

By late 1975, Senator Church's committee was ready to issue its report
on CIA assassination plots. This set off concerns in the White House that
the report could damage the reputation of the United States, perhaps even
lead to a United Nations investigation. At one White House meeting,
someone suggested the UN might formally accuse the United States of
genocide, or even expel America. By then, some of the findings had already been publicized through more than a year of steady leaks. But the
same information in an official American government document might
force foreign countries to take retaliatory action. Ford personally wrote to
Church asking him not to publish the report, or at least to let administration officials delete sensitive material before publication.

"Public release of these official materials and information will do griev-
ous damage to our country," the president advised the senator. "It would
most likely be exploited by foreign nations and groups hostile to the
United States in a manner designed to do maximum damage to the reputation and foreign policy of the United States."

Despite that plea from Ford, the Church committee voted to publish the findings of its investigation. The major conclusions were: The CIA had not actually been responsible for killing any foreign leaders, although there was evidence that it plotted or aided plots to kill Sukarno of Indonesia, Duvalier of Haiti, Trujillo of the Dominican Republic, Lumumba of the Congo, and Castro of Cuba. Further, the Church committee reported that the Kennedy administration had encouraged plotters to overthrow South Vietnam's president Ngo Dinh Diem. But, despite all that, it concluded, "No foreign leaders were killed as a result of the assassination plots initiated by officials of the United States."

Unlike its Senate counterpart, the House of Representatives committee investigating possible wrongdoing by the U.S. intelligence agencies voted to keep its findings secret. However, Dan Schorr, with the help of an anonymous source, obtained a copy of the House committee report. Schorr passed the report to the *Village Voice* in return for the promise of a cash contribution from the *Voice* to the Reporters Committee for Freedom of the Press. Schorr's arrangement was supposed to be a secret, but like most secrets in Washington, that one leaked too. Someone told the *Washington Post* about the deal.

"I deeply regret that the Reporters Committee has not been able to maintain the confidentiality of the arrangement," Schorr complained after the *Post* published the story. To his credit he added, "I am fully aware of the irony of my complaining about leaks." Schorr was suspended and then fired by CBS.

As a journalist for more than twenty years, I believe strongly in the First Amendment, a reporter's right to protect his sources, and the value of investigative journalism in exposing wrongdoing. However, I also believe that if the elected members of the House of Representatives vote to keep an investigative report secret for legitimate national security reasons, a lone journalist should not decide to exercise his contrary view and release the report.

About a year after the great uproar over CIA misdeeds, the intelligence agency volunteered a public admission of serious error. The CIA revealed publicly that for ten years or more it had badly underestimated the proportion of the Soviet gross national product being spent on its military. I took part in a flurry of White House meetings to prepare for the expected deluge of press queries. But reporters did not ask me a single question about the matter. Maybe the CIA's admission would have gotten a lot more press attention if we had arranged for an "anonymous source" to leak the story instead of revealing it ourselves in an official government document.

As an old Washington maxim says, "Nobody believes the official spokesman; everybody trusts the unidentified source."

25

Speech Writing or Speech Fighting

The president decided to formally announce his program for dealing with the nation's simultaneous inflation, recession, and energy problems in his first State of the Union speech to a joint session of Congress in mid-January 1975. He suggested to his speechwriters that they read the State of the Union speeches of President Franklin D. Roosevelt from the World War II years to catch the serious tone he wanted to project.

But first, the president decided to discuss the economy two nights earlier in a more informal fireside chat to the American people from the Lincoln Library in the White House. The decision to make the earlier, less formal talk grew out of a memo I wrote saying that some of the proposals Ford intended to make in his speech to Congress were leaking out and were being attacked by his opponents. I suggested he ought to announce and explain the proposals publicly as soon as possible. As always, there were arguments among White House staff members about the wording of the fireside chat. This fighting sometimes turned nasty and personal. During one acrimonious debate over rival speech drafts, Bob Hartmann, the author of one version, cursed the author of another version: "Fuck you." The rival author responded by calling Hartmann a "prick." Not exactly the level of decorum you would expect in the White House.

When Hartmann's speech-writing office sent its draft to Ford three days before the fireside chat, I privately used the word "abominable" to describe it. The language was flowery, it was too long, it was full of clichés, and it did not clearly make the points the president wanted to get across. I tinkered with the text before it was put on the teleprompter for Ford to rehearse, but it still didn't read like the call to action that the economic circumstances required. I went to Rumsfeld's office and told him and Cheney how bad I thought the draft of the fireside chat was. Cheney asked whether I thought it could be salvaged. I told him I thought it could be, but only with very heavy editing and rewriting.

Rumsfeld invited me to submit my own version of the speech. I went home and spent five hours writing my draft, finishing at 2 a.m. Unbeknownst to me, Rumsfeld also asked economic adviser Alan Greenspan and Robert Goldwin, the White House liaison with the academic community, to write a draft. And Rumsfeld himself came up with yet another version. One night while all this behind-the-scenes maneuvering over the speech was going on, Hartmann invited me to share his car for the ride home. He complained during the drive about White House staff members conspiring to undermine his speech-writing authority. He apparently did not know that I was one of the conspirators.

On Sunday, the day before the fireside chat, Hartmann made a tactical error. He failed to come to the White House, where Ford was rehearsing the speech. That gave an opening to Rumsfeld, Greenspan, Goldwin, me, and other senior advisers who did not like Hartmann's draft. After Ford read through that version on the teleprompter and watched a videotape playback of his performance, Rumsfeld suggested some changes in the text. Over a two-hour period, individual words were changed, then phrases, then sentences, then whole paragraphs. The resulting text amounted to a new speech.

The Super Bowl was being played that Sunday. So, in between rehearsals and revisions and reprogramming the teleprompter, Ford, Rumsfeld, Greenspan, Cheney, and I—all casually dressed—took the elevator to the First Family's residence on the second floor of the White House and watched some of the football game.

The wrangling over the competing versions went on almost until the moment that Ford begin his fireside chat to the nation. The president hated such feuding among members of his staff and consequently was in a foul mood during the days leading up to the speech. But his friendly personality would not let him crack down on the staff fighting. And Rumsfeld was too competitive to be able to bring the factions together. The ultimate version of Ford's fireside chat was a pasted-together combination of the Hartmann draft and the rival Rumsfeld-Greenspan-Goldwin-Nessen version.

"Without wasting words, I want to talk to you tonight about putting our domestic house in order," the president began. "We must turn America in a new direction. . . . We must wage a simultaneous three-prong campaign against recession, inflation, and energy dependence." After listing his specific proposals—new taxes to encourage less energy use; development of nuclear, geothermal, and solar power; tax rebates to individuals; and a threat to veto new government spending programs—Ford concluded, "We know what must be done. The time to act is now. We have our nation to preserve and our future to protect."

Not only did the fireside chat contain specific, well-conceived proposals to lift the country out of its economic troubles, but Ford delivered the speech better than any other address I had heard him give. "We did it! We did it!" I enthused to Rumsfeld as soon as Ford had concluded. The president knew he had hit a home run. When I approached him immediately after the speech and told him how well he had done, he took my hand, squeezed it hard, and held it a long time while receiving the congratulations of other staff members. Even normally critical reporters thought it was one of the best speeches Ford had ever given.

But there was no time to celebrate. The State of the Union speech to Congress was just forty-eight hours away. And preparing for it ignited a new round of skirmishing among staff members. The renewed fighting began when Hartmann delivered a speech draft that lacked any clear policy proposals or visionary message but contained much hackneyed rhetoric. Hartmann was capable of crafting memorial phrases, such as, "Our long national nightmare is over." But he didn't understand complex policy issues, partly because he boycotted the daily senior staff meetings where such issues were discussed. He refused to attend because his rival Rumsfeld presided. Ford's own reaction to Hartmann's draft was: "It was short on specifics and long on rhetoric; worse, it didn't have a clear and central theme."

Rumsfeld summoned to his office Cheney, Greenspan, Seidman, energy "czar" Frank Zarb, and me. For eight hours, we pieced together a rival State of the Union speech draft, while munching on cookies, peanuts, and steak sandwiches, washed down with beer. At 9 p.m. we took our speech draft and Hartmann took his speech draft into the Oval Office. Ford, irritated by the process, waved the two versions away and snapped, "Go back and give me one speech, not two speeches." We finished work on the final, combined draft about 3:30 a.m. and sent it up to Ford, who was impatiently waiting for it in the White House residence. He sent it back about a half-hour later with some final edits and his approval.

At one o'clock that afternoon, on less than three hours' sleep, Ford began his State of the Union speech in the House of Representatives chamber at the Capitol with words rarely if ever uttered by a president: "I must say to you that the State of the Union is not good. . . . I have bad news, and I don't expect much applause." Ford went on to elaborate on his proposals for combating both inflation and recession, reducing unemployment, overcoming the energy crisis, dealing with the final chapter of America's involvement in Vietnam, and facing the threat from the Soviet Union. The president concluded the speech with these words: "America needs a new direction, a change of course, which will put the unemployed back to work, increase real income and production, restrain the growth of federal government spending, achieve energy independence, and advance the cause of world understanding. We have the ability. We have the know-how. In partnership with the American people we will achieve these objectives."

In the months following Ford's first State of the Union speech, Congress approved the more popular parts of the president's economic and energy programs—tax cuts—and declined to deal with the less popular proposals—raising petroleum prices. There was some talk among the president's advisers that he should veto the tax cut because it was too big. But Ford decided it would be political suicide to veto a tax cut for working-class Americans just before he flew off to his annual Easter golfing vacation in the millionaires' enclave of Palm Springs.

A key figure in dealing with the nation's economic and energy problems was Treasury Secretary William Simon, a former financial industry executive and a carryover from the Nixon Cabinet. As part of the never-ending sniping among Ford's senior advisers, Simon's rivals floated rumors that he would soon be ousted. One day, when I wandered down to the Press Room, I encountered Helen Thomas, the UPI White House correspondent. In her usual blunt manner, she asked, "Is Bill Simon leaving?" I knew there had been discussions about replacing Simon, because in recent speeches he had publicly disagreed with some of Ford's energy and economic policies. But I couldn't confirm anything without talking to Ford first. Caught by surprise by Thomas's question, I said, "Well . . ." and then paused while I decided how to word my nonanswer.

She took the word "Well" and my long pause as confirmation. She filed a story saying Simon would be leaving the Cabinet soon "according to White House sources." Other reporters picked up the story.

Simon called me and said he needed a strong endorsement from the president, or else his authority to run the Treasury Department would be undermined. I asked Ford what he wanted me to say publicly about the Simon-is-leaving rumors. The president replied that he had not asked Simon to resign—something less than a wholehearted endorsement. I found out that Ford was unhappy with Simon's initial public opposition to his policies. But, eventually, Ford authorized me to issue a statement saying he had "full confidence" in Simon, the traditional Washington code for, "I mean it this time."

What really happened? I have no idea. Maybe it was Rumsfeld floating rumors because he wanted Simon's job. Maybe it was Simon floating rumors to force Ford to publicly endorse him. Maybe it was other enemies of Simon floating rumors to nudge him to resign. Maybe Ford originally contemplated replacing Simon, but decided that was not prudent when the government was trying to deal with major economic and energy problems.

The Simon-is-quitting-or-getting-fired rumors were only one part of a never-ending flood of often-contradictory rumors about top officials of the Ford administration: Simon was supposedly angling to be Ford's vice-presidential running mate in 1976; Rumsfeld was also making a pitch to be Ford's running mate; Kissinger would resign after the election; Rockefeller would be named the new secretary of state. Some observers suggested that Ronald Reagan supporters were generating the rumors to sow disunity in Ford's camp in order to advance Reagan's presidential ambitions. Whatever their origin, the rumors were spread by columnists and reporters, always without attribution.

The controversy over whether Simon would remain in the Cabinet was soon overshadowed by a much bigger controversy over whether Ford would run for election in 1976. It began when reporter Tom DeFrank came into my office and dropped a bombshell: *Newsweek* was going to run a story in its next issue saying Ford had told several friends and senior White House advisers that he was not going to run for election in 1976 because of Mrs. Ford's shaky health and because he didn't have the money, inclination, or energy to campaign for president. I immediately and strongly told the reporter I had never heard the president say anything suggesting he would not run. While DeFrank waited in my office, I went to see Dick Cheney and told him what the reporter was planning to write. Cheney checked with Ford, then came to my office and told DeFrank the story was "bullshit."

But *Newsweek* wouldn't back down. I telephoned the Washington bureau chief of the magazine and then the top editor in New York. I reiterated Ford's declaration that he was going to run. To no avail. I demanded to know who the source was. They refused to name him but said the source had been reliable in the past. I asked the *Newsweek* officials why they were sure their source wasn't using them for his own ulterior motives, hiding behind the cloak of anonymity to sabotage the Ford election campaign, perhaps for the benefit of another candidate. The magazine executives said they had gone back to their source four times, and he had stuck by his story. I told the *Newsweek* executives that publication of the story would have an insidious effect on the 1976 presidential race because supporters and contributors would be reluctant to sign on to a Ford campaign if they believed he wasn't going to run, while potential rivals for the nomination would be encouraged to crank up their own campaigns. But, despite our firm denials, *Newsweek* ran the article.

There were many postmortems theorizing about who foisted the story on *Newsweek* and why. The most popular theory was that it was an effort by someone connected to former California governor Ronald Reagan to sabotage Ford's campaign in order to give Reagan time to organize his own presidential bid. The day the *Newsweek* article appeared, Lou Cannon, a correspondent for the *Washington Post*, told me that someone had tried to peddle the Ford-won't-run story to his newspaper, but the *Post* wouldn't grant anonymity to the source of such a damaging leak.

The president himself may have inadvertently contributed to the flap when he told *CBS Evening News* anchorman Walter Cronkite during this period, "I have indicated that I intend to be a candidate. I have not made any categorical legal determination that I will be a candidate."

Another theory about the source of the *Newsweek* story—the one I tended to believe—was that a Ford supporter and friend, perhaps former congressman Melvin Laird, had leaked the story as a way of prodding Ford to announce publicly that he was running and to start planning his campaign, raising money, appointing a staff, devising a strategy, and so forth.

If that was the motive, it worked. Shortly after the *Newsweek* article appeared, Ford filed the official papers making him a candidate for a full presidential term in 1976 and read a short statement to the TV cameras: "I expect to work hard, campaign forthrightly, and do the very best I can to finish the job I have begun." He added that he was running "with the strong support of my family and my friends."

At about the same time this controversy flared up, several reporters came to me and said someone was spreading rumors that Mrs. Ford was dying of cancer and would be dead in a matter of months. *New York* magazine ran the rumor in its Intelligencer column. As proof, the magazine noted that when the Fords attended a recent performance at Ford's Theatre in Washington, White House physician William Lukash was seen in their box with his medical bag. The item failed to mention that the White House doctor's assignment was to always stay close to the president.

Sometimes I felt I needed a gigantic fire hose to douse the rumors that periodically enflamed the White House press corps.

26

Kicking Around Ron

After about six months as press secretary, I felt I was doing a better job than I had at the beginning. But the press corps had a different appraisal. There was a flood of media criticism, touched off when I imposed some mild sanctions on the *Washington Star* after it broke the embargo on publication of President Ford's first federal budget. The *Star* illustrated its story about the flap with a ludicrous photo that made me look absolutely deranged. The newspaper also recalled that I had promised to be a Ron but not a Ziegler, and then jabbed, "Well, live and learn." The New York Press Club unanimously passed a resolution condemning me for denying millions of people their right to the news, because I insisted on enforcing the traditional embargo against publication until the budget has been delivered to Congress. The *Chicago Tribune* also ran a story criticizing my performance as press secretary.

Then there was the nice young man from Yale who asked if he could follow me around for a week so he could write an article for the university newspaper. He said he had followed my work as a correspondent with admiration and was interested in doing a favorable article about me as press secretary. Naively trustful, I agreed to give him access to practically everything I did for a week. His article was probably the most viciously critical, cheap-shot, vile piece ever written about me. In one of the milder passages, he quoted a White House reporter as repeatedly referring to me as a "schmuck." Mike Wallace of CBS, smelling blood, wanted to do an interview with me. The *Columbia Journalism Review* announced that it would shortly publish an article about the White House Press Office, which I was sure would be another attack on my performance. And I learned that *Newsweek* was planning to do a story about me. One reporter told me he hoped Ford would lose all fifty states in the 1976 election "just to get rid of you."

Between the *Star* episode, the Yale episode, the *Chicago Tribune* article, the anticipated *Columbia Journalism Review* criticism, Mike Wallace's anticipated hostile interview, the anticipated critical *Newsweek* article, constant conflicts with the press corps, the eighteen-hour days, the seven-day weeks, the nonstop feuds among White House staffers, frustration over not being fully informed on what was going on in the White House, I was deeply depressed. I didn't think I could hold on for a year, much less the two years left in Ford's term. On a helicopter flight back to the White House after a speech in New York City, Ford commented that he had heard about the barrage of press criticism I was receiving. I started to explain, but the president cut me off by saying, "The hell with them." I started again to explain and again he cut me off by saying, "The hell with them." I was glad I had his support, but I still felt besieged.

And finally, I became fed up with press questions about trivial matters and leftover Nixon matters, fed up with allegations of misdeeds and cover-ups in the Ford White House, fed up with the reporters' lack of interest in and knowledge of important policy matters. I typed out an angry statement denouncing these and other news media shortcomings, which I intended to read at my briefing. I showed it to my staff. None of them raised strong objections. At my briefing, I told the reporters in a sarcastic tone that I was willing to wait while they phoned their offices and corrected their mishandled stories about the president's nuclear weapons policy. And then I read my statement harshly denouncing the press coverage of the Ford White House. For once, I didn't have any trouble persuading reporters to write about it. The Associated Press newswire flagged my statement as "urgent" news. Every newspaper ran stories about it. I was flooded with phone calls, mostly from reporters angry about my criticism. Some warned that my statement would have huge repercussions, severely damaging White House relations with the press. My friend Tom DeFrank, the *Newsweek* magazine correspondent, wondered whether I could continue in my job. I wondered the same thing.

I showed the wire service stories to Rumsfeld and Cheney to prepare them for what was becoming a huge controversy. Rumsfeld's advice was: "Don't apologize, and when the news media criticize your remarks, repeat them in even stronger terms." I did not take his advice. Instead, I invited fifteen of the top reporters to my office. I explained that my complaints were directed at the conduct of a few specific reporters at my briefings. I did not mean to make a blanket denunciation of the entire White House press corps. And I said my remarks did not refer to Ford's own relationship with reporters, just the atmosphere at my briefings. That seemed to reduce the heat and tension between me and the press corps a little.

Some members of my staff urged me to show Ford the wire service stories so he wouldn't be caught by surprise when he saw coverage of the controversy on that night's evening news shows on TV and in the morning papers. I resisted because I was afraid the president would be angry at me. But I was finally persuaded to give the president a heads-up about what was coming. By the time I got to the Oval Office, however, Ford had left for the day. I decided not to go to his living quarters to tell him what was coming. I sat around for a while commiserating with my staff. The atmosphere was like a wake. I drank a couple of beers. I thought about what I would do if I lost my job.

The next morning, the newspaper stories were not as bad as I had anticipated. Most of them focused on my squabbles with the White House press corps at the daily briefing. The stories did not portray my outburst as indicative of a broader antipress attitude in the Ford White House. And some of the stories named specific White House correspondents who were guilty of focusing on trivia or Watergate, who poisoned the atmosphere at my briefings.

When I went into the Oval Office for my daily meeting with the president, I greeted him by asking, "How are you?" He replied, "How are *you*?" From his tone, I knew he had read about my outburst at the previous day's briefing. Instead of rehashing the episode, I simply went through my daily routine with Ford, telling him the questions I anticipated at my briefing on other issues and writing down his suggested answers. At the end of our meeting, I said, "I guess you've read the stories about me." He said he had. And then he volunteered, "You're doing a goddamn good job." He said he knew my job was tough and that I was taking a lot of heat from the reporters. "But I want you to know that I think you're doing a great job, and I'm proud to have you on my team."

His endorsement bolstered my spirits greatly. Nevertheless, I knew that how my press briefing went that morning would probably determine my future as the president's spokesman. If I lost my temper again, or if I lost control of the briefing, I would probably be gone. A lot of reporters who didn't normally cover my briefing showed up that day. *Variety*, the entertainment industry magazine, sent a correspondent. Mark Russell, a comedian who specialized in satirizing the ways of Washington, attended. They were disappointed. The briefing went smoothly. Both I and the reporters were on our best behavior. Both sides obviously had decided that what happened the day before was not helpful to the process of dispensing and circulating information from the White House to the American people and the world.

Not that a couple of reporters didn't try to revive the previous day's confrontation. One reporter asked me if I was paranoid. However, the reporters who wanted to keep the controversy going were put down, not by me, but by other, more serious correspondents, including my former NBC News colleague Tom Brokaw. And after just thirty minutes—half the length of my recent contentious briefings—the senior wire service reporter, Frank Cormier of the Associated Press, ended the session by declaring, "Thank you, Ron." That night, at a party at the home of Ford's economic adviser, Bill Seidman, my confrontation with the White House press corps was a major topic of conversation. The wife of Attorney General Edward Levi said she wanted to give me a kiss for telling off the reporters.

By coincidence, that weekend I and my Press Office staff, along with our families, gathered for a long-planned retreat at Camp David. Naturally, ways to ease tensions with the White House press corps after my blow-up was the major topic of discussion. Jerry Warren, the wise and low-key director of communications—whose reputation was unsullied by his service in the previous administration—was the source of much good advice. Warren shared the lessons he had learned working in the Nixon White House. He was critical of my performance and the less pleasant parts of my personality. And he offered specific recommendations for what I needed to do to become a better press secretary. Warren advised me to maintain tighter control over my briefings, to exhibit humor, to drop the sarcasm. By the end of the retreat, the Press Office staff had decided on a number of steps to do a better job and improve relations with the press corps. We concurred that one step was to reassert the importance of the Press Office within the White House and reestablish my stature as one of the president's nine senior staff members. I and my staff left

Camp David and headed back to Washington with a renewed sense of our independence and importance in the White House, and with a renewed determination to improve our performance.

Privately, I worried that I had slipped back into a state of lacking confidence in myself, of losing my temper, of exhibiting other character flaws I thought I had outgrown. I considered revisiting my psychiatrist. I was smoking too much, eating too much. I felt depressed. I had a recurring fantasy of Ford firing me. One night, after a particularly punishing day at the White House, I shared my sense of defeat with my wife. She suggested that I stick it out as long as I could, then quit, get a less-demanding job, make some money, spend time with my family, play with my son, take vacations. It was a very appealing scenario.

Another thing that made me uncomfortable with my job was that I was required periodically to "send a message" with my answers at briefings. An example of this occurred as the endgame began in Vietnam in the spring of 1975. I was asked at my briefing if Ford was considering a resumption of American bombing raids or even the dispatch of American troops to stave off a Communist victory. I replied that Congress had passed legislation forbidding the president to take either of those steps. After the briefing, Henry Kissinger's National Security Council liaison with the Press Office, Les Janka, complained to me that I had closed the door too tightly on American action in Vietnam. He said my answer should have been more carefully nuanced so as to scare the Communists, or at least leave them uncertain, about renewed U.S. involvement. It wasn't the first time that Kissinger and his aides had tried to use my briefing to scare an adversary. Previously he had given me a statement to read and suggested answers to media questions that were designed to scare Arab countries about American intentions in the Middle East during the oil embargo. In both instances, I didn't like being used to frighten foreign countries because I knew my statements would also frighten the American people.

Ford understood that what I said at my briefings could have a big impact in the United States and around the world. As the economic recession grew worse, he instructed me not to be unduly optimistic in my statements. He said I should err on the side of pessimism. Then, when the economy finally did turn around, the press and the public would believe the good news because we had been honest about the bad news.

27

Testing the President's Resolve

Ford worried that the final U.S. withdrawal from South Vietnam and the conquest of that country by the Communists in the spring of 1975 would be interpreted by adversaries and allies around the world as a sign of American weakness and lack of resolve, particularly in Asia. He was concerned that America's allies in the region, like South Korea, the Philippines, and Thailand, might no longer trust America's commitment to come to their aid in case they were attacked. He was even more concerned that America's enemies would be emboldened to test his resolve. And on May 12, 1975, just two weeks after the fall of Saigon, that test came. A U.S. merchant ship, the ss *Mayaguez*, with a crew of thirty-nine Americans, was seized by Cambodian patrol boats in international waters about sixty miles off the Cambodian coast and forced to sail toward the port of Kompong Som.

Ford advised me of this development—what he referred to as "bad news"—when I went into the Oval Office that morning for my daily meeting with him. Oddly, he gave me this disturbing news in a whimsical tone and with a "can you believe this?" look on his face. And, even more oddly, he asked me—rhetorically, I assumed—what I would do about the capture of the *Mayaguez*. "Would you go in there and bomb the Cambodians and take a chance of the American crew members being killed?" he asked. "Would you send helicopters to rescue them? Would you mine every harbor in Cambodia?" I had no answers, of course.

While the president and his national security advisers deliberated over a response, we did not publicly reveal the capture immediately. Since reporters did not know about the episode, it did not come up at my morning press briefing. After the briefing, we told reporters they were free to go to lunch, that we did not foresee any more news from the White House before 3 p.m. But shortly after the White House reporters left for lunch, Ford and the National Security Council decided we needed to immediately issue a strong public statement, calling the capture of the *Mayaguez* an act of piracy and demanding that Cambodia release the ship and crew immediately or else face "serious consequences."

Since the United States had no direct communications with Cambodia, Ford directed Kissinger to ask the Chinese government to make sure Cambodia received his warning. Chinese officials in Washington and Peking refused. The president then decided to use the news media to transmit his warning to Cambodia, on the assumption that Cambodian officials would read the U.S. demands on the Reuters newswire, hear them on the BBC, or learn of them from other news outlets. So the Press Office staff got on the phone, called nearby restaurants, and told them to notify all reporters eating there that they needed to return to the White House immediately. It worked. Before 2 p.m., the president's warning had been distributed to the reassembled reporters and was being transmitted worldwide by wire services, radio and TV stations, and newspapers.

After filing their bulletins, some of the reporters drifted back to my office, curious as to why there did not seem to be an air of crisis in the White House as there had been when previous administrations faced international confrontations. I believed it was a reflection of Ford's own style—low-key and cool—when dealing with difficult situations. Whatever he was feeling inside, he didn't show it. By his demeanor, he discouraged a crisis atmosphere.

When there was no immediate response from Cambodia to the president's demand that it release the *Mayaguez*, Ford ordered American reconnaissance planes based in Thailand to find the exact location of the freighter. He dispatched an aircraft carrier and two destroyers to the scene, but it would take them two days to reach the captured merchant vessel. I went home about midnight, got a few hours sleep, and was back in my office before 6 a.m. because I knew the TV and radio networks needed fresh information about the episode for their early morning programs.

I found both Brent Scowcroft and Robert "Bud" McFarlane asleep in their NSC offices. Scowcroft looked like he was about to collapse from stress and exhaustion. They advised me that they had awakened Ford at 2:21 a.m. and told him the *Mayaguez* was being forced to sail to the Cambodian mainland. Ford had ordered a contingent of American marines to Thailand in case they were needed to free the ship. And, I was told, American B-52s based on Guam were being prepared to bomb Cambodia, if necessary. I wrote and distributed a statement to reporters for the morning programs and wire services, describing the ship's overnight movements, announcing that American reconnaissance planes were circling the *Mayaguez*, and reporting that the president had been awakened several times during the night with updates on the situation.

At another National Security Council meeting on the second night of the *Mayaguez* crisis, Ford was informed that American planes circling the freighter had spotted small boats shuttling between the ship and the Cambodia mainland, carrying what appeared to be "Caucasian faces"— presumably *Mayaguez* crew members. The president faced another hard decision. If he ordered U.S. planes to attack the small boats, the freighter's crew members might be killed. If he didn't order an attack, the crew members would be taken to the mainland, where it would be much more difficult to rescue them. The president directed the circling American planes to drop bombs and fire rockets and cannon shells into the water near the Cambodia boats, and to douse the boats with tear gas. The attack did not deter the Cambodians. They continued to sail toward the mainland with their captives.

By the third day of the *Mayaguez* crisis, a substantial America military force had finally reached the area—the aircraft carrier *Coral Sea*, the destroyers *Holt* and *Wilson*, and 1,100 marines. At a late afternoon meeting, the president issued his orders: Marines were to be lowered to the deck of the *Holt*, and then were to approach and board the *Mayaguez*. Other marines were to land by helicopter on an island off the Cambodian coast where the *Mayaguez* crew members were believed to be held. And jet planes from the *Coral Sea* were to bomb military installations on the Cambodian mainland to prevent reinforcements from being sent.

Early that evening, sitting in my office, I received a phone call from Kissinger, sounding highly agitated, almost yelling. He summoned me to his office. When I got there, he was dressed in a tuxedo for a state dinner starting shortly for the visiting prime minister of the Netherlands. Kissinger said he needed to use me to get a message to the Cambodians. He explained that the CIA had picked up and translated an announcement on the Cambodian government radio station offering to release the *Mayaguez* and its crew. But since there was no official channel through which the United States could tell Cambodia that we accepted its offer, we again decided to use the news media to transmit the message. Kissinger's plan was for me to immediately announce in the White House press briefing room that the United States had heard and accepted the Cambodian offer and would call off its military attack as soon as the ship and crewmen were released. Then I was to urge the AP, UPI, Agence France-Presse, Reuters, the BBC, and other international news services to report the U.S. acceptance immediately in hopes that the Cambodians would hear or read about it, or that their embassies in other countries would advise them of it.

I ran to the briefing room and started reading the statement spelling out the U.S. acceptance of the Cambodian offer. I read it very fast, because time was running out to call off the U.S. military operation. The reporters kept telling me to slow down so they could make notes. And they kept interrupting me to ask questions. I became agitated. "Listen to what I have to say!" I almost shouted. "There is some urgency in it!" The reporters caught the tone in my voice and let me read the rest of the statement without interruption. I explained that the White House believed their stories reporting the president's offer were the fastest way—maybe the only way—to get Ford's message to the Cambodians. "Go file!" I urged. I then went to Kissinger's office and watched the TV correspondents right outside his window reporting on the statement.

The state dinner for the visiting prime minister of the Netherlands was a disaster. Ford and Rumsfeld had to excuse themselves several times to deal with the *Mayaguez* matter. Defense Secretary Schlesinger left and went back to the Pentagon. Kissinger and Scowcroft made it to the dinner only at the very end. After the dinner, Ford, Kissinger, Scowcroft, Rumsfeld, and I gathered in the Oval Office to await the news from Cambodia. At first the news was bad. The marines who had landed on the island were under heavy fire. Eighteen were killed. Several American helicopters had been shot down. Twenty-three marines died in one crash. The marines who had boarded the *Mayaguez* had found all the crew members gone. But shortly after midnight, the white phone on Ford's desk buzzed. It was Schlesinger reporting from the Pentagon that the Cambodians, apparently fearful of an imminent air strike and/or marine landing on their shores, had set the *Mayaguez* crew free. The Cambodians had put them aboard a rickety fishing boat and told them they were free to go. The destroyer *Wilson* had picked them up. They were all safe.

"They're all out!" Ford shouted to the aides in his office. "They're safe! Thank God!"

But before we could announce Ford's successful resolution of a potentially dangerous international confrontation, the never-ending internal rivalries in the administration broke out again. Schlesinger's chief information officer announced the end of the *Mayaguez* confrontation from the Pentagon before the president could announce it from the White House, detracting from Ford's role in successfully resolving the crisis. Ford and his senior staff members milled around the Oval Office, grumbling and cursing the Pentagon for stealing the president's thunder. Then I said, "Hey, we've got something the Pentagon doesn't have. We've got the president." It was quickly decided that Ford would step outside the West Wing, where the TV cameras were massed, and announce to the nation and the world his successful—and peaceful—resolution of the *Mayaguez* episode. And he would have a huge audience of viewers—his statement would appear right in the middle of Johnny Carson's *Tonight Show*.

Back in the Oval Office, after Ford's statement to the TV cameras, no one was in much of a celebratory mood. We had had three long, hard, tense, and dangerous days. Ford looked exhausted. He said he was going home and to bed. The White House doctor told me later that Ford had taken a sleeping pill that night to help him unwind and fall asleep after the stresses of the confrontation. And the next morning Ford slept in until seven, two hours later than usual.

A few days after the successful rescue, the *Mayaguez* crew members visited the White House to express their appreciation to Ford. They told the president they believed they were released because the Cambodians feared a massive American attack. One of the crew members reported to Ford that as they were being set free, an English-speaking Cambodian captor anxiously said, "You will contact the American government when you get on your ship. Tell them to stop the jets."

About a month later, Ford received word that the Russian author Aleksandr Solzhenitsyn, exiled from the Soviet Union because of his anti-

Communist writings, wanted to visit the president. Some White House advisers and conservative members of Congress favored such a meeting. But Kissinger and Scowcroft opposed the idea, fearing that such a visit would anger Soviet leader Brezhnev, with whom Ford was scheduled to meet in less than a month to negotiate an arms limitation agreement. Others opposed a meeting because they thought it was a publicity stunt to help Solzhenitsyn promote his books. In the midst of the debate, Ford flew to Chicago to deliver a long-scheduled speech. In the president's hotel suite before the talk, Rumsfeld urged Ford to see Solzhenitsyn, arguing that not meeting with him could become a domestic political liability. I called Ford's attention to the editorials and letters to the editor in favor of a Solzhenitsyn meeting that were being published daily in many newspapers.

Ford declined to state clearly to Rumsfeld and me what his position was. If he were asked about the issue at a scheduled news conference after his speech, he said he would give a vague answer that wouldn't completely close the door on a meeting with Solzhenitsyn. But, to my surprise, none of the reporters asked Ford about the Solzhenitsyn controversy. After the news conference, Ford hung around and chatted informally with some of the reporters. I quietly suggested to Ann Compton of ABC that she ask the president whether he was willing to see Solzhenitsyn. She did. But Ford unexpectedly replied that the news conference was officially over and he wasn't going to answer any more questions. With that, he left the ballroom and returned to his hotel suite. Rumsfeld and I followed the president and pinned him down on the wording of a White House statement about the Solzhenitsyn matter that I would issue to reporters. It would say that if the president had been asked at his news conference, he would have said he was willing to meet Solzhenitsyn, but that such a meeting should not be interpreted as endorsing the Russian's views, and should not be seen as reversing his efforts to relax tensions with the Soviet Union.

It was a Saturday night, and I wanted news of Ford's willingness to meet with Solzhenitsyn to be in as many Sunday newspapers as possible. So I ran down to the temporary press room, which was being dismantled after the president's speech, and informed all the reporters I could find about the president's views concerning a Solzhenitsyn meeting. But in the end, the whole episode turned out to have been a waste of everyone's time. Solzhenitsyn decided he couldn't squeeze a meeting with the president into his schedule. I concluded that Ford had been right in his private description of the writer: "A goddam horse's ass."

The *Mayaguez* crisis and the Solzhenitsyn faux crisis apparently were all the crises the White House press corps could handle at one time. So, during this period, when construction equipment arrived at the White House and began digging a giant hole on the South Lawn for a swimming pool, the reporters didn't make much of a fuss about it. The Fords had a backyard swimming pool at their former home in suburban Alexandria. Ford had swum laps almost every day for exercise. For once the White House press corps accepted my truthful explanation that friends of the president were paying the full construction costs of the new White House pool so he could continue his daily workout regimen. No taxpayer money was being spent.

Months later, when the pool was completed and filled, reporters and TV crews clamored for an opportunity to witness Ford's first swim. I agreed. While the cameras rolled and the press corps scribbled notes, the president swam several laps. During this "photo opportunity," a reporter for a local TV station approached me and asked whether it would be all right if she put on a bathing suit, stood at the edge of the pool, delivered her report to the camera, and then jumped into the water. I usually tried to accommodate reporters' needs, but this time I said no.

28

Stumbles and Changes

In late April of 1975, Ford made his first trip to Europe as president, to attend a NATO meeting in Brussels and visit other capitals. The trip was the occasion for a new barrage of press stories, mostly attributed to anonymous sources, critical of Kissinger and suggesting that he might be on his way out of the administration. Rumsfeld recommended that Ford, rather than Kissinger, do the press briefings in Brussels, to emphasize that the president, not the secretary of state, was in command of American foreign policy. For the same reason, Rumsfeld also proposed that when reporters and cameramen were ushered into Ford's meetings with the foreign leaders, only the heads of state should be in the pictures, that Kissinger should be excluded. Then, a *New York Times* reporter phoned me and asked for my help with a story he was writing about incidents when Ford had rejected Kissinger's recommendations. I suspected that Rumsfeld had planted the idea with the reporter. The day before Ford departed for Brussels, the *Times* ran a story citing several episodes that the paper claimed demonstrated Kissinger was losing his influence with Ford.

On the flight to Brussels aboard Air Force One, I wanted someone knowledgeable to brief the press pool on what issues the NATO leaders would be discussing. However, Kissinger was not aboard, having gone to Brussels early for some preliminary discussions. So I suggested Rumsfeld brief the press pool, since he had previously served as America's ambassador to NATO. At the beginning of Rumsfeld's briefing, I made a lame joke to the press pool, which turned out to be a mistake. I said something like, "For this performance only the part of the Senior American Official [the phrase normally used to describe Kissinger when he briefed anonymously] will be played by Don Rumsfeld." The reporters took this not as a joke, but as a serious statement that Kissinger was losing his influence with the president on foreign policy issues while Rumsfeld was gaining influence with Ford.

In Brussels, Kissinger asked me to meet with him privately. He complained about the *Times* story and other stories that suggested his influence on Ford's foreign policy decisions was diminishing. He said he was sick and tired of such stories. He said his critics were crazy if they thought he was going to let himself be nibbled to death in the press. And he threatened to strike back if the leaks didn't stop. I assured Kissinger—truthfully—that I was not involved in the leaks, nor was anyone on my staff. He replied that he thought I was involved only "at the periphery." In fact, I had made a conscious decision to totally stay out of what I saw as a subtle campaign by Rumsfeld and others to reduce Kissinger's influence with Ford, and I had instructed my staff to stay out of it. One morning, when I was meeting with the president on another matter, I took the opportunity to assure him that I was not involved in the anti-Kissinger campaign. He asked me whether I thought anyone on the White House staff was involved. I replied that, honestly, I *did* think so. Ford reiterated how much he hated fighting among his staff members. He said it was the one thing that really made him mad.

I admired Kissinger for his knowledge of history, his grasp of complex situations, his innovative policy ideas, his quirky sense of humor. But one thing I found less than admirable was his willingness to stretch the truth or tell untruths if it advanced America's foreign policy goals. I encountered a major example of this during Ford's European trip. The president made a stop in Salzburg, Austria, to confer with Egyptian leader Anwar Sadat about the tensions between Israel and the Arab countries. While Ford was in Salzburg, the *Chicago Sun Times* published a story saying Ford had assured Sadat that the United States favored Israel returning to the borders that existed prior to the 1967 Israeli-Arab War, with some minor exceptions. The story accurately described what the president had told Sadat. Nevertheless, apparently fearful that the story would antagonize Israel, Kissinger flatly denied to reporters that Ford had said any such thing to the Egyptian leader. I noted in my oral diary that Kissinger's denial was "an outright lie." It was a demonstration of Kissinger's willingness to fudge the truth if it helped advance a foreign policy or national security objective.

The big news story during Ford's Salzburg visit, the story that had the most lasting impact on his public portrayal for the rest of his term and, really, for the rest of his life, was not about substantive issues or important meetings. It was about Ford stumbling and falling to the tarmac as he walked down the stairs from Air Force One. I didn't see his fall because I was still aboard the plane, making my way toward the exit door. So when reporters pounced on me and asked about the president's fall, I replied, "What fall?" They wrote that I had tried to deny Ford's stumble, when in fact I didn't know about it when they initially asked. At my first opportunity, I told Ford I was being bombarded with press questions about his fall. The president advised me not to worry about the reporters' preoccupation with his misstep. "If you don't let their questions get under your skin," he advised, "they'll realize they're just wasting time, and they'll start focusing on something else."

But the media preoccupation only got worse later that day when the president appeared to stumble twice on the steps leading to the Austrian chancellor's palace, where Ford was meeting Sadat. I didn't see that second episode either, so when reporters asked me about it, I again replied, "What stumble?" That evening I was called away from a dinner the Austrian chancellor was giving for Ford, Sadat, and their staffs to take a phone call from my assistants, Jack Hushen and Larry Speakes. They told me they were being bombarded by questions from reporters demanding to know what was the matter with the president. Was he ill? Why did he keep tripping? I went back to the press center and tried to quiet the hysteria. I explained that the president had tripped disembarking from Air Force One because it was raining, the steps were wet and slippery, and Ford's legs were somewhat stiff from sitting for many hours during his flight. As for the stumble entering the chancellor's palace, I explained that the steps were oddly shaped and also wet from the rain.

A reporter asked me whether Ford was tired. And I replied truthfully that, yes, Ford was tired, I was tired, the other staff members were tired, and I assumed the reporters were tired. One of the reporters recalled that he had once heard me say that Ford rarely got tired, and now I was reversing myself and acknowledging that he did get tired. Some of the more serious reporters, who were not taking part in this silly exercise, laughed at their colleagues. I didn't elaborate on why Ford was tired. But the night before, during a stop in Madrid, the Spanish authorities had provided Ford with a very small bed, much too small for his six-foot, muscular build, and with a very hard pillow. Ford got almost no sleep.

There always seemed to be some frivolous distraction that preoccupied the news media every time Ford was on an overseas mission. There was falling down in Salzburg. There were the short formal pants in Tokyo. There was Nicole in Martinique. I thought the problem was that many reporters did not have a good grasp of the complex foreign policy and national security issues being discussed at these international meetings and therefore focused on trivia in their stories.

Not long after the European trip, Rumsfeld summoned me to his White House office. When I arrived, I found him in an angry mood. He accused me and others in the Press Office of leaking negative stories about Kissinger and of suggesting to reporters that Vice President Rockefeller would not be Ford's running mate in 1976. I denied, truthfully, that I had leaked such stories about Kissinger and Rockefeller, and I told him I had given specific instructions on several occasions to the Press Office staff not to leak such stories. I reiterated my interpretation of the press secretary's role—to accurately report the president's actions and views. What I did not say to Rumsfeld was that I suspected *he* was the source of some of the anti-Kissinger and anti-Rockefeller stories. Nor did I enunciate my belief that he had ambitions for higher positions, and that the leaks might have been designed to discredit potential rivals. By the end of the meeting, Rumsfeld had calmed down. But I recognized that our relationship and my earlier admiration for him were cooling.

The chairman of Ford's election campaign, Howard "Bo" Callaway, a former governor and House member from Georgia, helped feed the rumor mill when he seemed to suggest at a news conference that Ford might not be 100 percent wedded to having Rockefeller as his VP running mate in the 1976 elections. He indicated that Ford might select a younger man. Callaway's statement was no doubt aimed at holding on to the votes of southern conservatives, who did not share the views of the liberal/moderate Rockefeller.

At one White House meeting, I noticed Rockefeller glaring at me. This was a day after Ford had issued a statement saying he favored Rockefeller for his running mate. Reporters had asked me about the endorsement.

And, sensing that Ford was somewhat ambiguous about Rockefeller being on the ticket, I responded that while the president wanted Rockefeller to run with him, it would be up to the convention delegates to decide.

After the meeting at which I had caught him glaring at me, Rockefeller asked me to join him in a small office just off the Cabinet Room. He informed me that he had a lot of friends in the press corps who told him I was the source of anti-Rockefeller stories. He accused me of doing Rumsfeld's dirty work, and he said the leaks about his not being Ford's running mate in 1976 were damaging the president.

I denied Rockefeller's accusations. But I thought to myself that I had probably contributed to the controversy when I quoted Ford to reporters as saying the Republican convention delegates would select his vice-presidential running mate. I promised myself that I would stop giving reporters guidance, hints, or leaks on personnel issues and the never-ending feuding among rival staff members. I recalled an old Vietnamese expression: "When the elephants fight, the grass gets trampled." When the elephants were Kissinger, Schlesinger, Rumsfeld, Rockefeller, Hartmann, Simon, et al., I definitely did not want to be the grass.

Over the next few months, Ford became convinced that Rockefeller's liberal/moderate position on issues was so unpopular with conservative voters that his presence on the Republican ticket might cost Ford the 1976 election. And given the likelihood that conservative Ronald Reagan was going to challenge him for the GOP nomination, Ford worried that he might not even be nominated if conservative primary voters and convention delegates believed Rockefeller was going to be his running mate. At a private meeting, Ford shared these concerns with Rockefeller. "To be brutally frank," the president said, "some of these difficulties might be eliminated if you were to indicate that you didn't want to be on the ticket in 1976."

Rockefeller got the not-so-subtle message and said he would immediately send Ford a letter saying he did not wish to run for vice president. Ford told Rockefeller, "Nelson, you are a hell of a team player."

The Rockefeller decision was announced as one part of a major personnel shake-up at the top levels of the Ford administration that became known as the "Halloween Massacre." The president had been under pressure from supporters and the press to finally get rid of the many Nixon carryovers who still filled most of the top positions in his administration. By the beginning of November 1975, Ford had determined whom he wanted to keep and whom he wanted to replace. He decided on the final personnel moves while confined to his White House residence suffering from a cold and sinus infection. During his illness, without the daily stream of Oval Office meetings and appointments, Ford had time alone to think through what he wanted to do. Alone in his bedroom, he made a flurry of personnel decisions:

- Take the National Security Council adviser position away from Kissinger, leaving him with just one title, secretary of state.
- Promote the deputy NSC adviser, Brent Scowcroft, to the top spot.
- Fire Defense Secretary James Schlesinger and replace him with Don Rumsfeld.
- Promote Rumsfeld's deputy, Dick Cheney, to the chief of staff job.
- Fire William Colby as director of the Central Intelligence Agency. While Colby was not implicated in the CIA assassination plots, Ford wanted his own selection in that vital job.
- Bring home George H. W. Bush from his post as America's diplomatic representative in China and make him head of the CIA.
- Bring home Elliot Richardson from his position as ambassador to England and make him commerce secretary, replacing Rogers C. B. Morton, who had health problems and wanted to spend more time working on Ford's 1976 election campaign.

Among White House staffers and other administration officials, firing Schlesinger was the most popular step in Ford's personnel shake-up. Schlesinger had a habit of lecturing people, including the president, acting as if he were a college professor talking to slow-witted freshmen. I once heard Ford tell some friends that he found Schlesinger "peculiar, strange, hard to get along with."

Ford intended to announce and explain all his personnel changes at one time. However, as with almost every major White House decision, bits and pieces began to leak to the press. Finally, Ford held a news conference to officially announce the top-level shake-up in his administration. The reporters' questions indicated they doubted the president's explanation that he was making the changes solely because he wanted his own choices in important jobs rather than inherited Nixon appointees. The journalists did not hide their suspicions that Ford must have some secret agenda or unspoken motive. In part, this suspicion was a residual attitude left over from Watergate and Nixon. Facing this open skepticism at his news conference, the president offered answers that were uncharacteristically terse, testy, and gruff.

Based on my experience, as a journalist and as press secretary, I knew that reporters didn't like surprises, such as Ford's staff shake-up. Surprises made them feel like they didn't know what was happening or was about to happen on their beat. And surprise announcements made editors and producers question whether their White House correspondents were plugged in. And so, surprises propelled journalists to look for hidden motives in order to cover their lack of advance knowledge. One theory advanced by skeptical reporters about Ford's personnel changes was that Rumsfeld was behind them in order to get his rival Kissinger out of the White House, to get his rival Bush out of contention for the 1976 vice-presidential nomination, and to get himself a Cabinet job. A *Washington Post* editorial complained that the firings and appointments had been done in an "abrupt and clumsy manner." And columnist Joseph Kraft said the staff shakeup had created new doubts about whether Ford "has the brains to be President."

A week after the "Halloween Massacre," Ford went on the NBC program *Meet the Press*, where he faced more suspicious questions suggesting various complex motives for the personnel moves. He explained to the panel that the simple truth didn't always seem to be the truth because it was so simple. "I told the simple truth," he declared, which was that he had made the staff changes primarily because he wanted his own people in key positions. Ford did acknowledge that Schlesinger had been replaced because his presence was causing tensions at national security meetings.

After his *Meet the Press* appearance, Ford invited me to ride back to the White House with him. I told him I lived close to the NBC studios, so it was more convenient for me to go straight home after the program rather than riding with him back to the White House. One of my staff assistants, Jim Shuman, told me later I should have accepted Ford's invitation because the president wanted someone to reassure him that he had done well on the program. "The president is a lonely man," Shuman commented.

Rumsfeld's departure from the White House to the Pentagon improved relations among White House staff members. The more easygoing Cheney did not generate a mood of rivalry. Hartmann, who had boycotted senior staff meetings when Rumsfeld ran them, started attending the meetings. I and other senior staff aides were able to spend more time interacting directly with the president.

29

To Helsinki and Beyond

At the end of July 1975, Ford took off on another diplomatic tour of Europe. The primary diplomatic purpose of the trip was for the president to meet in Helsinki, Finland, with the leaders of thirty-four other countries at what was called the Conference on Security and Cooperation in Europe, or CSCE. Some historians believe the CSCE began the process of loosening the Soviet Union's domination of Eastern Europe. Other stops on Ford's European trip included Poland, West Germany, Romania, and Yugoslavia.

In Poland, I went with the president when he visited Auschwitz, the Nazi concentration camp where more than a million Jews had been killed by Hitler's Nazi troops during World War II. The Poles had preserved the camp as a memorial. Relatives of both my mother and my father had died at the hands of the Nazis. Kissinger told Ford that members of his immediate family had perished at Auschwitz. I walked with Ford through the barracks where the condemned prisoners had been held while they waited to die. We looked at the railroad boxcars used to transport Jews and others to the death camp. And we stood in front of the cement gas chambers in which the victims had perished. It was silent. No one spoke. We were all overcome by emotion.

In Belgrade, Yugoslavia, Ford met with that country's president, Josip Broz Tito. Following their meeting, Ford and Tito went to the auditorium in a modernistic government building to give a press conference. An interpreter, translating Tito's words into English, quoted the Yugoslav leader as saying that his views and Ford's views on the Israeli-Arab confrontation in the Middle East "are quite identical." This was big news, since previously Tito had demanded that Israel give up territory it had taken in the 1967 Middle East War, while the United States had strongly supported Israel. After the news conference, as Ford and his entourage were leaving the building, the American ambassador to Yugoslavia, Laurence Silberman, came running after us, grabbed me, and said the translator had made a terrible error, which had to be corrected immediately. According to Silberman, what Tito had actually said was that his and Ford's views were quite identical on the *dangers* of the situation in the Middle East, not on *solutions* to the situation.

Before putting out a correction to the press corps, I decided to check with Kissinger. He advised me not to issue a correction for twelve hours, because the erroneous translation would give the impression that Ford had persuaded Tito to change his position on Middle East policy. In a decision I look back on with great shame and regret, I followed Kissinger's instructions and did not correct the translator's version of Tito's remarks until the next day.

This was only one of several occasions during Ford's European trip when I was unhappy with Kissinger because I believed he was bending the truth while talking to reporters in order to further his diplomatic goals. In addition to persuading me not to immediately correct the interpreter's error in translating Tito's remarks about the Middle East, Kissinger misleadingly told reporters in Helsinki that the status of Berlin was the topic of conversation at a private lunch Ford had with the leaders of the United Kingdom, France, and Germany. In fact, the topic discussed at that lunch was the world's economic problems. Kissinger also told reporters that a meeting between Ford and Soviet leader Brezhnev in Helsinki had made some progress on an arms limitation agreement, when actually the two leaders had made virtually no progress.

The CSCE meeting in Helsinki was the largest gathering of European heads of state since the Congress of Vienna in 1815. Initially Ford had been reluctant to attend, because he didn't see any likelihood that Moscow would soften its hard-line stance on various issues. But eventually he decided to go, after the Soviet Union indicated it was willing to ease somewhat its Cold War domination of Eastern Europe, allow more access to Berlin, and agree to joint Soviet-NATO troop reductions in Europe. In his formal speech to the delegates, looking directly at Brezhnev, Ford declared, "History will judge this conference not by what we say here today but what we do tomorrow, not by the promises we make but by the promises we keep." By signing the CSCE agreement in Helsinki, Ford, Brezhnev, and the other leaders pledged to cooperate with each other; respect the sovereignty, borders, and internal affairs of other countries; refrain from using force to settle disputes; and not violate human rights. Some historians believe this agreement encouraged Vaclav Havel in Czechoslovakia, Lech Walesa in Poland, and other democracy advocates in Soviet-dominated Eastern Europe to assert their rights and eventually to overthrow Moscow's rule.

But at the time, the CSCE agreement did not get much attention from the press. I thought the lack of coverage stemmed from the fact that the treaty had been quietly negotiated over a long period, and reporters had not known much about the low-visibility negotiations and didn't fully understand the complexities and significance of the document. I and other government officials were partly responsible for this lack of coverage because we failed to educate reporters about the history, importance, and impact of the agreement.

Some of my most vivid memories of Helsinki are not about the agreement or American-Soviet issues. Some of my most vivid memories are about the good food, the fine weather, the gracious hospitality, and the beautiful Finnish women.

At the CSCE sessions, a very attractive Finnish woman was assigned by her government to escort photographers in and out of the conference hall. Ford noticed her, flirted a little, and commented to me about how pretty she was. On a day when not much was happening in the formal meetings, a group of Finnish journalists—including a couple of beautiful female journalists—invited me to accompany them on an outing to a lake north of Helsinki. Dressed in bathing suits, we walked out on a long pier jutting into the lake and entered a wooden sauna built over the water. The temperature inside the sauna must have been well over 100 degrees Fahrenheit. The Finns explained to me that the procedure was to sit in the sauna as long as I could stand the heat, then to go out on the pier and jump into the water to cool off. I did as instructed. When my overheated body hit the cold lake water, I could practically hear my pores slamming shut. It was invigorating, to say the least.

Leaving Finland, I sat with the president and Mrs. Ford in their compartment aboard Air Force One. The president commented on the attractive Finnish women. "Next time, we leave the wives at home," he joked. "The hell you will!" Betty told him. She was smiling. But I think she meant it.

30

Nine Lives

In September 1975, Ford made two trips to California in a two-and-a half-week period. On both trips he was the target of assassination attempts, both times by women.

The morning of September 5 was sunny, clear, and warm in Sacramento. It was so nice that the president decided to walk the short distance from his hotel to a meeting with then-Governor Jerry Brown at the state Capitol building. As the president strode along a paved path across the grounds of the Capitol, he was accompanied, as always, by Secret Service agents. I walked on the grass a few feet to the side of the path and slightly ahead of Ford. The president stopped periodically to shake hands with spectators along the path. Suddenly, I saw the Secret Service agents close in around the president and start shoving him rapidly toward the Capitol building while other agents grabbed a woman in a bright red dress with a pistol in her hand.

Safe inside the Capitol building, Ford went directly into his meeting with Brown, apparently unfazed by his close brush with death. Neither the president nor anyone else told the governor about the assassination attempt on his front lawn. Brown and Ford talked for forty minutes about energy and economic issues. Only when Rumsfeld interrupted their meeting to give Ford a Secret Service report on the incident did the governor learn of the attempt to kill the president.

Meanwhile, the press corps was clamoring frantically for information about what had happened. At the time the woman pulled the gun on Ford, many of the White House reporters were still at their hotel or in the press room in the Capitol and had not witnessed the episode. After quickly gathering information from the Secret Service and local police officials, I faced a huge throng of reporters, photographers, and TV cameras. In a somewhat shaky voice, I reported that the would-be assassin's name was Lynette Alice Fromme, who went by the nickname "Squeaky." As soon as I imparted this information, I heard "ohs" and "ahs" from some of the reporters. I didn't understand their reaction until later, when I found out that "Squeaky" Fromme was well known locally as a follower of Charles Manson, the leader of the violent and anarchistic 1960s' hippie movement called Helter Skelter.

I informed the reporters that Fromme, standing beside the path outside the Capitol, had concealed a .45-caliber pistol in a holster strapped to her leg beneath her skirt. As Ford walked past her, she raised the pistol and pointed it directly at him from two feet away. Secret Service agent Larry Buendorf had grabbed the gun and wrestled it away from Fromme before she could fire. She was handcuffed and taken to jail.

Once my briefing was over and the reporters had raced off to file their stories, Rumsfeld complimented me on my performance. He was particularly impressed by how quickly I had pulled together the essential facts of the incident. Just thirty-two minutes after Fromme pulled the gun from under her skirt, I had stepped in front of the reporters to recount the facts of the attempted assassination. Jack Warner of the Secret Service said it was the most accurate report he had ever seen assembled under such circumstances. For that afternoon, at least, my journalistic background had helped me fulfill my press secretary's duties.

Ford remained amazingly calm and unruffled in the face of his close call. In addition to his meeting with Governor Brown, the president went through with a scheduled speech to the California state legislature. By coincidence the topic of his speech was crime. Rumsfeld thought it was important for the president to demonstrate that he was not hurt and not ruffled by his close call. So Ford held an impromptu news conference in the lobby of his hotel after the speech. He praised the Secret Service. And he declared that the episode would not deter him from traveling and mingling with the American people. A reporter asked for his personal thoughts. "Well, I was very thankful," the president replied.

Later that night, aboard Air Force One, flying back to Washington, Ford was more open about his personal reaction to the episode. In fact, he almost obsessively recounted over and over again his minute-by-minute recollections of the attempted assassination and of how he felt about it.

Robert Redford visits Ford . . . and the president's daughter, Susan, grabs a seat close to him

Enjoying an indoor game with some of the president's family members during one of Ford's vacations in Vail, Colorado

Working on—or fighting over—a presidential speech (with Robert Hartmann, at left, Henry Kissinger, right, and Brent Scowcroft, rear)

Sometimes the only chance to sleep was aboard Air Force One (yes, that's Cheney)

On Air Force One, from right to left, in front: Kissinger, Rumsfeld, and Cheney; opposite them, Nessen on the aisle and Appointments Secretary Terry O'Donnell in window seat

Ron Nessen, Don Rumsfeld, Dick Cheney conferring on Air Force One

Outside the Gates!

A lighthearted stroll on the South Lawn of the White House

Hitching a ride on the "press truck" during the 1976 election campaign

Sparring with
Helen Thomas

Working in my White
House office

My daily Oval Office meeting with Ford

Two big influences in my life—my mother and Jerry Ford

My daily White House press briefing, with Helen Thomas in the front row.
Time *photo by Dirck Halstead*

In Kansas City for the 1976 Republican nominating convention

Back in the press corps— interviewing Ronald Reagan for Mutual Broadcasting

"Old press secretaries never die . . .

And he did this for days afterward. Perhaps, by reliving the incident, he was releasing all the emotions he had kept to himself.

Attempts by the Air Force One crew to pick up local TV news coverage of the assassination attempt as we flew back to Washington from Sacramento were not successful. But White House communications technicians did radio to the plane the sound track of the *NBC Nightly News* story on the incident. The president listened intently. There was a lot of black humor on the flight. Someone suggested that the White House stewards had been farsighted to pack extra undershorts for Ford.

That night, back home in the Washington suburbs, I had a delayed emotional reaction. I awoke in the middle of the night, believing that my two-year-old son, sleeping between me and my wife, was dead. I felt his chest to see if he was breathing. I put my ear to his face to feel his breath. I tickled him to see if he would move. He was fine. But I lay awake for a long time.

After the Sacramento trip, I recorded this observation in my oral diary: "Now I'm worried about whether something else might happen on the next trip to California, although that's really silly and too much of a coincidence, except it's California."

Seventeen days later, during another Ford trip to the state, my fears came true. This time the episode occurred in San Francisco, well known for its large population of liberal, anti–Vietnam War, antiestablishment hippies. A TV cameraman I knew advised me, "Get him out of town as fast as you can. These are not good people." He pointed to a group demonstrating for various causes outside the St. Francis Hotel, where Ford was staying. Kennerly, the White House photographer, also worried about the demonstrators. He urged the Secret Service not to let Ford shake hands in the crowd. The Secret Service shared those concerns.

After speaking to an AFL-CIO meeting and attending a World Affairs Council lunch, Ford left the St. Francis by a rear entrance, on his way to the airport for the flight back to Washington. A crowd had gathered on the other side of the street to see him. The president followed the Secret Service admonition not to shake hands in the crowd. He headed straight for his limousine parked at the curb. But just before getting into the car, he raised his arm and waved to the crowd.

At that instant, I heard a loud popping noise. At first I thought it might be a firecracker. A Secret Service agent yelled, "Get him in the car!" The agents grabbed Ford, bent him over to make a smaller target, threw him onto the floor of the limousine, and piled on top of him for protection. I realized the pop was a gunshot.

I was walking out of the hotel beside Dr. Lukash, the White House physician, a few feet behind and to the left of Ford. When I saw the Secret Service agents bundle Ford into his limousine, I knew the motorcade was going to take off any second, leaving me standing on the sidewalk. I ran to the closest car in the motorcade and jumped in. It turned out to be the wire service car carrying the UPI's Helen Thomas.

The motorcade took off at high speed for the airport. Looking out the window, I saw police dragging a gray-haired woman out of the crowd, apparently the shooter. After witnessing two assassination attempts in California in less than three weeks, something in me snapped. "Goddamn California!" I yelled, pounding the door and the front seat with my fist. "These motherfuckers in California! Why the fuck did we ever come back here! I hope we never come back to this fucking state."

The next issue of *Time* magazine ran a chart showing the path of the bullet. It hit the facade of the St. Francis, ricocheted across the sidewalk, hit the curb, and bounced away. I calculated that the bullet had passed a few feet—or a few inches—in front of me.

After the presidential limousine had gone a few blocks on its way to the San Francisco airport, the president asked the Secret Service agents to let him sit up. "Will you guys get off? You're going to smother me," he complained. Ford also directed that all the agents on duty be notified via radio of his gratitude for their actions. And Ford asked that Betty, who was in Monterey visiting friends, be notified that he was fine. When Ford's motorcade reached the airport, the Secret Service wanted to hustle the president aboard Air Force One immediately. However, the president insisted on first thanking and shaking hands with all the policemen and other security people who had been assigned to protect him.

Aboard Air Force One, Rumsfeld, Hartmann, Kennerly, and I followed Ford into his compartment. Almost immediately, the president directed a navy steward to bring him a martini. And as soon as the drink arrived, he took a big gulp. I didn't blame him. When the steward served drinks to the rest of us, we all took big gulps. Always ready with an irreverent wisecrack, Kennerly asked Ford, "Other than that, Mr. President, how did you like San Francisco?"

We could not take off immediately because we had to await the arrival of Mrs. Ford from Monterey. Finally, she arrived, climbed the steps into the plane, and joined her husband and the rest of us at a table in the presidential compartment. "Well, how did they treat you in San Francisco?" she asked Ford. Could it be that no one had told the First Lady that someone had tried to assassinate her husband? "You mean you don't know?" Rumsfeld asked incredulously. "Know what?" she replied. The rest of us looked at each other. Who was going to tell her? The president didn't say anything. Finally, Rumsfeld started to tell her what happened, in a long and convoluted narrative, covering almost everything Ford had done that day. Hartmann cut in impatiently, "Why are you taking so long? Get to the point." Finally, Rumsfeld told Mrs. Ford, "Someone took a shot at your husband." I was looking intently at the First Lady's face when Rumsfeld informed her of her husband's close call. She had had a big smile on her face as Rumsfeld started his account. And her expression never changed when he got to the part about the gunshot.

From the very beginning of her marriage to Jerry Ford, Betty had tolerated the many rituals expected of a career politician's wife. She had stood by her husband's side, smiling, through victories and defeats. She had silently tolerated the vilification of her husband by political opponents and by the press. And she had learned to hide her personal reactions. Thus, it was not a total surprise that she suppressed the emotions she must have been feeling when Rumsfeld told her that someone had tried to shoot her husband.

On the flight back to Washington from San Francisco, we learned that the shooter was Sara Jane Moore, forty-five years old, another member of the San Francisco radical community. We also learned that a man standing near her, Oliver Sipple, had seen her raise the gun and had shoved her arm just as she pulled the trigger, sending the bullet into the wall of the hotel, saving Ford from injury or death. Sipple was a decorated marine veteran of the Vietnam War. News stories about the incident revealed that he was also gay. Ford later sent Sipple a letter of thanks, but did not invite him to the White House. Critics complained that Sipple was not invited to Washington to receive Ford's gratitude in person because the president was afraid of antagonizing conservative, antihomosexual supporters. I never knew if that was really Ford's motive for not inviting Sipple to the White House. But if it was, I disagree with the decision.

The mood aboard Air Force One on the flight back to Washington from San Francisco was a mixture of relief and hysteria. The booze and the black humor flowed. Someone asked if legislation granting equal rights to women included equal rights to take a shot at the president. Someone else wondered whether Ford was current on his life insurance premiums.

After about a half hour, I and the other staff people departed for the back of the plane and left the Fords alone in the presidential compartment. I found out later that the president and Mrs. Ford had called their children from Air Force One to reassure them that their father was fine. The president also took a nap during the flight, leaving a wakeup call for twenty minutes before landing at Andrews Air Force Base. I was amazed that Ford could fall asleep so easily after his close brush with death that day.

Safely back in the White House that night, Ford told reporters, "I don't think any person as president ought to cower in the face of a limited number of people who want to take the law into their own hands."

Nevertheless, after the two assassination attempts, the Secret Service insisted that Ford wear a bulletproof vest under his suit jacket when in public.

For a long time after that day, I periodically heard in my head the sound of Sara Jane Moore's gunshot, the instant of silence that followed, and the Secret Service agent yelling, "Get him in the car!"

Strange things kept happening to Ford. About a month after the San Francisco episode, a 1967 yellow Buick slammed into the side of Ford's limousine as he was leaving a fund-raising dinner at the Civic Center in Hartford, Connecticut. Thinking it was yet another assassination attempt, Secret Service agents surrounded the Buick, guns drawn. It turned out the driver was not an assassin, but a teenager who had run a red light.

That night I kidded Ford about his many close calls. He replied, "Well, the cat has nine lives."

31

"Ford to New York: Drop Dead!"

New York City almost went bankrupt in the fall of 1975. Too much spending and not enough revenue brought it to the brink of defaulting on its
debt. Ford decided not to provide taxpayer funds to the city, to let it sink
or swim on its own. I was on the phone with Treasury Secretary Simon
almost every day, getting his guidance on how to answer press questions
about New York City's troubles. Simon expressed anger at Vice President
Rockefeller, a former governor of New York State, for trying to persuade
the president to bail out the city financially. Simon argued that Rockefeller
ought to resign if he disagreed with the president's position.

Still recovering from a cold and sinus infection, Ford met with senior
administration officials in the Cabinet Room to evaluate the New York
City financial crisis and decide what action he should take, if any. Speaking in a weak voice and coughing frequently, the president asked whether
anyone at the meeting thought he should support legislation to prevent a
default by New York City. He paused. There was silence from the assembled officials. After about five seconds, Rumsfeld declared, "The answer is
not just 'no.' It's 'Hell no.'"

I was authorized to state flatly at my briefings that the president would
not take any action to prevent a financial default by New York City and
that he would veto any congressional legislation providing a bailout.
Ford's reasoning was that if the federal government bailed out New York,
the mayor, Abe Beame, and other city officials would have no incentive to
manage their finances more responsibly. He also believed that a federal
bailout of New York City would send a message to state and local officials
all over the country that they didn't have to match their spending to revenue, because the federal government would always be there to rescue
them. In a speech to the National Press Club in the midst of the New York

financial crisis, Ford asked rhetorically, "What restraint would be left on the spending of other local and state governments once it becomes clear that there is a federal rescue squad that will always arrive in the nick of time?"

The *New York Daily News* headline on the story of Ford's tough stance read, "FORD TO CITY: DROP DEAD." Congressman (later Mayor) Ed Koch called Ford's position "immoral." Congresswoman Bella Abzug accused the president of wanting to "pull the plug" on the city. Most of the news stories were critical of Ford and supportive of helping the city.

Then, someone, identified only as "an administration source," anonymously leaked a story to the TV networks and the *New York Times* saying that Ford would reluctantly sign legislation to help New York City out of its financial troubles if Congress approved it. The leaked story made me worry that I had been too strong in my declaration that Ford would not take action to stave off a financial default by New York City. I went to see Cheney about my concerns. He informed me that some of Ford's advisers had gotten "soft" in their opposition to aid for New York. Cheney, Hartmann, and I were concerned that any movement by Ford toward eventually offering federal help to the city would undermine the president's credibility and anger conservative voters. Hartmann declared, "If the president wants to win the election, he will *not* give aid to New York City. If he wants to lose the election, he *will* give aid to New York City."

Shortly afterward, Ford told a visiting group of magazine publishers that before he would agree to help New York City, he would need to see in writing a commitment from the city to manage its finances more responsibly in the future. Aware that this response was considerably softer than his original flat "no aid to New York" position, Ford asked me, "I didn't undercut you too much, did I?" I replied, "Oh, no, that's all right." In truth, his softer position on aid to New York did not match what I had been telling reporters. I noted in my oral diary that I felt "like a man out on a limb, out on the furthest branch of the limb, and the limb has been cut about three-quarters of the way through and is going to be cut all the way, and I'm going down with the limb."

I joked to some of my staff that I was going to start off my next briefing by declaring, "All previous statements on New York City are inoperative." What I actually did was carefully adjust my answers to reflect Ford's more nuanced approach to dealing with New York City's financial problems. It was a difficult line to walk. Ford didn't want me to signal that he would save New York City and other cities from the consequences of irresponsible financial management. But he did want me to signal that he would take steps to help if New York City committed to get its financial house in order. After one briefing, I told my friend Tom DeFrank of *Newsweek* that my statements on aid to New York City had been "the most orderly retreat since Napoleon withdrew from Moscow." That evening, on the *NBC Nightly News*, correspondent John Cochran, who frequently criticized my performance, told his viewers, "Ron Nessen is doing a very good job of giving us an accurate portrayal of the president's reaction" to New York City's financial crisis.

In the short term, the New York Teachers Union pension fund lent the city $150 million to see it through its immediate cash shortage. In the longer run, after New York City agreed to take specific steps to manage its budget more responsibly, Ford said the federal government would lend money to the city from time to time to cover short-term deficits, but only if New York paid back the loans at the end of each year, along with interest 1 percent higher than the prevailing rate.

Once the crisis had passed, I met with my Press Office staff to assess how we had done. I was surprised at the outpouring of concern about a much broader issue—that Ford was often slow to articulate in specific terms what he stands for on major policy issues. Did he have an overall plan for governing? What was he trying to accomplish by the end of the year and in the long run? Did he have a strategy for winning the 1976 election? These were some of the issues my staff raised. I mostly agreed with their concerns. I told them I would raise their questions with Ford.

32

State of the World, State of the Union, State of My Marriage

At the end of 1975, during a presidential visit to China, there was another apparent attempt on Ford's life. The president and his staff were awakened about 5:30 a.m. by the sound of gunfire close to our hotel in Beijing, or Peking, as it was called then. I counted about twenty shots. Then I heard more sounds of gunfire from farther away. When Secret Service officials asked the Chinese authorities about the shots, the Chinese denied there had been any gunfire.

Four years earlier, Nixon had visited China and reopened relations between the two countries, which had been severed when Mao Tse-tung and his Communist revolutionaries defeated China's American-supported Nationalist government in a civil war. Ford felt it was important to maintain and improve contacts with the Communist regime because of China's growing importance on the world stage. China was interested in improving relations with Washington for economic reasons and as a counterweight to its neighbor, the Soviet Union, with whom there were tensions over border disputes, treatment of ethnic minorities, and other issues.

While the president and Kissinger met with lower-level officials, the Chinese government refused to say when during Ford's four-day visit he would meet with Mao, or even whether there would be a meeting with Mao.

My job of keeping the press informed was made almost impossible because the Chinese demanded that no news at all be released about the content or tone of Ford's conversations. The reporters whose news organizations had sent them halfway around the world, at great expense, to cover Ford's visit were frustrated by the lack of information and took it out on me. All I could offer them were the menus from the official dinners

Ford attended, descriptions of the president's sightseeing tours around Peking, the size of curbside crowds watching the president's comings and goings, and innocuous adjectives about the official negotiations.

Even getting the Chinese officials to approve the nightly press announcement of the next day's schedule of meetings and coverage arrangements was a frustrating battle. After each night's official banquet, I would return to my temporary office on the tenth floor of the shabby Minzu Hotel and await a telephone call from the Chinese Information Ministry. Finally at midnight, or later, I would get a call from an English-speaking official of the ministry, Mr. Ma. He invited me to come down to his office two flights below. He introduced me to his boss, who spoke no English. Mr. Ma invited me to partake of a cup of tea or a soda. He made small talk. Finally, when he was ready, he informed me that the schedule and press coverage plans for the next day were approved and I had his permission to distribute them to the news media.

One morning, on short notice, Chinese officials notified the American delegation that Chairman Mao would meet with Ford. The Chinese decreed that the president could bring only Betty, their daughter Susan, and five aides. I was on the list. However, only the president, Betty, and Susan were allowed to actually approach Mao. The rest of us had to observe from a distance. After photos were taken, Mrs. Ford and Susan were ushered out, and the substantive discussions began. Ford and Mao sat next to each other in easy chairs during their ninety-minute meeting. Two women translators and a nurse sat behind them. I was close enough to hear Mao. He seemed to be speaking gibberish, not Chinese words. Yet the interpreters translated his gibberish into perfect English sentences. Mao was eighty-two years old then and in declining health. He died a year later.

As the Peking visit came to an end, Kissinger visited the press center to brief reporters, who were angry about the total blackout by Chinese officials on news about Ford's meetings. Kissinger announced that the Chinese had agreed to return the remains of two American airmen shot down during the Vietnam War, and to provide information on five other Americans missing in action. Kissinger also reported that Ford had told the Chinese he intended to continue improving relations with the Soviet Union despite Peking's objections. And Kissinger said he had informed the Chinese that while the United States wanted to improve and formalize diplomatic relations with the Peking government, it also intended to maintain a cultural and economic relationship with the Chinese Nationalist government on Taiwan. "We are satisfied with the visit," Kissinger informed the reporters.

In the days after Ford and his entourage returned to Washington, a flood of stories criticized my performance during the trip. I cut short a vacation in Florida with my family and returned to Washington to deal with the media's fault-finding. Typical was a column in the *Chicago Tribune* by Jim Squires complaining that I had come to the press room only twice during the Peking visit, "once to announce [I] had nothing to say and another time to say [I] had nothing to announce." It was maddening to be blamed for not releasing information on Ford's trip, when it was the Chinese officials who had imposed the news blackout and Kissinger who had insisted on abiding by the blackout.

After the China trip, Ford immersed himself in preparations for his State of the Union speech to Congress in January 1976, a speech that would be studied carefully as a preview of his 1976 election campaign. As always, drafting the speech set off bitter arguments among staff members. The fighting began when Hartmann and his speech-writing team returned to Washington from the restored colonial town of Williamsburg, Virginia, where they had retreated to write a first draft. Williamsburg was the place where Thomas Jefferson, Patrick Henry, and other heroes of the American Revolution wrote or uttered some of their most historic and inspiring words. There was nothing historic or inspiring about the document produced in Williamsburg by Hartmann's group. Their draft speech ran two hours. One senior White House adviser commented, "It would make us all ashamed to have the president deliver that speech."

Meanwhile, another group of White House staff members, including David Gergen and Alan Greenspan, had written their own version. As always the rival versions ended up on Ford's desk. "Neither constituted exactly what I wanted to say, but each included passages I liked," Ford recalled later. "If I took the best from each, I would have a pretty good speech. That's what I did." At a Saturday meeting in the Cabinet Room, I watched as the president went through the two drafts page by page, choosing a portion from the Hartmann speech, a portion from the Gergen-

Greenspan speech, while the rival teams sat around the table squabbling over which sentences should be retained and which deleted.

After the meeting had been going on for three hours and had gotten through only ten pages of the twenty-six-page speech, Ford lost his temper. He slammed his fist down on the table, startling all the aides seated around him and rattling our coffee cups. "Damn it, we've got to stop bickering over little details," the president shouted, madder than I had ever seen him. "We're just screwing around. . . . This has got to be frozen. There can't be any more changes. . . . We're too damn close to the deadline." Ford put Hartmann in charge of coming up with a final version, then stomped out to keep another appointment.

We took a short break to recover from the president's outburst. Then I proposed a plan to end the impasse. We would produce two versions of the State of the Union speech. One would be a longer text consisting of the best of the Hartmann and Gergen-Greenspan drafts pasted together. It would be distributed to members of Congress and the press. The other version would be shorter, for the president to actually read to the joint session of Congress. Gergen would be in charge of editing the shorter version from the longer version. But Hartmann correctly saw that idea as a thinly disguised scheme to minimize his contribution to the version that Ford would deliver to Congress. Speaking with a sneer, Hartmann rejected my plan and insisted that only he would draft the final version of the State of the Union address. The Gergen-Greenspan team gave up trying to produce a better speech for the time being and departed, leaving Hartmann and his team to draft the address.

The next morning, Sunday, the day before the speech was to be delivered, the rival groups reconvened and the fighting continued. Finally, late in the afternoon, Cheney went into the Oval Office alone to hash out with Ford the final version. While he was with the president, the rest of us watched the Super Bowl on TV. Just before halftime, Cheney came out of his meeting carrying a heavily edited final text of the State of the Union speech. In the end, the president dumped some of the Hartmann draft and adopted some of the Gergen-Greenspan draft.

One of the themes of the speech was that the nation and the world were in the midst of extremely difficult times, facing many problems that tested our determination. That idea came from Ford himself. Explaining why he adopted that theme, the president showed me an old paperback copy of writings by Thomas Paine, one of the Founding Fathers of the United States, which Jack Marsh had given him to read. Ford instructed Hartmann to include in the State of the Union speech Paine's famous declaration in *The Crisis*: "These are the times that try men's souls. The summer soldier and the sunshine patriot will, in this crisis, shrink from the service of their country; but he that stands it now, deserves the love and thanks of man and woman."

In accord with his conservative philosophy, Ford called in his State of the Union address for "a new realism," which would include an active government but also a vigorous private economy that would create jobs and hold down prices. "We must introduce a new balance in the relationship between the individual and the government," the president declared, "a balance that favors greater individual freedom and self-reliance." Specifically Ford proposed restraining the growth of the federal government, cutting taxes, providing incentives for private companies to expand, reducing government regulations, and easing restrictions that hindered the effectiveness of American intelligence agencies.

The success or failure of Ford's program depended to a great extent on how Congress, the press, and the public reacted to his federal budget proposal, issued shortly after the State of the Union speech. The federal budget was a massive document, almost a thousand pages, proposing dollar figures for what could be spent in the new fiscal year for every government department, agency, bureau, program, and employee. Traditionally, budget bureau experts had briefed reporters on the tens of thousand individual expense items. But as 1976 began, Ford decided to present the press briefing on his budget himself. It would be another opportunity to counter the never-ending portrayals of the president in the press and by comedians as a dullard, not too bright, not mentally up to the task of running the government. In fact, he was an expert on the federal budget, having served more than twenty years on the House Appropriations Committee and having spent more than one hundred hours in the White House putting together the new budget.

The president conducted his budget briefing for reporters in the State Department auditorium. Several hundred journalists packed the place. It lasted for ninety minutes—three times longer than a normal presidential news conference. After explaining the details of his budget, Ford answered fifty-six questions. Looking back, Ford wrote later, "I felt that my appearance had done more to convince members of the press of my competence to be president than almost anything else I'd done."

Although I didn't start smoking cigarettes until I was in my twenties, by the time I became press secretary, I was a heavy smoker, going through two or three packs of filtered Marlboros a day. I was hoarse and coughed constantly. Once I had such a coughing fit during a meeting in Rumsfeld's office that he was afraid I was going to collapse. It wasn't my only unhealthy habit. The long hours in the White House left no time for exercise. And to relieve the stress of my job, I ate too much and drank too much. At a healthier point in my life, I weighed 175 pounds. But now my weight had ballooned to 212 pounds.

One day I saw an advertisement in the *Washington Post* for a smoking cessation program called SmokEnders. Along with five members of my Press Office staff, I attended the course, one night a week for six weeks. Essentially, attendees smoked fewer and fewer cigarettes each week, switched to milder cigarettes, and kept their cigarette butts in a water-filled glass jar where the resulting ugly mess was supposed to remind us of what we were inhaling into our lungs. The day the course ended was the day we were supposed to give up cigarettes entirely. It worked for me and two of my colleagues. The other three reverted. It turned out that my first day without any cigarettes under the SmokEnders program was an especially hectic day at the White House. As I dropped off to sleep that night, I thought to myself, "If I could get through a day like today without smoking, I'm cured." I was. I've never smoked another cigarette.

I was mostly faithful to my wife while I served in the White House. That wasn't entirely because I had grown and matured and understood the need for faithfulness in marriage. I also was afraid that if a reporter found out and exposed an affair, it would embarrass Ford and almost certainly result in my dismissal. There was also a practical reason for not cheating on Cindy. I worked such long days and long weeks there was no time to fool around. However, I did revert to my old habit with one woman, a TV cameraman's wife. On the nights I went to see her, I would ask the White House driver to drop me off on a street corner near her house. Then I would walk into an alley and wait until the limousine had pulled away so the driver wouldn't see where I was going. When the car had departed, I would come out of the alley and walk to her house for our liaison. After engaging in this surreptitious sneaking around a couple of times, I realized it was too dangerous and unseemly even for me. I was faithful to Cindy for the rest of my time in the White House.

33

"Live from New York"

In March 1976, Ford attended the annual black-tie banquet of the White House Correspondents Association. A big-name entertainer is engaged each year to perform after dessert. And that year the entertainer was comedian Chevy Chase, whose portrayal of Ford as a stumbling, bumbling, air-brain on the new NBC satirical television show *Saturday Night Live* had attracted a large audience and much comment. While the band played "Hail to the Chief" and the president and Mrs. Ford watched from the head table, Chase entered the huge banquet hall from a distant doorway and made his way across the room in what was supposed to be an imitation of a clumsy Ford, falling and bumping into tables every few steps. Once he reached the head table, he pretended to bang his head on the podium. The audience laughed at parts of Chase's Ford routine, of course, but there was an uncomfortable feeling in the room.

Traditionally, the only kind of humor that really went over in Washington was self-deprecating humor—making fun of yourself, not making fun of others. Chase didn't understand that tradition. Or, if he did, he decided to break with it.

Once the hired entertainer has finished his act at the correspondents' banquet, the president speaks. Unbeknownst to the audience—or to Chase—a former Hollywood producer and writer named Don Penny, who was working in the White House speech office, had helped prepare the president for his response. Ford was introduced. As he stood up to move to the podium, he followed Penny's coaching by pretending to pull his place mat off the table. The audience laughed. Then he placed a pile of papers, supposedly his speech, on the podium and pretended to knock the pages to the floor. The audience roared. They got the joke. Ford was making fun of himself. It was self-deprecating humor at the highest level. It won over the audience and made Chase's harsh put-downs seem unfriendly and out of place.

Nevertheless, Ford and Chase somehow hit it off. They discovered they both loved to play tennis. So Ford invited the comedian to come to the White House the next day to play a few sets on the tennis court just outside the Oval Office.

I had met one of the *Saturday Night Live* cast members and writers, Al Franken, the previous month in New Hampshire, where Ford was making an early campaign tour. Franken explained to me that the program wanted to recruit non–show business guest hosts, and he asked me if I was interested. I was intrigued but leery. I received several phone calls from the program's producer, Lorne Michaels, over the next few weeks urging me to come on the show. After witnessing Ford's superb self-deprecating performance at the Correspondents Association dinner, his comfort level with people making fun of him, and his hospitality toward Chevy Chase, I agreed to host the program on Easter weekend of 1976. I even accepted Michaels's invitation to come to New York City a few days early to participate in writing the show. It was not a totally foreign experience for me. The *Saturday Night Live* offices and studios were in the NBC headquarters at Rockefeller Center, where I had often originated stories for the *Huntley-Brinkley Report* and the *Today* show when I was an NBC News correspondent. I knew and had worked with many of the technical crew and studio crew for *Saturday Night Live*.

Ford was familiar with the program. He had children in their teens and twenties who kept him current on popular culture. In keeping with his genial personality, Ford even agreed to videotape a few bits for the show. Standing before an NBC camera set up in the Cabinet Room, Ford intoned, "Live from New York, it's Saturday night," and "Ladies and gentleman, the press secretary to the president of the United States," and "I'm Gerald Ford and you're not."

Saturday Night Live had been on the air for only six months. In addition to Al Franken, the cast of performers that first season included John Belushi, Dan Aykroyd, Jane Curtin, Garrett Morris, Laraine Newman, Gilda Radner, and, of course, Chevy Chase. The guest entertainers the night I was on the program were comedian Billy Crystal and the first of the punk rockers, Patti Smith. Smith and I were assigned adjoining dressing rooms.

The aroma of marijuana wafted from her dressing room into my dressing room.

In my opening monologue—some of which I wrote myself—I began by saying that some viewers were probably wondering why the press secretary to the president of the United States was appearing on a live comedy show. The punch line was, "Well, this is not so very different from my daily press briefing."

My monologue was interrupted by a young man walking onto the stage carrying a red telephone. He informed me that the president was on the line. I held the receiver to my ear and pretended to respond to Ford:

" . . . You're watching the show . . ."

Pause

" . . . You heard my monologue . . ."

Pause

" . . . Betty liked it . . ."

Pause

" . . . I'm fired . . ."

Throughout the program, dressed in the appropriate period costume, I did a series of one-liners pretending to be the press secretary for various historic figures. For instance, wearing a toga as the press secretary to Oedipus, I announced that henceforth the Queen Mother would be known as the Queen Wife. And wearing colonial garb, I announced that President Thomas Jefferson denied having "six thousand close relatives who enjoy picking cotton twenty hours a day."

In many of the skits, I played myself interacting with Chevy Chase's impersonation of a clumsy, clueless President Ford. For instance, in one skit I briefed Chase/Ford on his daily schedule.

Nessen: You'll be awakened at 5:30 a.m. in the usual manner.

Chase: Ron, Betty and I are getting sick and tired of the twenty-one-gun salute. . . . Couldn't someone just speak in my ear or set the alarm clock?

Nessen: We tried the alarm clock in the beginning, if you'll remember, sir.

When it rang, you answered the telephone and broke your ankle.

If I was expecting Washington-style self-deprecating humor on the *Saturday Night Live* program I hosted, I was extremely naive. There was nothing self-deprecating about Chase's portrayal of Ford, there was no gentle ribbing, no well-intended satire, no good-natured spoofing. A lot of it was nasty, and all of it was designed to denigrate Ford.

In books written later, cast members owned up to going out of their way to harshly portray Ford because they disagreed so vehemently with his political philosophy and his actions in the White House. Chase told *Playboy* magazine that Ford "never gave a shit about people." He told the *Washington Star*, "I think he's a terrible President." He told the *Washington Post*, "He's never supported any legislation to help people in his life."

Saturday Night Live began a new era of political humor, a nastier, angrier era of put-downs. In the years since then, the political humor on *Saturday Night Live* and on other programs has grown even harsher. A recent example of this new, nastier political humor is the imitation of Sarah Palin by Tina Fey, a *Saturday Night Live* veteran. The good-natured ribbing of public figures by a Bob Hope or a Jack Paar is ancient history.

After the *Saturday Night Live* program I hosted, there was a party at a restaurant in Rockefeller Plaza for cast members, studio and control room crew, friends of the cast, hangers-on, and advertisers. And then there was a smaller party-after-the-party at the Central Park West apartment of singer Paul Simon, a friend of producer Lorne Michaels. The heavy aroma of marijuana was in the air. In fact, I took a couple of tokes myself. What I did not detect, but read about later in books by cast members, was the amount of cocaine being snorted at that party.

Back at the White House on Monday, the president told me he had watched the show at Camp David, where he had spent the weekend. He said he laughed at some skits, didn't like others, and couldn't understand some. (Perhaps the mock commercial for a carbonated vaginal douche?) Mrs. Ford told the Associated Press, "I thought the White House material was very funny and so did the president. We both laughed at it and had a good time." However, she also said she found some of the skits "distasteful."

Jack Ford, the president's son, then twenty-five years old, sent me a hand-delivered note scrawled in red ink on White House stationery: "I thought as Press Sec. you're supposed to make *professional* decisions that get the Pres. *good press.* If you get a min., I'd be happy to explain to you that your job is to further the Pres. interests, not yours or your family's."

The press coverage of my appearance was almost universally negative. The *Chicago Sun-Times* ran a banner headline across the top of the front page reading, "REPORT FORD TURNED OFF BY HIS ROLE IN TV SKIT." The lead on the Associated Press story also said Ford was unhappy about my appearance on the program. Buried down in the middle of the story was a quote from an unnamed White House staff member saying Ford was *not* displeased. Even Rona Barrett, who covered show business and celebrities, thought she had a scoop on my future. On ABC's *Good Morning America* program, she told her audience, "Usually reliable sources in Washington report that Ron Nessen's days at the White House are numbered thanks in great measure to President Ford's negative reaction to NBC's *Saturday Night*."

One of the few reporters who looked past the news media's common wisdom and took a contrarian view of my appearance and Ford's appearance on *Saturday Night Live* was John J. O'Connor of the *New York Times*. He wrote, "Perhaps President Ford has defused the 'clumsiness issue' by good-naturedly joining his detractors." Indeed, my goal in agreeing to appear on *Saturday Night Live* had been to counteract the portrayals of Ford as clumsy and not very bright, by demonstrating that the president and his staff could laugh at themselves, could even participate in the fun. It did not work.

While I never said this publicly, I worried privately at the time about whether I had made a mistake by going on the program. Had I been duped by the cast and producer, whose real goal in inviting me to appear was to gain wider attention for their demeaning portrayal of the president? Had I put my own interests ahead of Ford's interests? Had my ego driven me to do it? Should I resign? I decided to stay and be the best press secretary I could be as Ford faced a major challenge in the 1976 election from within his own party.

34

Ford vs. Reagan

As the 1976 election year began, Ford and his advisers knew he faced a tough battle. First he had to win the Republican presidential nomination in a contest with Ronald Reagan, who had officially declared his candidacy at Thanksgiving. It was rare for a politician to challenge a sitting president of his own party. Ford and his staff took the challenge seriously. We knew that there were a lot of Republicans in the country who would rather lose with a conservative candidate than win with a moderate candidate. Assuming Ford won the nomination from Reagan, he would then have to overcome lingering public displeasure with his pardon of Nixon, a bad economy, and a tense international situation in order to defeat the Democratic candidate in the November election.

The first head-to-head primary race between Ford and Reagan was in New Hampshire. Both the state's governor and the publisher of the influential *Manchester Union-Leader* were strong Reagan supporters. And I idiotically answered a reporter's question in a way that caused a huge furor in the state and could have cost Ford the primary there. The episode started when a reporter asked me if Ford intended to ski in New Hampshire in the weeks before the primary. I had recently heard Ford comment privately that when he attended Yale Law School he had tried skiing in New Hampshire but didn't much like the conditions there. So, sure that I was accurately reflecting Ford's views, but without considering the political consequences, I responded to the reporter's question by saying Ford preferred skiing in Colorado because he found the New Hampshire slopes icy and the snow uncertain.

My comments were a huge story in New Hampshire, where ski resorts are a major industry. I was denounced in editorials and columns and cartoons in the state's newspapers. One ski resort at Mount Sunapee even named an icy section of one ski run for me. I was afraid that if Ford lost the New Hampshire primary, I would be blamed. To offset any effect on voters of my ill-considered remark, I wore a large badge reading "Ski New Hampshire" when the president made his first campaign trip to the state.

At a news conference in Manchester, Ford told the reporters, "I am surprised that some of you haven't asked about my good press secretary Ron Nessen's comment." So, a reporter asked, "Is he going to ski?" Ford responded—jokingly, I hoped—that he was thinking about taking his press secretary up to the top of the mountain and "throwing him over."

Ford's real anger during the New Hampshire primary campaign was directed at Reagan. At a town meeting–style event in the Keene High School gymnasium, the president was furious over a question he thought had been planted by the Reagan campaign. The question suggested that Ford and other politicians had engaged in duplicity to achieve pay raises for federal government officials and members of Congress.

The question really riled the president. When he came off the stage, he ordered me to get on the phone right away and find out what pay raises Reagan had received and what pay raises he had approved for state employees when he was governor of California.

Ford did not think highly of his competitor. He wrote later, "I didn't take Reagan seriously. . . . Several of his characteristics seemed to rule him out as a serious challenger. One was his penchant for offering simplistic solutions to hideously complex problems. The second was his conviction that he was always right in every argument."

I was not happy with the press coverage in New Hampshire. Some reporters seemed more interested in covering the press coverage than in covering the campaign. News organizations assigned correspondents full time to report on the media coverage of the campaign. I believed this focus was the result of the popularity of *The Boys on the Bus*, a best-selling book by reporter Timothy Crouse examining in great detail the press coverage of the 1972 presidential race between Nixon and Democratic senator George McGovern.

The media's interest in trivia was another problem. One day, the first nine paragraphs of a story in the *Detroit Free Press* were devoted to a brief heckling episode during a Ford campaign stop. The tenth and last paragraph reported what the president said in his speech. And the *Washington*

Star ran a story on the campaign with this lead: "While President Ford's motorcade swept north yesterday on Interstate 95, an accident occurred in the opposite lane which police said had nothing whatever to do with the motorcade."

As a result of this lack of attention to issues, and a belief by many of the president's advisers that most reporters were biased against Ford, anti-media sentiment grew and spread among the White House and campaign staffs. I referred to some reporters as "the muggers of the press corps." Even the president himself, normally very tolerant of the press, was irritated by some of the coverage, particularly by TV correspondents.

Ford's campaign in New Hampshire was hampered by severe limits on how much it could raise from contributors and how much it could spend. These limits were imposed by a federal campaign law enacted as a result of Nixon's electioneering abuses. The limitations hurt Ford more than Reagan because the president was required to travel with, and pay for, a large entourage, while Reagan could campaign with a minimal staff.

The spending limitations were so severe that at one point it appeared the campaign did not have enough money for Ford and his staff to stay overnight in New Hampshire. Campaign chairman Bo Callaway had to ask the telephone company to return the campaign's deposit so the money could be used to pay other campaign expenses. During another Ford campaign trip, the spending limits meant we could not afford to pay for lighting and sound equipment at two events. And the campaign staff informed me that it could not afford to pay eighty cents apiece to print photos of the president for press kits.

Another serious threat to Ford's campaign to win the primary was the announcement that Richard Nixon had accepted an invitation to visit China just before the voting in New Hampshire. Such a trip would remind voters of the Watergate scandal and, particularly, of Ford's unpopular pardon of the former president. As the *New York Times* put it in a front-page headline, "NIXON TRIP REVIVES ISSUE VEXING TO FORD IN THE PRIMARY." During an informal conversation among senior White House aides, Jack Marsh referred to Nixon as an albatross around Ford's neck. More bluntly, Brent Scowcroft—normally a soft-spoken, polite man—referred to Nixon as "a shit." After stories by Reuters and the *New York Times* suggested that Nixon's toast at a banquet in China was critical of several Ford foreign policy steps, the president with uncharacteristic venom declared, "If he keeps this up, we're going to crack him."

The results of the New Hampshire primary voting were slow coming in. Finally, at 3 a.m., with Ford trailing Reagan in the limited tabulation of ballots, I stretched out on the couch in my office to get a little sleep. Cheney also slept on the couch in his office. Ford retired to his residence and slept in a real bed. At 6:30 a.m., my deputy, John Carlson, shook me awake. We went to the newswire machines and found that the president had defeated Reagan by 1,587 votes—a margin of less than 1 percent—but still a victory. I went to Cheney's office, woke him, and gave him the good news. We phoned Ford. He had gotten up an hour earlier, turned on the radio, and heard the happy results.

However, our celebratory mood was dampened by the suspicion that Reagan would try to convince the press corps that the outcome was actually a moral victory for him, since a sitting president had won by such a tiny margin. Ford decided the best way to convince the press corps that it was indeed a victory for him was to act like we considered it a victory. I was authorized to tell my press briefing the morning after the New Hampshire vote that when Ford walked into the 8 a.m. senior staff meeting he was greeted by a standing ovation for having won in New Hampshire. And I relayed to the reporters that Ford had told his staff he intended to use his New Hampshire victory as a "great springboard" toward winning the nomination and the election. It worked. The reporters treated Ford's victory, no matter how narrow, as a victory.

The outcome in New Hampshire was good news for me on a personal level. Voters in the ski areas cast their ballots overwhelmingly for Ford. My thoughtless remark about poor snow conditions in the state hadn't lost votes for the president after all.

There wasn't a lot of time to bask in the glow of victory. Coming up in a couple of weeks were primaries in two big and important states. Ford's strategists believed that if the president could win in the southern state of Florida and in the midwestern state of Illinois, having won in the New England state of New Hampshire, Reagan would be forced to give up his challenge.

I tried a little media manipulation during the Florida campaigning by telling a reporter that Ford was trailing Reagan badly in the state, even though I knew he wasn't. My goal was to make a Ford victory in the Florida primary look even more impressive by convincing reporters that he had overcome an early deficit.

Ford's main campaign tour in Florida—a six-hour motorcade from Palm Beach to Fort Lauderdale with fourteen stops for speeches and handshaking—was marred by nonstop rain. Standing and waving in the open roof hatch of his limousine, Ford was soaked to the skin by the downpour, his wet hair plastered to his head.

The president beat Reagan in the Florida primary by a comfortable margin.

Then it was on to Illinois. While the president was campaigning there, the press corps reported an ethical lapse by his campaign chairman, Bo Callaway, which could have harmed Ford's primary run in the state. The news stories said Callaway had used his former position as army secretary to pressure government agencies to approve an expansion of a ski resort he owned in Colorado. Dick Cheney decided the Ford campaign could not tolerate such a scandal. Cheney informed Callaway he had to resign. During a campaign trip aboard Air Force One, Callaway went to the president's compartment and told Ford he was quitting. The president did not try to talk him out of it. After that conversation with the president, Callaway, normally a tough politician, returned to his seat on the plane and cried. Despite the Callaway episode, Ford won the primary in Illinois, again by a comfortable margin.

Having lost the first three primaries, Reagan was under great pressure to drop out of the race for the Republican nomination. But Reagan refused to abandon his campaign.

Meanwhile, I and a few others in the White House and on the campaign staff thought Ford ought to call off *his* primary campaigning and return to his Oval Office duties, announcing that voters would judge him based on his ability to deal with the nation's domestic and foreign problems, not on his skills as a campaigner. But Ford was afraid that if he did not meet Reagan's challenge head-on, he might lose the nomination.

The Reagan campaign got a boost when Reagan won his first primary, in North Carolina. It was the first time in a twenty-seven-year political career that Ford had lost an election. Reagan's success in North Carolina was partly because of a tough half-hour TV commercial he ran accusing Ford of dangerously weakening America's defenses, giving in to the Soviet Union, and negotiating away America's rights to the Panama Canal.

At the White House, we decided that I should be perfectly honest with reporters in describing the president's reaction to his first primary loss, rather than trying to downplay it or offer some weak excuse. "The president had expected a close race, but he expected to win," I told the press corps. "So, naturally we are disappointed. The point is we lost, and there are no excuses and no alibis."

Week after week after week, for the rest of the primary season, Ford and Reagan fought it out. Ford won in some states. Reagan won in some states. On the night of the Texas primary, after returning from the annual black-tie banquet of the White House Correspondents Association, Ford invited Cheney, photographer Kennerly, and me to follow the returns on TV with him and Mrs. Ford in their living quarters. Before joining the Fords, I stopped in my office to check the AP and UPI newswires. The news was bad. Ford was trailing Reagan in every district in Texas. When I reached the second-floor presidential living room, I tried some lame humor to soften the news: "Mr. President, in the old days the kings used to shoot the messenger who brought bad news."

"Do you have bad news?" the president asked.

I showed him the wire copy from Texas. As more returns came in, Ford's mood alternated from angry to profane to glum to silent. By 11:30 p.m., the bad news had turned to disastrous news. Reagan had won all ninety-six delegates from Texas. He had carried every district in the state. I tried to cheer up the president by reminding him that when he played college football, his team had been behind in games and came back to win.

And then the news got really bad. Ford lost the primaries in Alabama and Georgia and Indiana and Nebraska. *Newsweek* magazine ran a cover story headlined, "A PRESIDENT IN JEOPARDY." As the list of primary losses grew longer, Ford's temper grew shorter. When a balloon drop at a Ford rally in Indiana failed, the president, in a testy voice, threatened that the next time something like that went wrong in the campaign, he was going to drop his chief event organizer, Red Cavaney, from the ceiling instead.

Big things and little things plagued the Ford campaign. During the primaries, a new Watergate book by Bob Woodward and Carl Bernstein called *The Final Days* was published, and a movie based on their previous Watergate book, *All the President's Men*, opened, reminding voters of Nixon, Watergate, and the pardon.

Among the minor distractions: At one campaign stop on a farm in rural Wisconsin, Ford got cow dung on his sleeve and on his pants leg while walking through a barn. Reporters used the incident as a peg for yet another round of stories about Ford's alleged clumsiness.

Ford's opponent was not subjected to the same scrutiny. One night, watching TV footage of a Reagan campaign stop, I noticed that Reagan bumped his head getting out of his car. The correspondent never said a word about it in his script, nor did anyone else in the press corps report the incident. If Ford had bumped his head, I believed, it would have been widely reported.

In response to the series of primary defeats for Ford, the White House and campaign staffers turned on each other. In stories leaked anonymously to the press, some blamed Kissinger, some blamed Cheney, some blamed Hartmann, some blamed the people handling the campaign's advertising, some blamed me, and some blamed Ford himself. I attended meetings at which rival factions on the staff literally screamed at each other. The situation got so bad that at one point the president assembled his senior staff and ordered his aides to stop "sniping" at each other.

In a depressed mood, I recorded in my oral diary that if Ford lost the nomination, the epitaph for his campaign ought to read that his presidency died "as a result of multiple self-inflicted gunshots in the foot." I blamed myself for some of the "gunshots." I wondered if my appearance on *Saturday Night Live* had contributed to Ford's unpopularity with voters. I also worried that I had hurt Ford's chances by not being a better press secretary. I had taken the job with great hopes, with great confidence. Now my confidence had turned to self-doubt. I wondered whether Ford, Cheney, and other senior staff members wanted me to resign. When James Reichley, an editor at *Fortune* magazine, was hired as a counselor to the president, I wondered whether he was my replacement-in-waiting. When I wasn't invited to attend a campaign planning meeting, I interpreted it as yet another sign that I was on my way out.

On a couple of occasions, I told Ford I was willing to resign so he could pick a new and better press secretary. Each time he told me he wanted me to stay. Rumsfeld called me one day during that period and told me I had looked very glum, almost whipped, at a White House reception the night before. He cautioned that my appearance could send a signal to my staff and to others in the White House that I was pessimistic about Ford's chances. Rumsfeld worried that this could cause a panic among the staff. I promised to try to act more upbeat.

I recorded in my oral diary at the time, "This White House is not showing grace under fire." I described those weeks of primary losses and finger-pointing as "a cannibalistic, self-devouring period." I also noted, "The White House doesn't seem to be as much fun anymore. . . . It seems to be all hard work, long hours, little fun."

During this period, the president's son Jack came to see me again to complain about how badly the White House staff generally and the Press Office specifically were serving his father. "I wonder how people around here can go home at night and sleep when they realize how they're letting my father down," Jack declared.

"I don't have any trouble when I go home to sleep because I work down here sixteen or eighteen hours a day for your father," I shot back. "When I get home, I'm pretty well tired from all that work, and I don't have any trouble sleeping at all." The angry conversation went on for two hours. By the end, I had not convinced Jack that I and the other staff members were working hard, competently, and enthusiastically for his father.

On top of all the problems I confronted daily at the White House, my three-year-old son Edward almost choked to death during this period. On a rare night when I got home from the White House before his bedtime, I was playing with him when he started coughing and gagging. A piece of hard candy he had been chewing on had become lodged in his throat. I grabbed him by the feet, held him upside down, and pounded on his back. He regurgitated the candy. I was shaken. If I had not been home, if I had worked my normal hours that day, my son might have died.

An event in the midst of the primary races gave Ford a unique opportunity to emphasize his role and stature as president. July 4, 1976, was the nation's bicentennial, celebrating the two-hundredth anniversary of the Declaration of Independence. Over a five-day period, Ford delivered a series of bicentennial speeches at the National Archives, where the Declaration of Independence and the Constitution were on display; at Valley

Forge, Pennsylvania, where General George Washington and his troops wintered during the Revolutionary War; at Monticello, Thomas Jefferson's home; and at Independence Hall in Philadelphia, where the Declaration was signed. I thought the speeches Ford delivered at these and other bicentennial events were the best he had ever given, with the exception of his inaugural speech. They were nonpolitical. They celebrated the two-hundredth anniversary of the Declaration of Independence as an inspiration to people all over the world, as a landmark in man's quest for freedom. The networks and the newspapers largely ignored them.

I joked to David Gergen that if Abraham Lincoln had to deal with today's press corps, the Associated Press would have devoted most of its story on the Gettysburg Address to Lincoln's political motivation for dedicating the Civil War battlefield and to his ill-fitting clothes, and would have summed up Lincoln's words in one sentence at the end of the story.

A much-less-historic event during the primaries allowed Ford to display his human side and his sense of humor. It was the annual Gridiron Club dinner, an affair dating back decades at which the president and senior officials of his administration mingle with the cream of Washington's journalists and pundits. After dinner, the journalists put on satirical skits, and the president delivers a humorous speech. With the help of speechwriter Don Penny, Ford used the occasion to take a couple of playful jabs at both his Republican and Democratic challengers.

"The primaries are really narrowing down the candidates," the president began. "The Democrats are down to twenty-eight, and the Republicans to one and a half." It got a laugh. "Governor Reagan did stop in at the White House not too long ago. He wanted to take a look around. He said he couldn't stay long. I said, 'You better believe it.'" That got an even bigger laugh. Then Ford aimed some humorous barbs at one of the contenders for the Democratic presidential nomination, former governor Jimmy Carter of Georgia, who also was attending the dinner. "There's the governor over there," the president said, pointing. "It's easy to see where he sits. Now if we could only figure out where he stands."

Returning to the White House after the dinner, Ford was feeling so elated about his performance that he invited Cheney, his military aide Robert Barrett, and me to come up to his living quarters for a celebratory nightcap. The navy stewards, who usually are on duty to take care of the

First Family's needs, had departed for the night. So Mrs. Ford mixed the drinks. We sipped and relived the dinner and recalled campaign experiences and relaxed for about two hours. In the midst of our celebration, the Fords' daughter Susan returned from a night out with friends and joined us. She was very excited about having met a handsome Washington Redskins football player named Rusty Tillman. "He's just gorgeous!" Susan enthused.

One of the key primaries was in Michigan, Ford's home state, where there was a sizable population of conservative voters who might be attracted to Reagan. If Ford could not win in Michigan, he almost certainly could not win the nomination. As in New Hampshire, a shortage of funds hampered the Ford campaign. Some Ford-friendly Republican politicians in the state wanted Ford to make a whistle-stop train tour. Initially, campaign officials said there wasn't enough money. But somehow they scraped together the funds. The campaign train was dubbed "The Presidential Express." The whistle-stop tour across the state attracted large crowds. And perhaps even more important, it attracted heavy news coverage. The large turnouts of home-state fans also bolstered Ford's spirits.

Late in the afternoon on the day of the Michigan primary, the networks were projecting a Ford victory over Reagan based on exit polling. But there was no time to celebrate. Ford and his senior staff aides had to attend a fancy white-tie-and-tails banquet given by the visiting French president, Giscard d'Estaing, in a tent on the grounds of the French embassy in Washington. Throughout the dinner, updates on the vote count were passed to Ford and circulated among his staff. By the time the banquet was over and we returned to the White House, the results of the Michigan primary were conclusive. Ford had beaten his challenger by a two-to-one margin. We watched Reagan being interviewed on TV. He said he was satisfied with the results. Smiling broadly, Ford commented, "I hope we can keep him that pleased in the other primaries."

As a result of Ford's primary victory in Michigan, the gloomy mood in the White House lightened a bit. Ford seemed less tense. Some of the staff members stopped sniping at each other. My own spirits rose. My concerns about Ford losing the nomination faded. But Reagan wouldn't give up. The Ford campaign was so low on funds during the primary campaign in California that we had to barter a deal with the local public TV station in Anaheim—the station would provide lighting and sound equipment for a Ford campaign event in return for an exclusive interview with the president.

Using his presidential powers to win delegates, Ford promised to build a veterans hospital in one state, approved a nuclear power plant in another state, designated a national landmark in a third state. A joke circulated that the president tried to win one New Jersey delegate by inviting him to attend a White House banquet for visiting Queen Elizabeth. The punch line was that the delegate, still undecided between Ford and Reagan, asked, "What's for dinner?"

Week after week after week, for four months, Ford and Reagan battled it out in state primaries all over the country. And when the final votes were counted in the final primary, the president was slightly ahead in total delegates, but he did not have enough to claim the nomination. The Republican candidate would be chosen at the party's national nominating convention in Kansas City in August. The long, hard slog through the primaries, and the inconclusive outcome, took their toll on Ford. The president was irritable and impatient, testy and tense. He couldn't seem to relax. He had a perpetual frown on his face. During one campaign trip to Ohio, Ford snapped to his appointments secretary Terry O'Donnell, "I don't want to see one more person!"

I and the other staff members tried to maintain a sense of humor, even playfulness, to survive the stresses and long days and disappointments of the primary campaign. The First Family sometimes took part in the stress-relieving fun. After one campaign stop in Michigan, Betty Ford and daughter Susan entered the presidential compartment on Air Force One wearing big black paper mustaches. Ford was so preoccupied that it took him several minutes to notice that his wife and daughter had sprouted (fake) facial hair.

One of the chief jokesters was Major Robert Barrett, the president's military aide, who was always close to Ford, carrying "the football"—a briefcase containing the codes needed to launch a nuclear attack. One day Barrett showed up carrying "the football" in one hand and a tiny leather pouch in the other hand.

"What's in the little pouch?" I asked him. "The codes for starting a small conventional war," he responded.

Some of the White House staff arranged a birthday party for me one night in San Jose, California, while Ford was campaigning there. Among the decorations were balloons filled with helium. After the president had left the party, and after I and the other staff members had consumed quite a few drinks, we amused ourselves by untying the balloons, inhaling the helium, and then talking to each other in the high-pitched Donald Duck voices caused by the gas. Under the circumstances of a long and grueling primary campaign, that was what passed for humor.

35

"One Actor Is Enough"

In August, one month after the Democratic convention at Madison Square Garden in New York City nominated former Georgia governor Jimmy Carter as the party's presidential candidate and Senator Walter Mondale of Minnesota as its vice-presidential candidate, the Republicans met at the Kemper Arena in Kansas City, Missouri, to select their candidates.

The weekend before the Republican convention opened, Ford went to Camp David. Cheney and I and some other staff members went with him to help prepare him for the convention. Although he did not have enough committed delegates to be assured of winning the party's presidential nomination, Ford practiced an acceptance speech and considered his possible choices for running mate. A podium and videotaping equipment had been set up for Ford's rehearsals. The president also filmed some sequences for campaign commercials and for a movie about his life and career that would be shown at the convention. The president didn't hit it off with the film's producer. He griped that the producer was trying to turn him into a movie actor. "One actor in the campaign is enough," the president commented.

Stringent spending limitations imposed by campaign regulations hampered the last-minute efforts by the Ford campaign to win over uncommitted convention delegates. The spending ceiling forced the president and his entourage to put off their arrival in Kansas City until the day before the convention opened. This was not altogether a bad thing. It emphasized that Ford *was* the president, with heavy responsibilities in Washington. Concerned about the campaign's financial status, the Crown Center Hotel demanded payment in advance for the Ford entourage's rooms, including the president's $350-a-day suite. The White House advance team stayed at a fleabag motel to save money. In order to gain free TV exposure, we timed Ford's arrival in Kansas City to coincide with the TV networks' convention-eve broadcasts. The networks were forced to carry live the enthusiastic welcome by thousands of screaming Ford partisans and the president's speech to them.

The Reagan campaign employed its own clever tactics. Reagan announced in advance that if he won the presidential nomination, he would select as his vice-presidential running mate Richard Schweiker, a moderate Republican senator from Pennsylvania. The choice was designed to balance Reagan's conservatism and appeal to moderate delegates. The second part of the Reagan strategy was to ask the convention to pass a resolution requiring *all* candidates to name their vice-presidential running mate in advance. The idea of forcing Ford to name his vice-presidential candidate before the presidential nominating convention was that no matter whom he selected—liberal, moderate, or conservative—it would lose him the votes of some delegates who disagreed with his choice. After heavy lobbying by Ford and his aides, the convention rejected Reagan's resolution by a narrow margin.

A final ploy by Reagan was to propose a "Morality in Foreign Policy" plank for the party platform. The plank criticized agreements with the Soviet Union, praised Aleksandr Solzhenitsyn for his courage and morality, and denounced "secret agreements" with other countries. When I showed Ford the wording of the proposed plank, he reacted angrily. "I don't like it," the president snapped. "I'll fight it." But eventually Ford decided not to oppose including the plank in the platform. To fight and lose would be worse than to grudgingly accept it. As Cheney put it while we were bouncing through the streets of Kansas City in a van on the way to attend a reception for delegates, "We're going to take a dive. Principle is OK up to a certain point, but principle doesn't do any good if you lose the nomination."

Since the end of the primary voting, both the Ford and Reagan campaigns had engaged in intense backroom maneuvering to win the votes of the remaining undecided delegates and thereby clinch the nomination. That maneuvering increased in Kansas City as the first roll call approached. Both campaigns focused particular attention on winning the thirty delegate votes from Mississippi. When the Mississippi delegation announced it would vote solidly for the president, the contest was over. Ford finally had enough pledged delegates to clinch the nomination. However, Reagan's tenacious challenge hurt Ford's chances of winning the presidential election in November.

Ford and his staff watched TV coverage of the convention vote in his temporary office. We allowed thirty or forty reporters, cameramen, and photographers to watch with us. Ford clutched in his hand a slip of paper on which he had written "1,179," the number of delegate votes he expected to win. He actually received 1,187. Reagan got 1,070. "I hope nobody demands a recount," Ford joked when the final tally was announced in the convention hall. Friends and staff members crowded around the president, congratulating him. The TV sets showed a jubilant Mrs. Ford at the arena being congratulated, hugged, and kissed by friends and well-wishers.

It was after 1 a.m., but the long and stressful day was not over yet. Ford and Reagan had agreed before the balloting that the winner would go to the loser's hotel immediately after the vote for a unity meeting. Such a public display of unity was necessary if Ford had any hope of winning the votes of Reagan's conservative supporters. So the president and his entourage piled into a motorcade and drove to the Alameda Plaza Hotel, where Reagan and his aides had taken over an entire floor. We got off the elevator and walked down a long corridor toward a meeting room where Reagan was waiting. I noticed that many of the hotel room doors were open, and inside some Reagan staff members were weeping.

When we reached Reagan's suite, Ford shook hands with his defeated challenger and told him, "Governor, it was a great fight." He added, "I just wish I had some of your talents and some of you tremendous organization." After the initial greeting and handshake for the cameras, Ford and Reagan sat side by side on a sofa, talking privately. Afterward, the president described the meeting as awkward. "The tension of our long contest permeated that room," he said.

While Ford and Reagan talked, I and other members of the two staffs stood uncomfortably at the other end of the large room, out of earshot. I found myself standing beside Lyn Nofziger, a longtime Reagan aide who had the reputation of being a tough, even mean, political hardball player. After a few minutes of uncomfortable silence, Nofziger asked me if I wanted a drink. Without thinking how my reply would sound, I replied, "Gee, Lyn, that's the nicest thing you've ever done."

Many years later, I was told that a member of the Reagan staff had asked Nofziger what kind of demeanor to display toward the Ford staff. Nofziger supposedly replied, "De meaner de better." One precondition Reagan had imposed before agreeing to the meeting was that Ford would not offer him the vice-presidential nomination. Reagan didn't want the nomination and didn't want the discomfort of turning it down if Ford offered it. The president kept his promise and did not ask Reagan to be his running mate. Ford and Reagan did discuss other possible vice-presidential candidates.

Reagan told Ford he thought Kansas senator Bob Dole would be an excellent choice. Some Reagan critics believe he made that suggestion because he knew Dole on the ticket would cost Ford the November election, opening the way for a Reagan presidential run in 1980.

By the time the president got back to his hotel, it was after 3 a.m. Ford sat down at the conference table in his hotel suite with a group of aides, former congressional colleagues, friends, and trusted advisers to consider who his running mate should be. They discussed a long list of possibilities, including Dole; Don Rumsfeld; Mel Laird; Anne Armstrong, the U.S. ambassador to London, who would have been the first woman VP candidate of a major party; and Senator Edward Brooke, who would have been the first black VP candidate of a major party. Finally, at 5 a.m., Ford suggested that they adjourn, get some sleep, think about who would make the best running mate, and reconvene at 9 a.m. to finalize his choice.

When the vice-presidential selection meeting reconvened, it was immediately obvious to the participants that Ford had made up his mind. His choice was Dole, a conservative who, Ford hoped, would appeal to Reagan's conservative delegates and voters. My personal choice—not that Ford asked me—was Anne Armstrong. Ford wrote later that if he had had the decision to make over again, he might have "gambled on Anne." While her selection would not have pleased the most conservative wing of the GOP, I believed she would have appealed to moderate Republicans, independents, and especially to women, who might not otherwise have voted for Ford.

Part of the Ford team's strategy was for the president to use his acceptance speech to reach a large national audience on prime time television. It would, no doubt, be his biggest audience for any event during the campaign. But the die-hard Reaganites had a nasty trick up their sleeves. Before Ford was introduced at the convention to accept the nomination, Reagan's supporters cheered and demonstrated, demanding that their candidate be allowed to speak before Ford. The convention chairman invited Reagan to come to the podium. He declined. The Reaganites continued their demonstration. The convention chairman again invited Reagan to come to the podium. Again Reagan refused. The Reagan demonstration went on and on as prime time slipped away. The deadline for morning newspapers was fast approaching.

Watching the Reaganites' delaying tactic on TV in his hotel suite, the president grew increasingly grim and tight-jawed. "Damn it!" he shouted. Ford ordered Cheney to contact the convention chairman to tell him to "get this thing under control."

Then he had an idea to regain the initiative, and the media's attention. He ordered me to call as many reporters as I could reach and tip them off that in his acceptance speech Ford was going to challenge Carter to a series of televised debates during the campaign. The TV and radio networks cut away from their coverage of the Reagan demonstration to report on Ford's debate challenge. And it was big news in the morning newspapers.

The Reagan demonstrations finally subsided, and the president was introduced. It was twenty minutes before midnight—long past prime time in the East—when Ford stepped to the podium to accept the Republican presidential nomination and launch his campaign. The acceptance speech had been meticulously written, and Ford had carefully prepared to deliver it. The aim was for him to convince the voters that he was more qualified than Carter to lead the nation as president. From the very beginning, the president fulfilled this goal.

"I seek not a Republican victory, but a victory for the American people," he proclaimed. "You at home listening tonight, you are the people who pay the taxes and obey the laws. You are the people who make our system work. You are the people who make America what it is." In a clear shot at Carter, Ford told the convention audience and the TV audience, "My record is one of progress, not platitudes. My record is one of specifics, not smiles. It is a record I am proud to run on."

Then, as prearranged, hundreds of delegates rushed out of their seats and swarmed over the podium to congratulate Ford. Amid the celebration, the president motioned Reagan to join him. Reagan came. And as planned, the challenger spoke—longer than was appropriate, self-servingly, using lines that probably were part of what he thought would be *his* acceptance speech. But, at the very end, Reagan urged the delegates to put aside the past and get behind Ford. "Go forth in unity," he urged.

Following this closing session of the convention, ABC gave a party in a park across the street from the Crown Center Hotel. After the long months of primaries and the stresses of convention week, I was ready for a party to unwind and relax. I got back to my hotel room at dawn, one hour before Ford's motorcade was scheduled to depart for the airport. I decided I needed a brief nap. Of course, I overslept. I had only a few minutes to pack, shave, shower, dress, and make the motorcade. Somehow I made it.

After the convention, Ford and his staff flew to Vail to map detailed plans for the campaign. I was disturbed because I was not invited to most of the meetings. Thinking it was important for me to know what the plans were so I could deal with news media queries, I attended the sessions anyhow. It seemed to me that reporters didn't trust me because they thought I was spinning the White House line, and Ford's campaign staff didn't trust me because they thought I was too cozy with the press corps. My paranoia was further fanned when David Gergen and other media relations specialists began playing a larger and larger role in the campaign. And my paranoia really got a boost when a new wave of stories and columns appeared reporting that I would be replaced as press secretary after the election.

A reporter for the *Washington Star*, Lynn Rosellini, interviewed me for a profile she was writing for her newspaper. I suspected it was going to be critical. At one point during the interview, she seemed to be hemming and hawing and clearing her throat. She finally said, "I don't know how to ask you this, but some people say you won't be here after the election." I joked, "Maybe it's wishful thinking." Then, more seriously, I answered her the same way I always answered that question: "That's up to the president."

I wasn't the only one feeling unwanted. At Vail, the president's pollsters and strategists advised him that he was trailing Carter badly in their surveys. The polls also showed that a disturbingly large number of voters questioned whether Ford was smart enough for the job. Nevertheless, the campaign planners informed him, "We firmly believe that you can win."

36

Swine Flu and Other Maladies

When Ford returned to Washington from Vail just before Labor Day to formally launch his campaign, bad news on many fronts was waiting for him.

David Gergen, Alan Greenspan, and deputy budget director Paul O'Neill came to my office to discuss what they called "a matter of some urgency." They advised me that statistics to be released the next day would show unemployment had increased for the third month in a row, to 7.9 percent. This would be the next to the last unemployment report before the election and the last report before the Ford-Carter debate on economic and domestic issues. It was bad news for the president's campaign.

An even worse problem involved an outbreak of swine flu. Government scientists and doctors advised Ford that there were signs the outbreak in the United States could become as bad as the 1918 flu epidemic, which killed half a million Americans and twenty million people around the world. The head of the government's Center for Disease Control and a panel of independent scientists recommended that the president order a $135 million program to vaccinate every American against swine flu. The mass inoculations began on October 1. We allowed reporters and TV cameras to witness Ford receiving his swine flu shot. Within two weeks, reports started flooding in of people suffering serious side effects after receiving their shots. Some became temporarily paralyzed. And twenty-five people had died from the shots. The mass vaccination program was canceled. Although Ford had followed the advice of experts in and out of the government, the fiasco was blamed on the president's supposed incompetence—not a good image in the midst of a tough presidential election.

Then there was the Earl Butz problem. Ford's agriculture secretary was known for his indiscreet comments. He had once mocked the pope's opposition to birth control by saying, "He no play-a the game, he no make-a the rules." And, in the midst of the 1976 election campaign, *Time* magazine quoted him telling a friend, "The only thing the coloreds are looking for in life are tight pussy, loose shoes, and a warm place to shit." After this statement set off a firestorm of outrage, Butz kept phoning me and asking what he should do. Some in the White House thought the secretary ought to ride out the storm because he would help Ford win rural and southern voters, while firing him probably would not win the president votes from blacks or liberals. No matter how Ford responded to the Butz indiscretion, it was going to make one group or another unhappy.

Ann Compton, the ABC White House correspondent, phoned me shortly before the network's evening newscast and, in a flip tone, asked, "Well, is he going to go? Is Ford going to boot him out tonight, or is he not going to boot him out tonight?" I was offended by Compton's tone. Having spoken to Butz by phone four or five times, I knew how anguished he was. He had made a terrible mistake and regretted it very much. But to Compton it was just a news story she needed to pull together by airtime. I told her that regardless of how badly Butz had chosen his words, he was a human being suffering greatly for his indiscretion. "Yeah, yeah, yeah, I don't need to hear that," she said. "I just want to know whether Ford is going to boot him out before I go on the air or not."

Ford summoned Butz to the Oval Office. In a meeting that lasted only five minutes, Ford expressed his strong displeasure and called the slurs unacceptable. Butz, with tears in his eyes, submitted his resignation. The president informed Cheney and me later that Betty had said she and other women were as offended by the sexist tone of the Butz comments as by the racist tone. Butz came to the Press Room to announce his resignation to the reporters. Walking down a White House corridor afterward, he put his arm around my shoulders, and I put my arm around his shoulders. He was a government official who had made a thoughtless mistake for which he had been punished. But he also was a human being in great pain who needed the consoling presence of a friend.

Even the Butz episode wasn't our worst problem. Labor Day is the traditional starting date for presidential campaigns. However, Ford's campaign was in such disorder that his strategists had no plans for a major speech by the president that day, or for almost two weeks after Labor Day.

Rather than let two critical weeks go by with no campaign events, it was decided to buy a half-hour of network TV time the day after Labor Day to show an edited version of Ford's convention speech. Reporters picked up on the campaign's shortcomings. Major newspapers began carrying stories saying the Ford campaign was so disorganized that the president and his advisers couldn't even decide where and when to formally launch his election effort. At one point, Stuart Spencer, the tough, blunt deputy campaign chairman, who was an old friend, told Ford, "You're a great president, but you are a fucking lousy campaigner."

The so-called Communications Group held a meeting at the White House every morning to review the news reports of the day, Carter's schedule, what the Democratic candidate was saying, and how the Ford campaign should respond. The problem was that whatever the meetings decided the president's campaign should do and say was rarely carried out. Statements the meetings decided should be issued didn't get written. Briefings and news conferences the meetings decided should be held didn't get arranged. Events the meetings decided should be staged weren't scheduled. I and other staffers who were upset about these problems went to Cheney to tell him of our concerns. He instructed us that every morning after our Communications Group meeting, we should report to him what action steps we had decided on, and he would make sure the steps got carried out. And if someone who was supposed to carry out decisions of the Communications Group didn't carry them out, Cheney said we should report that to him. After that, the situation improved somewhat. But not a lot.

On top of all those problems, feuding and finger-pointing among Ford's aides resumed. Staff members didn't share information with other staff members, were suspicious of each other's motives, spread malicious rumors about each other, leaked negative stories to the press.

I and others in the White House were frustrated because reporters seemed reluctant to pursue allegations of misdeeds by Carter. There was little or no coverage of the Democratic candidate's failure to publicly release his income tax returns. There was little or no coverage of his campaign's payment of $150,000 to a group of black ministers who then endorsed his candidacy. The press didn't look into charges that Carter had illegally used corporate jets for campaign travel, that foreign governments had paid for his overseas trips, and that he had vacationed for free at lodges owned by large companies. *Playboy* magazine ran an interview with Carter in which the candidate confessed, "I've looked on a lot of women with lust. I've committed adultery in my heart many times." But, at least from the perspective of the White House, reporters didn't make a big deal out of what would have been damaging quotes if they had been uttered by Ford.

Part of the Ford strategy was for the president to limit his time on the campaign trail. He was to remain in the White House, above the fray, working on official business, demonstrating his competence at running the government, looking and acting presidential. This was known as "The Rose Garden strategy." Dole and other "surrogates" would do the hard campaigning and, particularly, the attacks on Carter. However, Dole was hampered in playing that traditional role, and was put on the defensive, by the revival of old allegations that in past senatorial campaigns he had taken illegal campaign contributions from Gulf Oil. At news conferences and in media interviews, reporters bombarded Dole with questions about the Gulf Oil allegations. Instead of smoothly sidestepping the questions and shifting the focus back to the current election, Dole conscientiously answered queries about the charges, keeping the story alive.

Another disappointment in the early stages of the campaign was Vice President Rockefeller. He was designated by the Communications Group to answer Carter's first campaign speech after Labor Day. Rockefeller declined. Other "surrogates," including Reagan and John Connally, also remained largely inactive in the campaign.

Ford finally delivered the speech "officially" launching his presidential campaign at the University of Michigan, in mid-September. And, like so much else in the campaign, it generated controversy, disunity, and incompetence. The president's speech was scheduled for 7:30 p.m., too late for coverage by the TV network's evening news programs. The campaign could have bought network time to broadcast the talk, but there wasn't enough money.

Ford had graduated from the University of Michigan. Many of the students, however, were determined to demonstrate against the president's delivering a speech at the school. This was the seventies, a time of campus protests against the Vietnam War, against many traditions of American society, against the government, against authority generally. A vicious editorial in the University of Michigan newspaper suggested that Ford opening his presidential campaign at the University of Michigan was like "Adolf Hitler giving the first contribution to the Jewish Bond Fund." Thousands of students packed Crisler Arena to watch Ford officially launch his campaign. Some booed and heckled the president. More applauded and cheered.

"The question in this campaign of 1976 is not who has the better vision for America," Ford told the audience. "The question is who will act to make that vision a reality." On the way back to Washington, I was authorized to tell the reporters on Air Force One that the president was "very pleased" with how he was received by the students at his alma mater.

With Ford trailing Carter in the polls, we were counting on the series of three televised debates between the candidates to turn the tide by winning over undecided voters and Carter supporters. The first debate, in Philadelphia on September 23, would focus on economic and domestic issues. Ford's advisers had originally pushed for starting the debates sooner, hoping to catch Carter unprepared. But they realized that delaying the first debate until late September would be more beneficial by encouraging voters to keep an open mind until they had seen the candidates debate face to face.

37

Does the Soviet Union Dominate Eastern Europe?

Before the debates could proceed, the two campaigns had to negotiate the ground rules. That proved to be difficult. The Carter team demanded that the panel of journalists who would question the candidates address the president as "Mr. Ford" instead of "Mr. President" to avoid placing Carter at a disadvantage. The negotiators finally decided to let the journalists address the candidates as they pleased. The Carter negotiators then demanded that Ford, who was six feet, two inches tall, be required to stand in a depression on the stage so that he would not tower over the five-foot, ten-inch Carter. When the Ford team stopped laughing, that idea was dropped.

In preparation for the confrontations with Carter, the president's advisers developed a list of seven "talking points" that he was told to mention at every opportunity, no matter what question was asked. The "talking points" included: America had recovered from Vietnam, Watergate, and economic recession during Ford's presidency; he would not be satisfied until every willing worker had a job; and he would veto legislation that contributed to inflation. Ford also rehearsed some memorable phrases we hoped the reporters would quote, including, "There is no button in the Oval Office marked 'maybe,'" and "A president cannot be all things to all people."

The moderator for the first debate was a former colleague of mine at NBC News, Edwin Newman. The panelists were Frank Reynolds of ABC News, James Gannon of the *Wall Street Journal*, and Elizabeth Drew of the *New Yorker*. The first question went to Carter. What were his specific plans to reduce unemployment? He stammered and hesitated in his answer, offering only generalities. For his rebuttal, the president declared in a forceful and confident voice, "I don't believe that Mr. Carter has been any more specific in this case than he has been in many other instances."

It was the response he had rehearsed to deliver no matter what his opponent said.

With eight minutes left in the debate, the audio on the TV coverage went out because of a technical breakdown. Ford and Carter stood stiffly and silently at their podiums, not sure what the cameras were showing or when the sound would come back. I and other members of the Ford team realized that the TV networks needed to fill the dead air. So we rushed to the lobby, where the television correspondents pounced on us and did interviews while technicians tried to fix the sound problem on stage. Naturally, our spin was that Ford was winning the debate, that Carter was performing badly. It took Jody Powell and other members of the Carter entourage about ten minutes to realize what was happening and to start giving their own interviews.

After nearly a half hour, the TV sound was restored. The two candidates launched into their prepared closing statements.

In most of the post-debate polls, a plurality said they thought Ford was the winner. This was especially good news, since the economy and domestic issues were supposed to be liabilities for the president. The polls also suggested that Ford benefited by counteracting his image among some voters of being slow-witted and a plodding speaker. In the first Gallup poll after the debate, Ford had cut Carter's lead in half and trailed by only eight points.

All that good news was wiped out in the second debate on October 6 in San Francisco, which focused on foreign and defense policy. The president's good performance and Carter's stumbling in the first debate made us a little overconfident. Ford did not spend as much time preparing as he did for the first debate. And he was distracted by the Butz affair.

The moderator this time was Pauline Frederick, another former NBC News colleague who was then with National Public Radio. The panelists were Max Frankel of the *New York Times*, Henry L. Trewhitt of the *Baltimore Sun*, and yet another former NBC News colleague, Richard Valeriani. After the debate had been under way awhile, Frankel said he wanted to explore America's relationship with the Soviet Union during the Ford administration. Referring to the accords Ford had reached with Brezhnev at the Helsinki conference, Frankel declared, "We signed . . . an agreement that the Russians have dominance in Eastern Europe." His odd question was, "Is that what you would call a two-way street in Europe?"

Inexplicably, Ford replied, "There is no Soviet dominance of Eastern Europe, and there never will be under a Ford administration." What the president *meant* to say—a phrase frequently employed by White House press secretaries—was that the United States would never *accept* or *recognize* Soviet domination of Eastern Europe. But it didn't come out that way. Frankel gave Ford a chance to nullify has gaffe: "Did I understand you to say, sir, that the Russians are not using Eastern Europe as their own sphere of influence and occupying most of the countries there and making sure with their troops that it is a Communist zone?" Ford passed up this chance to retrieve his mistake: "I don't believe, Mr. Frankel, that the Yugoslavians consider themselves dominated by the Soviet Union. I don't believe the Romanians consider themselves dominated by the Soviet Union. I don't believe the Poles consider themselves dominated by the Soviet Union."

Carter jumped on Ford's poorly worded answer: "I would like to see Mr. Ford convince the Polish-Americans and the Czech-Americans and the Hungarian-Americans in this country that those countries don't live under the domination and supervision of the Soviet Union behind the Iron Curtain."

There was no immediate red flag that Ford had committed a campaign-altering mistake. I was watching the debate in a room behind the stage with Helen Thomas of the UPI, Frank Cormier of the Associated Press, and Tom DeFrank of *Newsweek*. None of the reporters said anything to suggest that they thought Ford's answer was a huge gaffe. And in a conference call among Ford staff aides in San Francisco and Washington beginning about fifteen minutes before the debate ended, there was no mention of the president's inexplicable denial of Soviet domination in Eastern Europe. In the presidential limousine after the debate, Ford and Cheney discussed the event, but no mention was made of the Eastern Europe answer. Kissinger phoned the president to offer his congratulations, and he did not mention the Eastern Europe answer.

After each debate, top Ford campaign and White House aides held a briefing for reporters—what is called a "spin session"—to influence press coverage by exalting about how well our guy had done. After the San Francisco debate, the briefing was in a ballroom of the Holiday Inn, the press center for the debate. In the lobby before the briefing, Brent Scowcroft of the NSC finally forced Cheney, me, and other staffers to face the facts. "Before we go in there and try to explain it away," Scowcroft advised, "we ought to understand . . . the president made a bad mistake." And my deputy, John Carlson, who had watched the debate with the press corps, warned the Ford team that the reporters were in an uproar over the president's answer on Soviet domination. Ford was staying at the home of a friend in Pacific Heights. Before facing the post-debate press briefing, one of us should have phoned the president and told him we were going to clarify his answer about Eastern Europe. For some reason, none of us made that call. Instead, we faced the press and denied that the president had made a mistake with his answer.

The next day, as the uproar gathered steam, Ford flew to Los Angeles for more campaigning. In a private meeting, Cheney and I urged the president to acknowledge his misstatement about Soviet domination of Eastern Europe. He replied in a steely tone, "I'm not inclined to do that." The president wrote later about the episode, "I can be very stubborn when I think I'm right, and I just didn't want to apologize for something that was a minor mistake."

Public opinion polls taken immediately after the debate showed that a majority thought Ford had won. But as the media frenzy over the Eastern Europe gaffe continued, later polls indicated that voters had changed their minds and a majority now said they thought Ford has lost the debate. Aides in the White House and at the campaign headquarters phoned in a panic, saying the gaffe could cost Ford the election by alienating Americans of Eastern European ancestry. Finally, the president grudgingly agreed to back off his Soviet domination remarks at an early morning breakfast meeting with a Chamber of Commerce group in Los Angeles. But his choice of words there only made the controversy worse. Ford talked about the Soviet Union's "alleged domination" of Eastern Europe. This new bobble drove the reporters into an even greater frenzy. Carlson phoned me in a panic, saying reporters were racing around the Press Room laughing, playing tapes of Ford's new misstep, and filing bulletins saying the president had put his foot even deeper into his mouth.

After his Los Angeles speech, we decided that Ford should try one more time to end the controversy. But by then most of the reporters had boarded the press bus parked about two blocks away. We scrambled to get them back. But we were able to assemble only three camera crews and a handful of reporters. Someone had the very good idea to pick up the president's mea culpa on a walkie-talkie radio and feed it to a walkie-talkie on the press bus.

Speaking slowly and carefully, the president read his statement: "I was perhaps not as precise as I should have been. I recognize there are Soviet [military] divisions in Poland. I regret it. And I am very proud of the courageous attitude of the Polish people who want freedom. There are several other countries in Eastern Europe that tragically have Soviet military forces. I hope and trust that my observations will put an end to a misunderstanding. It was a misunderstanding." And Ford took one other step to put the episode behind him. He telephoned the vice president of the Polish American Congress and apologized. That did end the controversy. But it certainly tarnished Ford's image and hurt his chances of winning the election. And it left the president and his staff bitter about the press coverage of his slip.

Cheney commented that the reporters had exacted their "pound of flesh." And Ford told a meeting of newspaper and broadcast executives later, "Ninety percent of what has been written [about the debate] involved one sentence. . . . There was such a concentration on that one point, ignoring virtually everything else, that I think the news media didn't give a full and accurate picture of the substance in many of the questions and many of the answers."

The final Ford-Carter debate, on October 22 on the campus of the College of William and Mary in the restored colonial town of Williamsburg, Virginia, was an anticlimax. Barbara Walters, yet another former NBC News colleague, was the moderator. The panelists were columnist Joseph Kraft, Robert Maynard of the Washington Post, and Jack Nelson, Washington bureau chief of the Los Angeles Times. While the president was testing his microphone and podium a few hours before the final debate, Mrs. Ford mischievously left a handwritten note on Carter's podium. It read: "Dear Mr. Carter—May I wish you the best tonight, I'm sure the best man will win. I happen to have a favorite candidate—my husband President Ford. Best of luck, Betty Ford."

The last debate was uneventful, with both candidates focused primarily on not making a mistake. With the debates finally over, Ford and Carter launched their final run to the finish line.

38

The Race to the Wire

Less than a month before Election Day, the president's campaign finally got some good news. Charles F. C. Ruff, a Justice Department special prosecutor who had been investigating allegations of illegal contributions to Ford's previous congressional campaigns, issued a statement saying he had found no violations and "the matter has therefore been closed." Ford telephoned me at home and directed me to assemble a news conference right away. A huge crowd of reporters and camera crews jammed into the auditorium of the Old Executive Office Building next door to the White House for the hastily arranged session.

"I am very pleased that the special prosecutor has finally put this matter to rest once and for all," Ford told the journalists. "The one thing that means more to me than my desire for public office is my personal reputation for integrity." He added that he hoped Ruff's findings would "elevate" the presidential campaign to a level "befitting the American people and the American political tradition."

Not likely. In the closing weeks of the campaign, John Dean of the Nixon White House made what the president called "preposterous allegations" that Ford had tried to block the Watergate investigation. At a private meeting, Ford blasted Dean as "a little snake in the grass who'll say anything about anyone." The president snarled that Dean was "a low-down, no-good son of a bitch, a sniveling bastard."

Carter tried to take advantage of Dean's unsupported allegations by demanding, "I call on the American people to force Mr. Ford to tell the truth, the whole truth, and nothing but the truth." Another nasty trick of Carter's was to refer constantly to the "Nixon-Ford administration." Because of such slurs, Ford began making personal accusations against Carter, which was not his usual approach to politics. Some of his charges:

"Jimmy Carter will say anything anywhere to be president of the United States"; "He wavers, he wanders, he wiggles, and he waffles"; and unlike Teddy Roosevelt, "Jimmy Carter wants to speak loudly and carry a fly-swatter."

As a result of the wide circulation the news media gave to Dean's allegations, the White House and campaign staffs, and Ford himself on occasion, developed a bitter and resentful antipress attitude. The president and his aides believed that reporters were following a double standard, vigorously pursuing allegations of misdeeds by Ford and largely ignoring allegations of misdeeds by Carter. For instance, the press did not pursue rumors that Carter once had a mistress. But the reporters did write stories saying the Ford campaign had used dirty tricks by spreading the rumors that Carter once had a mistress. The name of the alleged mistress was Irene. One campaign official suggested, half-jokingly, that Ford supporters could pressure reporters to check out the rumor by attending Carter campaign rallies and singing loudly, "Goodnight, Irene . . ."

Ford campaign officials also resented the fact that the press accepted Carter's depiction of himself as a poor peanut farmer from Georgia when he was, in fact, a multimillionaire agribusiness executive. And when a former co-chairman of Carter's National Steering Committee, Herb Hafif, spent eight thousand dollars of his own money to buy an ad in the *Los Angeles Times* to deliver "a personal warning" about electing Carter, there was a small Associated Press story but no coverage at all by the TV networks or the major newspapers. I and others in the Ford camp believed there would have been huge coverage if a high-visibility Republican campaign official had spent eight thousand dollars to buy an ad denouncing the president.

When Ford campaigned in the New York City area, the *CBS Evening News* anchorman Walter Cronkite joined the president's press contingent. Ford indicated to me that he would like to shake hands with Cronkite and have a picture taken with the anchorman. Cronkite wanted to bring a camera crew to the meeting. I explained to him that it wasn't an interview, just a courtesy call. Cronkite said he only wanted some silent footage to show that he had met with the president. My deputy John Carlson argued that I ought to grant Cronkite's request. I told John that I didn't trust Cronkite to keep his promise not to try to interview Ford. Carlson said,

"How can you not trust Cronkite?" The anchorman was known in those days as the most trusted man in America. As soon as Cronkite sat down next to Ford, he said, "You don't mind if we record this, do you?" So much for trustworthiness. I asked Cronkite why he had pushed so hard for the interview. He replied, "Well, you know the name of the game, don't you?" I replied, "What is it? Beat Barbara Walters?" And Cronkite said, "That's it." In those days, Barbara Walters was the aggressive co-anchor, with Harry Reasoner, of the ABC *Evening News*, which was in head-to-head competition for viewers with Cronkite's newscast. Cronkite told me there were "new rules" for the competition among network newscasts, "and you'd better learn to live with them."

The final days of the campaign were a blur of nonstop travel: Richmond, Virginia; Raleigh, North Carolina; Columbia, South Carolina; Burbank, California—and that was all in one day! San Diego, Seattle, and Portland, Oregon; Pittsburgh, Chicago, Atlantic City, Philadelphia, Syracuse, and Baytown, Texas; Buffalo, Akron, Detroit—and on and on and on.

The long days and minimal sleeping time, the hostile media stories, our outrage at some of Carter's tactics, and the contemplation of possible rejection by the voters caught up with me and others in the campaign entourage. We were tense and on edge. We huddled together in our own tight little circle. The fatigue and stress caused us to become flaky. For instance, we dreamed up an imaginary newspaper story: "In his sharpest attack yet on his Democratic opponent, President Ford today ordered air force F-4 Phantom jets to shoot down Jimmy Carter's airplane. Democrats immediately charged that this was another Republican dirty trick."

At one stop, Ford was assigned to a hotel room that had a plaque on the door reading "The Emperor Suite," which seemed inappropriate for a man with Ford's simple, down-to-earth tastes. So Terry O'Donnell taped a piece of cardboard over the plaque and wrote on it in felt-tip pen, "Jerry Ford's Room." David Kennerly conjured up a scenario in which Ford got so mad at NBC News for its hostile campaign coverage that the president would use the antitrust laws to dismantle the network. And members of the president's staff developed a little stunt in which we concealed "Ford-Dole" campaign stickers in the palm of our hands, put our arms around the shoulders of reporters, and surreptitiously glued the stickers to the back of their jackets. The reporters also grew flaky near the end. Jim

Naughton of the *New York Times* somehow rented a chicken costume and wore it to a Ford news conference in the airport at one campaign stop. The president joined in the gag. After answering some press queries, Ford pointed to Naughton and said, "Yes, that chicken back there, you have a question?"

The night before the nation voted, Ford ended his campaign where he had begun it, in his hometown of Grand Rapids, Michigan. He was cheered by thousands of friends and supporters. Ford was exhausted, his voice hoarse, from months of hard campaigning. "When I was sworn in, I asked for your prayers," Ford recalled to his hometown fans. "But tomorrow I ask that you confirm me with your votes. I won't let you down. I promise that." The final Gallup poll had Ford ahead by one point. The final Harris poll had Carter ahead by one point.

After voting, the president participated in the dedication of a mural at the Grand Rapids airport depicting highlights of his life. Ford called it the most special moment of the campaign. He began to cry when he talked about his mother and father and how much he owed them. People in the audience cried. I and others on the staff cried. And I was shocked to see that even hard-as-nails UPI reporter Helen Thomas was crying!

And then the president and Betty, the staff, and the press corps flew back to Washington to await the returns.

39

The End

In the second-floor residence at the White House, the returns were followed on TV by the Fords and their children; family friends; members of the White House and campaign staffs; singer Pearl Bailey; Joe Garagiola, a former major league baseball catcher and later sportscaster who had campaigned and filmed commercials for Ford; Bob and Liddy Dole; former congresswoman Edith Green; Senator Jacob Javits; Cheney; Kennerly; Bob Barrett; pollster Bob Teeter; and many other Ford friends and supporters. The guests nibbled from a buffet table while watching the returns. Many TV sets were scattered around the rooms and hallways of the residence, tuned to the various networks. Betty and Pearl Bailey sat on the floor in front of one of the TV sets, their arms around each other, watching the results. For some reason, the coverage on NBC drew the most attention. Its election maps were color-coded; the states Ford won were depicted in blue, while the states that went for Carter were shown in red. I drifted back and forth between my office, Cheney's office, and the residence.

Initially, the news was not good. Carter was sweeping the Deep South. Ford was ahead in only a handful of states. Garagiola walked over to the president, put his hand on Ford's shoulder, and said, "It's all right, Prez. We've given up a couple of runs, but the ball game is only in the top of the fourth. We've got a long way to go." As more and more ballots were counted, the outlook for the president improved. He appeared to have captured Connecticut, Virginia, New Jersey, New Hampshire, and Vermont and was ahead in New York. One of the networks, which had awarded Oregon to Carter, reversed itself and said Ford had won the state. At midnight, campaign officials told Ford that if he carried the states where he was leading and won Ohio, California, and Hawaii, he would be elected. But in the early morning hours, things took a turn for the worse. Carter won New

York when the ballots from Manhattan were counted. Pennsylvania didn't look good. Texas, which Ford thought he would win, went for Carter. Ford had asked Reagan to campaign for him in Texas. Reagan had refused.

By 2:30 a.m., the outcome depended on the final count in four states: Ohio, where Ford was leading by a tiny margin; Hawaii, where Carter was ahead by four thousand votes; Mississippi; and Wisconsin.

At 2:57 a.m., the UPI newswire ran a "flash," the highest level of urgency: "Washington—Carter wins presidency." I ripped the "flash" off the machine and hurried to the residence. When I got there, I found the president bidding his guests goodnight. He squeezed my arm and said, "I'm going to bed. If I'm going to be worth a damn tomorrow, I'd better go to bed." He was exhausted. He had almost no voice left. I didn't have the heart to show him the UPI story declaring him the loser. Instead I took it to Cheney's office, where a number of senior White House and campaign officials were gathered. Robert Teeter, the president's pollster, advised that if all the remaining undecided states went for Ford, and if one of the states in which Carter had been declared the winner actually was carried by Ford, the president would win the election by a very narrow margin. A long shot, at best.

We decided that I would tell reporters the president would have nothing more to say until later that day when the returns would presumably be more definitive. At my briefing, I was asked whether I thought the president could still win. I said "yes." As dawn approached, Gergen and I were about the only ones left following the returns in the White House. I told him it felt like we were there to plan a funeral. He said he had, in fact, already drafted a telegram of concession for the president to send to Carter if Carter was officially declared the winner.

I went home about 5 a.m. to change clothes and get a little sleep. I was back in the White House by 8:30 a.m. I went straight to Cheney's office, where a number of senior staff people had already gathered, including Greenspan, Teeter, Jack Marsh, campaign chairman James Baker, and others. We went over the returns state by state and concluded that Carter, indeed, had won the election, though by a tiny margin. Was there enough suspected voter fraud in various places to justify demanding a recount? One of the White House lawyers made a phone call, came back, and reported that there wasn't. "Gentleman," Cheney proclaimed, "we have to hoist our flag—the white flag of surrender."

David Kennerly was the first one to give Ford the bad news when the president awoke a little after 9 a.m. Ford later recalled his reaction: "I was terribly hurt and disappointed, but at the same time I was proud of the effort we'd made." The president phoned Carter about 11 a.m. and congratulated him. Then the president and Mrs. Ford came to the briefing room, where a huge crowd of reporters had assembled.

The Ford children stood on the podium behind their parents, Susan weeping, the three boys fighting back tears.

Whether from emotion or from the months of campaign oratory, Ford's voice was a barely audible croak. So Betty had to read the concession statement I had written:

> The president . . . wants to thank all those thousands of people who worked so hard on his behalf and the millions who supported him with their votes. It has been the greatest honor of my husband's life to have served his fellow Americans during two of the most difficult years in our history. . . . The president urges all Americans to join him in giving your united support to President-elect Carter as he prepares to assume his new responsibilities.

I looked directly at the president as Betty spoke. His face was a mask of pain and bitter disappointment. There was a haunted, hurt look in his eyes. I will never forget that look.

After Betty had read the statement and Ford's congratulatory telegram to Carter, they stepped off the podium and mingled with the crowd of reporters. Some of the reporters were crying. As Ford and his wife made their way back to the residence, the White House corridors were lined with staff members offering their condolences, many of them weeping. The feeling in the building was like there had been a death in the family. I went back to my office, locked the door, and cried for a long time.

One effect of Ford's loss was that I and other White House staff members suddenly had a much lighter workload. We were basically caretakers for the next two and a half months, until Carter's inauguration. I noted in my oral diary, "I felt a great emptiness in my life. My days had been filled with excitement and decisions and clashes and important work on historic matters. Now there was a void. I realized I had to fill it by reviving a private life which had been abandoned during my White House service."

My sixteen-hour days became eight-hour days. I got home in the evenings while my son Edward was still awake. He had been an infant, a year and a half old, when I became press secretary and virtually disappeared from his life. Now he was a bright little boy almost four years old. I was determined to make up to him for my long absence. And I was able to spend more time with my wife Cindy, to try to restore our relationship, which had been strained by my workload. I suddenly had the time to watch TV, ride my bicycle, read for pleasure.

The press corps shifted its focus from the lame-duck Ford White House to the incoming Carter administration, so I didn't hold briefings every day, and when I did they were short, pleasant, nonconfrontational. My bedside phone didn't ring at 3 a.m. with news of a new crisis. The beeper I wore on my belt to alert me to some White House emergency rarely went off.

Some of the correspondents and columnists who had previously been critical of the president found some nice things to say after the election. For instance, David Broder wrote in the *Washington Post*, "In an odd, inexplicable way, the truth has begun to dawn on people in the final days of Gerald R. Ford's tenure that he was the kind of president Americans wanted, and didn't realize they had." A *New York Times* editorial said, "Mr. Ford today enjoys the respect and affection of his fellow citizens. Moreover, he leaves the country in better shape than he found it." Privately, in a bitter tone, Ford wondered why he didn't get this journalistic praise when it might have swayed voters.

There were also some articles describing me and my Press Office operation in more sympathetic and favorable terms than had been the case during the previous two and a half years. Like Ford, I wondered why these favorable appraisals weren't published and broadcast previously.

Carter's press secretary, Jody Powell, came to visit me about ten days after the election. He wanted to look over the Press Office setup, talk about the daily routine, get any advice I might have. Some of the White House correspondents found out he was in the building and requested that he come to the briefing room to talk to them. Jody said he didn't want to. Noting that I had already done my daily press briefing, he said, "One feeding a day is enough." About ten reporters walked into my office anyhow and started asking Jody questions.

"This is my office and this is my guest," I protested to the invading reporters. "We're trying to do some business, and Jody has already said he doesn't want to be interviewed."

Phil Jones of CBS, a competitor when I was an NBC News correspondent and a frequent critic after I became press secretary, retorted, "This is not your office, so just go away and leave us alone." "What do you mean, this is not my office?" I asked Jones incredulously. "It's not your office," he answered. "It's the taxpayers' office." After some previous confrontations with Jones, I had vowed to myself not to let him set me off again. But given my short fuse, it was predictable that I would lose my temper one last time. I told Jones I was going to call the White House guards if he didn't leave my office. All the other reporters in my office were making notes on my blowup.

I recalled that once, when I vented my frustrations with Jones to Cheney, he had told me that one time before the end of the Ford administration I could tell the correspondent to "fuck off." I decided this was that occasion.

"Phil," I said, "why don't you fuck off."

Late in November, Carter came to the White House to meet Ford as part of the transition. Mrs. Carter was supposed to come with him to meet with Mrs. Ford, tour the private living quarters and public rooms in the White House, and learn about the First Lady's responsibilities. Early on the morning of the Carters' visit, I got a call from the White House physician, Dr. Lukash, advising me that Mrs. Ford was ill with an intestinal ailment, possibly caused by antibiotics she was taking for an infection, and might not be able to meet with Mrs. Carter. Lukash promised to call me back before my 11:30 a.m. press briefing to give me a final answer.

When Cheney, Marsh, and I went to the Oval Office to discuss the impending visit by the Carters, the president said Betty was so upset about Carter winning the election that she couldn't stand the thought of Mrs. Carter inspecting their private living quarters. But in the afternoon, after taking a nap, Mrs. Ford was feeling well enough to show Mrs. Carter around. The president, however, set limits. He said he was perfectly happy to have Mrs. Carter taken on a tour of the public rooms in the White House, but, "We're just not going to have her in the residence, that's all there is to it."

When the motorcade bringing the Carters to the White House arrived at the South Lawn, President and Mrs. Ford were there to greet them. Carter kissed Betty on the cheek. I wondered how she felt about receiving an uninvited kiss from the man who had defeated her husband and was about to evict her and her family from their home. Ford did not kiss Mrs. Carter. After the Carters had left following their orientation meetings, Cheney, Marsh, Kennerly, and I met to discuss how things had gone. It was agreed that Carter had asked all the right questions, mostly about foreign policy.

As Ford's presidency neared its end, I was offered a new position. A public relations firm wanted to pay me twenty-five thousand dollars to become the international media spokesman for a new movie about to open, *Superman*. I turned it down. I was contacted by a lecture bureau in New York, which offered to book a series of lectures about my White House experience. The agency estimated I could earn about one hundred thousand dollars from a year of lecturing. I accepted. I was also offered a contract to write a book about my experiences in the White House, which I also accepted.

In the last weeks of my tenure in the White House I decided to take advantage of a perk I had never exercised before—visiting the underground bunker complex inside Mount Weather, Virginia, to which the president and senior government officials—including me—would be evacuated in case of a Soviet nuclear attack. I was transported by helicopter to the secret facility forty-six miles west of Washington. Access was through a long tunnel bored into the side of the mountain. In the event of a nuclear attack, huge steel doors, several feet thick, would be closed once the evacuees were inside. I felt like I was in a science-fiction movie. I was shown the president's office and living quarters, my office, and facilities for a small number of reporters who would be evacuated with the president. I was informed that there were no plans to bring the families of evacuees to Mount Weather, except for the president's wife and children. Privately, I concluded that if a nuclear attack was imminent, I would stay with Cindy and Edward rather than go with the president.

A few weeks before the end of Ford's presidency, I was invited to give a farewell speech to the Gridiron Club. I joked self-deprecatingly that Jody Powell should emulate three rules I had followed in the White House: "(1) Don't be charming. (2) Learn to accept compliments with grace. I got one once. (3) Don't worry about your temper. You'll find one in my office. I lost it there many times."

I also was invited to deliver a speech to the National Press Club looking back on my tenure as press secretary and appraising the relationship between the White House and the press corps. Again, I began with some self-deprecating humor: "When I look over all the various people who have served as spokesmen for famous figures in history, I will be ranked somewhere in the middle," I told the gathering. "Not as unpopular as Joseph Goebbels, but not as well remembered as, say, Saint Peter."

More seriously, I recalled that when I took the press secretary position, the relationship between the press and the White House was not good. As Ford's presidency came to an end, I said, that relationship "is good and healthy. And I am proud of the role I have played in making it good again." I noted that Ford held 39 news conferences in 29 months, gave 200 media interviews, and took part in 133 other events involving the press corps. I recalled some unprecedented improvements in relations with the news media—allowing the author John Hersey to spend an entire week in the Oval Office observing Ford's every activity for an article in *New York* magazine; agreeing to have Ford answer questions on NBC's *Meet the Press* program, the first president to do so; and making a major improvement in presidential news conferences by permitting follow-up questions. I acknowledged and apologized—and jokingly granted myself a pardon—for my shortcomings: losing my temper; having a thin skin; being sarcastic; being impatient with reporters; saying New Hampshire's ski slopes were too icy; being unavailable in China; giving a briefing at midnight in Korea; and for "all other minor idiocies, blunders, oversensitivities, and shortcomings." I ended by saying, "If you want to sum up my term as press secretary, I would hope that you would say 'he left the White House better than he found it.'"

On Ford's last night in the White House, I and my Press Office staff, all feeling sad, gave ourselves a farewell party. First we downed several bottles of champagne purchased for the occasion. When that was gone, we drank all the liquor we could find in our cabinets and closets. And when that was gone, we even consumed an old bottle of fizzy white wine brought home from a Ford visit to Romania. We dimmed the lights to match our mood.

A small group of Carter press aides had moved into an office next to mine, where they were typing and copying the incoming president's inauguration speech. The names of Carter staff members were already being attached to the push buttons on the telephones.

On his last morning as president, Ford awoke early, as always, at 6 a.m. Two hours later, he came to the State Dining Room, where seventy-five Cabinet members and senior White House staff members were gathered for a farewell buffet breakfast. I wore a black suit, a sign of mourning. The president moved around the room, shaking hands and exchanging a few words of good-bye with each aide. Some of the staff members were in tears. When Ford got to me, I was too emotional to say anything. After Ford had spoken to each person, Vice President Rockefeller, the master of ceremonies at the breakfast, rapped for quiet.

"Mr. President, this is the proudest moment of our lives," the vice president declared. "Your presidency has brought a restoration of faith. Pride has been brought back to our country. It is typical of your thoughtfulness to have us to breakfast."

"I'm not very good at putting words together on an occasion like this," Ford began his farewell speech, looking around the room at the people who had worked most closely with him during his presidency. "I've enjoyed the White House mainly because of the fine people. The days were long, but they were lightened by the people. You all contributed to an administration which I think was good and which history will treat kindly. I hope to see you all again. I believe the friendships we made here will go well beyond January twentieth."

By then almost everyone in the room was weeping. Ford moved toward the door, shaking a few more hands. At the door, he stopped, waved, and shouted in a very loud voice, "Good-bye, everybody! Thank you all very, very much." I think he shouted those last words so loudly so he wouldn't cry himself.

I began my last press briefing—number 583—after the breakfast. Dozens of reporters, TV camera crews, and photographers had descended on the White House to cover Ford's final hours and Carter's first hours. I described Ford's morning activities and promised to keep the reporters informed of what the president did until the moment he departed. Then I invited questions. "When did the president take his last swim in the White

House pool?" a reporter asked. "Last night at 5:45 p.m.," I replied. After a few more desultory questions, Frances Lewine of the Associated Press asked, "Do you have anything else, Ron?"

"Not right now, Fran," I answered.

"Thank you," she said, ending my final briefing. I stood at the podium awhile longer, anticipating that some of the journalists—my former colleagues—might wish me luck or ask what I was going to do next or thank me for my service. But the reporters just drifted away, saying nothing.

Back in my office, I looked around one last time at the place where I had spent ten to sixteen hours a day, six or seven days a week, for almost two and a half years. I looked at the red and gray sofa where I had slept at night during crises. I wrote a note to my successor, Jody Powell, and attached it to the blue brocade bulletproof vest I had received from friends in the Justice Department. "Jody—I hope you won't need this. Good luck.—Ron"

And then it was time to go to the U.S. Capitol for the passing of the torch, for Ford to end his presidency and for Carter to take his oath. A motorcade was lined up in the driveway on the north side of the White House to take the outgoing and incoming presidents, their families, and their staffs to the inauguration. The last person Ford said good-bye to was Freddie Mayfield, a veteran White House doorman. Tears welled in Mayfield's eyes.

When the motorcade reached the Capitol, I discovered that no seats had been provided for the Ford staff members at the swearing in, so we found an inconspicuous place to stand at the rear of the platform.

Carter began his inaugural speech with these gracious words: "For myself and for our nation, I want to thank my predecessor for all he has done to heal our land."

When the Carters entered the Capitol building for the celebratory post-inauguration lunch, the Fords, the Rockefellers, and few members of their staffs made their way to across the Capitol grounds to a helicopter parked near Pennsylvania Avenue. We climbed into the chopper for the trip to Andrews Air Force Base, where the Fords would board a plane for the flight to their new home in Palm Springs. Ford's only comment as he prepared to leave his long career in Washington behind him was, "Whew, it's cold."

The helicopter took off and made a low pass over the terrain where Ford had spent the last twenty-eight years of his life—the Capitol, Pennsylvania Avenue, the White House, buildings housing the government departments. While Kennerly snapped dozens of photos, Ford stared down at the city through the helicopter windows. All at once it hit him that his career in the capital city was over. Ford turned to Rockefeller and grasped his hand, hard. Ford couldn't speak. His lips were squeezed tightly together. Tears welled in his eyes.

After passing over the city's landmarks, the helicopter was supposed to head for Andrews. But Kennerly yelled at the pilot to make one more pass over the White House. He had missed the shot he wanted. "No, let's not waste any time," Ford grumbled. But the pilot listened to Kennerly and made one more pass so the photographer could get his shot.

At Andrews, a crowd of several hundred White House staff members, administration officials, secretaries, wives, and children had gathered to bid the Fords good-bye. Some carried signs wishing them good luck in their retirement and expressing thanks for their service. A red carpet was laid out on the tarmac. An honor guard marched past. A battery of howitzers fired a twenty-one-gun salute. A band played "God Bless America."

Finally, the Fords climbed the stairs to the door of the plane, turned, waved one last time, then entered the aircraft that would carry them into retirement. Despite the words of praise for Ford in his inaugural speech, Carter refused to permit the outgoing president to fly home on Air Force One. Instead, the new president consigned the Fords to one of the backup jets. The plane taxied away, speeded down the runway, and took off for California. I stood on the tarmac and cried.

My adventure of a lifetime was over. My one experience as a participant had ended. It had not been an altogether happy experience. I had not performed as well as I wanted to. But facing the daily challenges in the White House had boosted my self-confidence and given me insights that reporters normally don't get. I would carry that confidence and those insights with me as I returned to the more comfortable role of being an observer, a journalist. I believed that what I had learned, how I had matured "making the news," would make me better at "taking the news."

About the Author

Ron Nessen was White House press secretary for President Gerald Ford from 1974 to 1977. Prior to joining the Ford administration, Nessen served as a correspondent for NBC News, including five reporting tours in Vietnam during the war. He is the author or co-author of several books, including *It Sure Looks Different on the Inside*, published by Playboy Press in 1979.